The Flight of a Butterfly
or *the* Path
of a Bullet?

USING TECHNOLOGY TO TRANSFORM
TEACHING AND LEARNING

LARRY CUBAN

HARVARD EDUCATION PRESS
CAMBRIDGE, MASSACHUSETTS

Paperback ISBN 978-1-68253-137-2
Library Edition ISBN 978-1-68253-138-9

Library of Congress Cataloging-in-Publication Data
Names: Cuban, Larry, author.
Title: The flight of a butterfly or the path of a bullet? : using technology to transform teaching and learning / Larry Cuban.
Description: Cambridge, Massachusetts : Harvard Education Press, 2018. | Includes bibliographical references and index.
Identifiers: LCCN 2017046603| ISBN 9781682531372 (pbk.) | ISBN 9781682531389 (library edition)
Subjects: LCSH: Internet in education—California. | Education—Computer network resources. | Web-based instruction. | Education—Effect of technological innovations on—California. | Teaching—Computer network resources. | Educational technology—California. | Educational change—California. Education—Aims and objectives—California.
Classification: LCC LB1044.87 .C79 2018 | DDC 371.33/44678—dc23 LC record available at https://lccn.loc.gov/2017046603

Published by Harvard Education Press,
an imprint of the Harvard Education Publishing Group

Harvard Education Press
8 Story Street
Cambridge, MA 02138

Cover Design: Wilcox Design
Cover Image: David Arky/Getty Images
The typefaces used in this book are ITC Legacy Serif and Frutiger.

I have been blessed with deep and close friendships
that have lasted a lifetime. These dear friends have,
over the decades, given and received love.

This book is dedicated to:

Joel "Yus" Merenstein
Dave Mazer
Sam Balk
David Tyack (1930–2016)

The path of educational progress more closely resembles the flight of a butterfly than the flight of a bullet.

—PHILIP JACKSON, Life in Classrooms

Contents

Contents

Introduction

For over thirty years, I have examined the adoption and use of technology in the classroom (*Teachers and Machines*, 1986; *Oversold and Underused*, 2001; *Inside the Black Box*, 2013).[1] I looked at the policy hype, overpromising, and predictions accompanying new technologies in each decade. The question I asked was: *What happens in schools and classrooms after the school board and superintendent adopt a reform-driven policy of buying and deploying new technologies to improve schooling?* In books, articles, and my blog (https://larrycuban.wordpress.com/), I moved back and forth between policy and practice.[2]

In these decades, champions of digital technologies in schools have believed deeply that the traditional goals of tax-supported public schools—building citizens, preparing graduates for a labor market, and making whole human beings—could be achieved through new electronic devices. They believed that hardware and software would, if not transform, then surely alter classroom teaching; they would improve students' academic performance and prepare graduates for an entirely different workplace than their parents faced.

In my research during these decades, I described and analyzed computer use in schools and classrooms across the United States. I tracked how these high-tech advocates and donors were often disappointed in how little school and classroom practice changed in the direction they sought, the anemic results in student achievement, and uncertainties in getting the right jobs after graduation, given the claims accompanying these new technologies.

I also documented occasional instances where individual teachers thoroughly integrated laptops and tablets into their practice and moved from teacher- to student-centered classrooms. And there were scattered cases of schools and districts adopting technologies wholesale and slowly altering cultures and structures to improve how teachers teach and students learn.[3] I found these occasional exemplars of classroom, school, and district integration important, although puzzling in their isolation from mainstream practices.

LITERATURE ON DIGITAL TECHNOLOGY IN SCHOOLS

In doing all of this research, I became intimately familiar with nearly all that had been written about digital technology in schools.[4] Researchers, policy advocates, and practitioners have created an immense literature on access to, use of, and effectiveness of technology in schools and districts. However, this literature, particularly as it deals with effectiveness, is stacked heavily at the *success* and *failure* ends of a continuum. Academics call this clustering at either end of the spectrum a *bimodal distribution*, with many fewer studies at the center of the continuum than at either pole. In short, the spectrum has two peaks, not the familiar, normal *bell curve* distribution.[5]

In this distribution, *success* refers to studies, reports, and testimonials about how technology has improved teaching and learning. Between the 1990s and early 2000s, researchers, commission reports, and reporters accumulated upbeat stories and studies of teachers and schools that used devices imaginatively and supposedly demonstrated small to moderate gains in improving test scores, narrowing the achievement gap between minority and white students, increasing student engagement, and achieved other desired outcomes. These stories, often clothed as scientific studies (e.g., heavily documented white papers produced by vendors; self-reports from practitioners), beat the drum for more use of digital technologies in schools.

At the other end of the continuum, the *failure* peak comprises a collection of studies that show disappointing results in students' academic achievement, little closing of the gap in test scores between whites and minorities, and a lack of substantial change in teaching methods during and after use of new technologies. Accounts include tales told by disgruntled teachers, irritated parents, and disillusioned school board members who authorized technological expenditures.[6]

Hugging the middle between these peaks are occasional rigorous studies by individual researchers and meta-analyses of studies done over the past half-century to ascertain the contribution (or lack thereof) of technology to student and teacher outcomes.[7] But even with these studies, the overall literature has yet to develop a stable and rich midpoint between success and failure. I would like this book to occupy the center of this continuum by documenting both successes and failures of going from policy to practice in using new technologies in classrooms, schools, and districts.

Such a bimodal literature results from questions researchers, policy makers, and practitioners asked about access, use, and effects of digital technologies. Most of the reports and studies were initially interested in answering the questions of who had access, how devices were used in lessons, and whether they "worked" (that is, raised test scores and influenced academic achievement). The resulting answers created each peak. Other questions about computer use in schools, however, went unasked.

A FUNDAMENTAL DILEMMA AND UNASKED POLICY QUESTIONS

In reading the literature, I noticed that top decision makers and funders seldom acknowledged the essential dilemma facing policy makers seeking to alter how teachers teach: They are asking the very people whom they regarded as the cause of the instructional problem to put new and different classroom practices into their daily lessons. Reform-minded decision makers, policy entrepreneurs, researchers, and advocates for this or that innovation—including use of new technologies—either dodged, neglected, or shunned this dilemma and the essential questions accompanying any new instructional policy.

But it is crucial to answer these policy questions if we are to understand the role that technology plays in public education when it comes to teaching and learning. And this is why I am writing again on the use of new technologies in classrooms, schools, and districts.

Reform-driven policy makers, entrepreneurs, donors, researchers, practitioners, and parents have sought substantial changes over the past three decades to transform schooling to improve student outcomes. Yet too often they either avoided the inevitable steps that need to occur for such changes to materialize in schools, or they skipped over the intricate interplay between the four basic questions that capture the necessary steps in going from adopted instructional policy to classroom practice:[8]

1. Did policies aimed at improving student performance get fully, moderately, or partially implemented?
2. When implemented fully, did they change the content and practice of teaching?
3. Did changed classroom practices account for what students learned?
4. Did what students learn meet the intended policy goals?

These straightforward questions must be asked of reforms aimed at improving student academic performance—creating small high schools, launching charter schools, adopting Common Core standards in states and districts, and instituting competency-based teaching and project-based learning. Most important for this book, these questions pertain not only to making digital technologies accessible to every student but also to expecting teachers to regularly use those technologies in lessons. To current advocates of using technology to transform teaching as, for example, personalizing learning, these questions are must-asks.[9]

Question 1 concerns the vital first step of actually implementing a policy adopted to improve classroom practice and student outcomes. Reform-driven instructional policies are not self-implementing.

Achieving policy aims requires leadership, political support, resources, technical assistance, staff development, and cooperation between administrators and teachers. Because teachers are the classroom gate-keepers—the ones who actually put a policy into practice—ample and clear evidence that teachers are in fact implementing new programs is key. If a policy is not being fully or moderately implemented, there is not much sense in pursuing the other questions. Evidence of teachers putting intended policy into classroom practice is essential to determining the degree to which an instructional policy is effective (or ineffective).

Once a policy's implementation in schools and classrooms is proved, then it is time to ask question 2: *Have teaching practices changed?* This linchpin question gets at the nexus between teaching and learning that is taken for granted in US schools: *Improve teaching, and then student learning will improve.* This has been the belief (or theory of action) driving reform-minded policy makers and leaders of university-based teacher education programs seeking to improve student outcomes since the introduction of tax-supported public education nearly two centuries ago. Determining the degree to which teaching practices have changed in the desired direction and which have remained stable is indispensable in moving from policy to practice.[10]

Question 3 closes this circle by getting at what students have actually learned as a consequence of altered teaching practices. In the past half-century, federal and state policy makers have adopted numerical measures of desired student outcomes (e.g., test scores, graduation rates, attendance, engagement in lessons) and established accountability structures to secure these outcomes. These measures, however, assume that teaching practices have indeed changed in the desired direction. Evidence of such changes is required.

Question 4 returns to the immediate, midterm, and long-term purposes of an adopted policy. It asks for an evaluation of its intended and unintended outcomes. Immediate purposes might have concentrated on annual student test scores and high school graduation rates. Midterm purposes perhaps sought college completion rates and graduates' annual salaries a decade after completing school. Long-term purposes

look for achievement of overall goals for tax-supported public schools
such as civic engagement, job and career history, measures of individual
independence, and mindful participation in the community.

ARGUMENT

My reasoning begins with the tight linkage between policy makers'
adoption of reform-driven policies aimed at altering how teachers teach,
their implementation, and changes in teaching practice—the first two
questions. Without classroom changes in the desired direction—the
final two questions—student learning remains largely untouched. Thus,
looking carefully at those instances where technology use in classrooms,
schools, and districts has become common and praised for its seamless
integration into daily lessons can get at determining what happens in
classrooms. Such studies, combined with other examples of stability in
practices and failed classroom use, can inform those eager to leverage
computers in improving teaching practice and student learning.

The essence of my argument is contained in two questions:

- Have classroom, school, and district exemplars of technology
  integration been fully implemented and put into classroom
  practice? (See the appendix for how I define *exemplary* and the
  criteria I used to identify teachers, schools, and districts in
  Silicon Valley).
- Have these exemplary teachers, schools, and districts altered
  classroom practices?

To answer the first question, I look at instances of where individual teachers, schools, and districts in Northern California have fully
implemented programs that integrated devices and software into
daily practice. Some of these exemplars are clearly part of larger policy-driven reform efforts to improve schools over the past three decades.
They include charter and traditional schools where expanded parental
choice has produced a marketplace of school options. The instances I

have selected aim at helping students learn more, faster, and better in particular classrooms, schools, and districts. Answering this question will unfold various meanings of the phrase *technology integration* in these best cases and explore what has happened to these efforts—whether they have become permanent in schools and districts or eventually faded away.

The second question asks whether such exemplars have led directly to desired changes in classroom practice—and it's one that policy makers and major philanthropists too often fail to ask. Determining whether and to what degree teachers have altered their routines, embraced changes in content and skills, and displayed these changes to students and observers is harder than one might expect. First, instructional policies seeking to change teaching practices do not necessarily mean improved lessons. Improvement is in the eyes of the beholder. Surely, a mother and father divorcing and having joint custody of their children is a change. Whether it is an improvement depends on who makes the judgment: the parent who initiated or opposed the proceeding or the children. Evidence of change in schools, depending on the interpreter, can mean improvement. But it may simply mean making changes to maintain stability in existing practices—not an outcome most policy makers or donors would applaud.[11]

There is also the teachers' frequent answer to the above question: "Yes, I have changed how I teach as a result of using these new technologies." A researcher or policy maker may disagree after observing those teachers in the classroom. Moreover, discrepancies in answers may result from differences in how researchers, policy makers, and students define "change" in teaching or what policy makers want as a result of shifts in classroom practices. Spelling out these different perspectives on changes in teaching is necessary before this question can be fully answered.

In this book, I will refer to student outcomes (one measure of improvement) and the degree to which changes in teaching practice are connected to short-term gains in test scores, graduation rates, and the like. However, I will not investigate the degree to which teachers, schools, and districts produced these short-term outcomes or how they did it. Focusing on student outcomes is another book unto itself.

WHY SILICON VALLEY?

This book's focus, then, is on the degree to which district instructional policies directed at teachers integrating digital technologies have altered daily classroom practices. Without such changes in practice, linkages to student outcomes become a story of other factors affecting how students perform academically. The place that I have looked for these exemplars is in Silicon Valley (the San Francisco Bay region stretching from south San Jose to north of San Francisco and across the water to the East Bay running from Berkeley to Milpitas in the South Bay). The area is home to over 3 million residents, of whom nearly two-thirds are minority. The median household annual income is over $110,000 (far higher than state and national averages). It contains seventy-seven school districts in four counties with over eleven hundred elementary and secondary public schools.[12]

Why here? The short answer is that these schools are located in the birthplace of computer hardware and software. Apple, Cisco, Intel, Google, and Facebook, whose names and icons have become internationally familiar, began and grew in the Valley. The area is characterized by technological innovation, a can-do spirit, and an entrepreneurial culture that prizes creating new devices, software, taking risks, and creating "unicorns"—a culture that encourages people to "think different" and to "make the world a better place." Silicon Valley has become the epicenter for technological progress.[13]

Another reason I've chosen the original Silicon Valley is the pervasive, heady optimism that digital technologies will improve life in general and education in particular. The ever-present social and mainstream media that hype each new "next thing"—from Google Glasses and driverless cars to home robots—breed a widespread, upbeat climate, implicitly demanding that schools keep pace with the innovations spilling out of Valley start-ups and established companies. Observers, then, might expect schools in Silicon Valley to have far more access to and extensive use of new technologies than most other locales.[14]

A longer answer to the question of why I chose Silicon Valley involves an in-depth look at the youth-driven work culture of these companies, the wealth that has accrued in the Valley, along with sharp demographic changes and gentrification of once poverty-wrapped neighborhoods, the impact of these companies on the labor market, and growing inequality in incomes that characterize this multicounty area. It is a region of deep economic, social, and political contrasts shaped in part by the growth of this technological cornucopia.

An extended answer also encompasses how the work culture, innovative spirit, and entrepreneurial risk-taking characteristic of Silicon Valley have spread to Austin, Denver, New York, Boston, and dozens of other places across the United States. Now Silicon Valley has become a metaphor for far-flung places where investors risk their monies on start-up companies promising the next best thing, the "killer app" that will make a fortune for its investors and first-generation employees and, of course, "make the world a better place." The long answer to the question getting into the innards of Silicon Valley has been fully explored by others. I will stick to selected classrooms, schools, and districts in the Valley.[15]

Reforming public schools is seldom far from the agendas and talking points of Silicon Valley CEOs and billionaires who made their fortunes here. They want public schools to be stronger than they are now and a pipeline of knowledgeable and skilled employees. They have shown concern and about what happens in classrooms, schools, and districts. Nor have they been shy in funding both public and private schools in and out of Silicon Valley.[16]

So this is why I selected Silicon Valley schools. I reasoned that most residents, visitors, and workers would expect intuitively that in the mecca of technological innovation for the nation, schools would have not only integrated the newest of the new devices and software but also benefited from access to the expertise, products, and dollars these internationally acclaimed corporations (and start-ups) have created.

And many local districts and schools have indeed profited from this proximity. School districts in Silicon Valley, for example, have received free beta versions of computer products for decades since 1984, when Apple's Steve Jobs donated one Apple II machine and software to each of over nine thousand schools in California. A slogan plastered on walls in Facebook's Menlo Park site captures the spirit of getting software and devices out the door to consumers: "Done Is Better Than Perfect." New devices and software have been tried out in these districts time and again.[17]

More recent examples of both gifts and collaboration include Google's donation of $600,000 to over six hundred teachers who requested grants to help them in their classroom—from funding an Oakland teacher to buy graphic novels to help his students read to buying tablets and a whiteboard.[18]

Facebook's relationship with Summit charter schools (seven schools in the Bay Area) provides another example. Since 2014, Facebook's software designers have met with Summit principals and teachers to create a "next-generation model of personalized, student-directed learning for the US public school system." Facebook's support and assistance come at no cost to Summit.[19]

Or consider Milpitas Unified School District, at the southern end of Silicon Valley. This nearly ten-thousand-student district of largely low-income and minority students introduced blended learning through teachers and administrators that took advantage of high-tech devices and software and models easily available in the Valley. District superintendent Cary Matsuoka launched the design process in 2012 and, with a coalition of parents and supporters of the school, convinced district voters to pass a $95 million bond referendum to build new schools, renovate old ones, and underwrite an effort to integrate technology across all schools.[20]

Schools in Silicon Valley, then, have benefited from the resources available, the climate of techno-optimism that pervades the region about change being an unalloyed "good," and access to beta products, software engineers, and money. Many districts and schools, both new and old, have adopted instructional policies geared to altering traditional classroom practices.

CHANGE AND STABILITY IN SCHOOLS

With all of these changes occurring in Silicon Valley schools, keep in mind that changes in public schools are historically embedded in an institutional contradiction.[21] In their multiple goals, public schools are both committed to change and stability. To understand the relative slowness of US schools, even in Silicon Valley, to embrace and deploy new technologies, I need to elaborate further this important and historical contradiction. Although schools are essentially conservative institutions committed to preserving core community and national values, they are also committed to changing individuals and improving society. The Valley's ubiquitous technological optimism pressures schools to embrace new ideas and practices. Because voters and taxpayers provide funds for public schools and parents, many of whom work for Silicon Valley companies, they want modern equipment in schools that can prepare children and youth for an information-driven workplace while instilling and reinforcing family and community values. So here, enthusiasm for transforming classroom practice spills over districts, leading many (but far from all) educators to accept beta versions of new software, buy laptops and tablets, and call for teachers to use devices and software in their daily lessons. It is this inherent paradox of change amid stability that explains the robust hold new devices have on Valley parents, teachers, students, and voters.[22]

For all of these reasons, I will focus on public schooling in Silicon Valley, particularly those classrooms, schools, and districts that have created exemplars of integrating technology into daily practices, places where technology is no longer in the foreground of teaching and learning but in the background, helping teachers and schools meet Common Core standards and skills needed for students to graduate high school and enter college or a career.

THE CALIFORNIA SYSTEM OF SCHOOLING

But Silicon Valley is not an island; it is part of California's state-funded and policy-driven system of schooling. A few words about that state system give a sense of the larger context in which Valley districts and schools operate.

In the 1950s and 1960s, California schools offered staffing and services that few places in the country could match: counselors, arts programs, school libraries, access to medical services, after-school programs, and other benefits that could turn out-of-state educators green with envy. State residents could go to two-year community colleges, four-year colleges, and universities virtually cost-free. What sounds like a "golden age," however, was far less glowing for most Mexican immigrants and blacks, who received inferior schooling even in those flush times.[23]

But times changed.

Today, California has eleven hundred districts with ten thousand schools enrolling a predominately minority 6 million students. Overseeing those students are nearly 300,000 predominately white teachers. In a few decades, California's schools sank to the bottom of national rankings in high school graduation, funding, and class size, among others. California ranks:[24]

1st	Number of students
4th	Teacher salaries
33rd	High school graduation rate
43rd	Per-pupil expenditures
49th	Students per teacher[25]

Most accounts of both successes and failures of California public schools target 1978 as the turning point. During Jerry Brown's governorship, state voters approved Proposition 13, which radically changed the assessment of property taxes, reduced the allocation of monies for public schools, and moved funding and policy-making authority from local school boards to the governor and legislature.

Soon after Prop 13 passed, decline set in. Schools went downhill fast, startling long-time residents.[26] Not only did property tax revenues for schools fall, but the state's economy went into recession. At the same time, immigration from Mexico, Southeast Asia, and elsewhere climbed sharply, increasing the numbers of children attending public schools. Subsequent governors and legislatures further reduced spending on schools, resulting in staff cuts, larger classes, decaying buildings, and erosion in academic achievement across the state, including districts in the emerging Silicon Valley. Unsparing blasts of criticism from civic and business leaders about the declining quality of schools further eroded public confidence in the public education systems.[27]

Amid the backlash over Proposition 13 and lack of school resources, Bill Honig ran for State Superintendent of Public Instruction on a platform of turning around the state's schools, preaching a gospel of traditional schooling. Anticipating the *Nation at Risk* report, he pressed for rigorous academic courses, a coherent state curriculum, and more academic demands on students and teachers. His reform message resonated with corporate leaders, parents, and ultimately voters—not once, but three times. Elected in 1982 and reelected in 1986 and 1990, Honig launched a subject-centered reform movement heavily endorsed by the state's business community, including tech entrepreneurs in Silicon Valley, that yielded higher and more graduation requirements, new curricula, and state tests tied to curriculum requirements. He also was instrumental in getting a fiscal floor for school funding into the state Constitution (Proposition 98).[28]

Between Proposition 13 and Honig's reforms, California became a more tightly aligned system of state-funded schools that hewed more closely than before to what governors and legislatures could agree on for the schools, such as new graduation requirements, state curriculum standards, and accountability. Successive administrations initiated reforms mirroring their values and voter wishes. That rollercoaster of reforms occurred every time there was a political change in Sacramento. It has persisted into the twenty-first century, even as the state's school population became predominately minority and academic performance in the eight large urban areas deteriorated even further.

The dream of putting new technologies into California schools and thereby revolutionizing teaching and learning appealed to corporate leaders and public officials from both political parties. Here was an instructional policy that political leaders and the California Business Roundtable endorsed sufficiently to pry open the public purse. As State Superintendent of Public Instruction Delaine Eastin put it in 1996:

> Technology is an essential part of education as we approach the twenty-first century. Ninety percent of the jobs created from this moment on will require advanced technological training. To compete for these jobs, our children will have to be skilled in the use of information technology . . . If we allow our educational system to fall behind the tide of change in the larger world, we prepare kids for bit parts at best. As the marketplace changes, so do the skills that all students require. Today, the want ads for coal miners in Pennsylvania call for laptop computer skills.[29]

With economic prosperity producing budget surpluses, California lawmakers authorized ever-larger appropriations for schools to get wired, buy machines, distribute software, and train teachers to use the equipment in their classrooms. Silicon Valley entrepreneurs rushed to deploy new technologies. In 1997, Governor Pete Wilson and the legislature appropriated over $100 million for the first year of Digital High School grants, equal to $300 per student, to install computer networks in each of the state's 840 high schools over the next four years.[30]

Few California reforms have seen such a powerful yet loosely connected coalition of public officials, corporate executives, parents, and educators who agreed on the task of getting teachers and students to use computers in schools. And nowhere has that coalition support for such disparate purposes of making schools more productive, revolutionizing teaching and learning, conserving traditional values, and securing skilled workers attained virtual unanimity than in Silicon Valley.

The school reform rollercoaster continued in the initial decades of the twenty-first century. Since 2011, for example, when Governor Jerry

Brown returned to Sacramento, the State Board of Education, superintendent of instruction, and a friendly state legislature have enhanced funding formulas to increase money for schools and students, decentralized budgetary and staffing decisions previously exercised by state officials back to districts, and pushed for more integration of technology into teaching and learning.[31]

The context, then, for understanding what happened in Silicon Valley before, during, and after the surge of technology enthusiasm requires knowing that the state of California and its governor, legislature, and state superintendent have enormous influence on the funding and policies that guide what over a thousand districts, including the seventy-seven in Silicon Valley, do in their schools and classrooms.

OVERVIEW OF CHAPTERS

Two central questions guide this study of exemplary classrooms, schools, and districts in Silicon Valley that have made technology a seamless part of their lessons. In part 1, I focus on the first of these questions: *Have classroom, school, and district exemplars of technology integration been fully implemented and put into classroom practice?* To answer this question, part 1 looks at exemplars of integrating computers into classrooms, schools, and districts in Silicon Valley. (I have included an appendix that defines what an *exemplar* is—that is, criteria determining "best cases"—and how I recruited teachers and administrators to open their classrooms, schools, and districts to me. I also lay out the pros and cons of the methodology.)

In chapter 1, I present selected vignettes of forty-one teachers I observed who integrated digital technologies into lessons. Analyses of these exemplary teachers document their determined efforts to acquire resources, design lessons, and implement them within their classrooms. These Silicon Valley teachers will be compared with national surveys and case studies of teachers who have integrated technologies into their lessons in low-income to affluent schools.

As complex as it is for an individual teacher to mix daily use of high-tech devices and software into routine classroom practices, technology integration across a school is even more complex. In chapter 2, I explain why that is (e.g., changes in structures and cultures) and then segue to schools I observed in Silicon Valley that have integrated new technologies across the entire school, expecting teachers to teach lessons using particular hardware and software. Descriptions of teachers and analyses of these schools will comprise most of the chapter. I end the chapter by synthesizing national research studies of other schools that have also integrated new technologies and compare and contrast them with those I have analyzed.

Chapter 3 considers the technology integration programs at the district level. The difficulty of integrating technology into individual classroom work or whole school policy pales in comparison with trying to get an entire district's structures, culture, and activities to seamlessly— without any dropped stitches—act as a unit in integrating new technologies into instruction across many schools and hundreds or more classrooms. While most US districts have "technology plans" for using computers to make administration and instruction more efficient, only a few have fully implemented their technology plans and actually built the infrastructure and culture, tying both to curriculum and classroom instruction, while also creating professional development for teachers to implement integrated practices into classroom lessons (e.g., Mooresville, North Carolina). Through the history of two districts, including vignettes of lessons, I concentrate on how a school system integrates technology across its classrooms.

In chapter 4, I identify one of the overriding purposes of instructional policies pursuing technology integration: creating personalized learning, or the tailoring of individualized lessons to differences between students. I place the exemplars of classrooms, schools, and districts described in chapters 1 to 3 in the context of historical and contemporary struggles among reformers (the two wings of educational progressives then and now) over how best to school America's children and youth. I then create a continuum of personalized learning and locate the classrooms, schools, and districts I visited in 2016 along that spectrum. I explain how these "best cases" of integrating technology contain features that were apparent a century ago, when reformers struggled over how schools should improve (e.g., efficiency-driven versus whole child reformers). I then compare and contrast past and present reform efforts to highlight how technology integration today in the Silicon Valley embodies arguments between reformers then and now. I end with a discussion of the paradoxical issue of stability in practice amid obvious changes.

Part 2 explores the second critical question addressed in the book: *Have these exemplary teachers, schools, and districts altered classroom practices?* Turning an instructional policy into practice is a long drawn-out process and requires hard work on the part of both administrators and teachers. And what occurs in classrooms is not always what policy makers and administrators expected. In looking at "best cases" in Silicon Valley, technology integration had already been put into practice and what I observed and heard spanned both rhetoric and action.

Chapter 5 summarizes the results of teachers responding to my questions: Has technology changed how you teach students? If yes, how? If no, why not? I explore the near unanimity among my sample of forty-one teachers that they have altered (and "improved") their practice and in what ways they have made changes. I then explore the differences between a teacher's perspective about what constitutes change and "improvement" and the perspectives of researchers, especially historians, who see the same classroom and answer the questions differently.

This chapter gets at the complexity of the question of what *change* means when it comes to classroom practice and how different criteria teachers and researchers use come into play; continuity in some practices and changes in other complicates any answer to the question. Nonetheless, I offer an unambiguous answer to the question.

Finally, I review the accumulated changes I have seen in Silicon Valley at three organizational levels.

Chapter 6 summarizes the degree of change and stability in my sample of Silicon Valley classrooms, schools, and districts that have been designated exemplars of integrating new technologies into lessons. I answer succinctly the two central questions that I asked at the beginning of the book. Finally, I ask the "So what?" question and look at the policy implications of these findings for reform-minded decision makers, practitioners, researchers, and parents: *Have new technologies "succeeded" or "failed" in altering lessons that teachers typically teach?* I end in pointing out that the path of school reform using new technologies is closer to the flight of a butterfly than the path of a bullet.

If policy implementation occurred (the first four chapters) and if classroom practices changed (which I take up in chapters 5 and 6), then the meshing of new digital technologies into daily lessons made a difference in how these teachers taught. And if teaching practices did, indeed, change, then whether these altered practices made a difference in student learning becomes the next big question. While I will not answer that question in this book, determining what has changed in daily lessons in these "best cases" of classrooms, schools, and districts is the critical question that all reform-driven policies aimed at altering how teachers teach must answer first.

PART 1

Exemplars of Integrating Digital Technology into Classrooms, Schools, and Districts in Silicon Valley

ONE

The Classroom

Peek into the classroom of second-grade teacher Jennifer Auten, a thirteen-year veteran who teaches in the Cupertino, California, school district at Montclaire Elementary School, less than four miles away from Apple headquarters.[1] I observed her eighty-five-minute class one morning in April 2016.[2]

The carpeted room is festooned with student work, wall charts, guidelines for students to follow in different activities, mobiles hanging from ceiling, and tables for two to four students arranged around the room in no particular pattern.

Twenty students enter the room at 8:30 a.m. and immediately pick up iPads and earphones stowed in a corner. They open the devices and go to an app where they sign in as present for the day and choose a regular or vegetarian lunch. This means that Auten can move ahead with the lesson without stopping to take attendance or ask about lunch choices. Students know the routine.

Auten calls the class to order and brings up on the whiteboard a YouTube video that shows teenagers stretching, dancing, and singing. The seven-year-olds are familiar with the video; they cluster in the center of the room and jump up and down in time with the teenagers on the video. For the next ten minutes, they see and imitate additional videos of singing and stretching.

When I asked Auten whether this was a warm-up for the lesson, she told me that the state requires so many minutes of physical education, and while she does take students outside to exercise for thirty minutes, three times a week, she still wants her seven-year-olds to stretch every day.

After the videos, she gathers the class on the carpet in front of her and goes over what they will do in the morning. They will write a "research paragraph" that contains three important details. Carrying her laptop in one hand, she projects slides (she uses Apple TV and a ceiling-mounted projector to throw the image on her laptop screen to the whiteboard). She shows a sample paragraph on plants—she told me that all her second-graders can read. She reads the paragraph aloud and points out that it contains description of seeds, roots, and stems. She wants students to work together and write a practice paragraph on a topic they choose from an online folder called "Student Project Choice." Each pair or trio of students will choose the topic they want to research—dinosaurs, bicycles, planes, etc.

She asks the class, "I am looking for a presentation that that has how many details?" Most of the students hold up three fingers. She then turns to the assessment students will use to determine the quality of the paragraphs they write. She flashes it on screen and goes over each part (e.g., topic sentence, details, eye contact for presentation, neatness, etc.) asking students to hold their thumbs up or down to show if they understand. Auten goes over each part of the rubric (see figure 1.1). When she asks students whether they understand, most respond with a thumbs-up.

She then summarizes tasks for the class: research the topic, read materials using apps, take notes, prepare the presentation, and check the rubric before they turn the paragraph in. Auten then goes over the apps students will be using to research their topic, pointing out which ones work well. After a few students identify other apps, the teacher points out which ones might cause a device to crash. She asks if there are any questions, and three students ask about different apps and what to do if the program crashes. She answers their questions and explains that if students load too many visuals using Seesaw, the program may crash.[3] To an observer, it is clear that this class has done reports before.

FIGURE 1.1   Rubric for checking quality of research presentations for Jennifer Auten's second-grade class at Montclaire Elementary School

	1	2	3	4
Topic & conclusion	We don't have a topic or conclusion.	Either the topic or conclusion are missing or don't make sense.	We have a topic and conclusion that make sense.	Our topic and conclusion make sense and are not the same words.
Yellow: Details	We have fewer than 2 yellow details that support our topic.	We have 2 yellow details that support our topic. We have 3+ yellow details but they are not all expanded sentences.	We have 3 yellow details that support our topic, and they are all expanded sentences.	We have more than 3 yellow details that support our topic, and they are all expanded sentences.
Red: Explain/ examples	We have written incomplete sentences. We don't have reds for all our yellows.	We have fewer than 2 reds for each yellow. We have 2+ reds for each yellow, but they are not all expanded sentences.	We have 2 reds for each yellow, and they are all expanded sentences.	We have more than 2 reds for each yellow, and they are all expanded sentences.
Illustrations	We have fewer than 2 illustrations that support our details.	We have 2 illustrations that support our details.	We have 3 illustrations that support our details.	We have more than 3 illustrations that support our details.
Sources	We listed fewer than 2 sources we used.	We listed 2 sources we used.	We listed 3 sources we used.	We listed more than 3 sources we used.
Questions	We didn't include questions.	We included 1 on-topic question we still wonder about.	We included 2 on-topic questions we still wonder about.	We included 3+ on-topic questions we still wonder about.

When I asked Auten about this, she said they had been assigned an animal and are still working on that report.

She then asks students what they want to do first: choose a topic or choose their partners. Auten lets students decide by asking them to hold up one finger for choosing topic or two fingers for partners. Most students vote to choose partners first, and do so. The children then scatter to different tables and discuss which topics they will research and create a presentation on. Students walk around holding their iPads and discuss with classmates what they have chosen and what they are taking notes on.

For the rest of the period, students work in small groups and pairs. No one works individually. Auten moves from table to table answering questions, inquiring about topics students chose, readings on their iPad they had finished, and notes they have taken. Some students go across the room to two baskets sitting on a ledge that hold notecards and pencils. Three boys are sitting on carpet as they read and take notes.

Auten raises her arm and quiet descends on class as students raise their arms in reply—another signal that students have been socialized to follow. She praises students for how well they have been working on project and reminds them that they have twenty-five minutes left to work on the projects before morning recess. Groups return to work.

I walk around and ask different groups what they are working on—planes, dinosaurs (three trios), bicycles. I asked a seven-year-old in another group what a rubric is, and she explains that the rubric tells her whether she has done all parts of the report and what she has to do on each part of the presentation to get a high grade on the report. Auten continues to check in with different groups at tables.

Chimes toll for recess. Students line up with balls and other equipment they use during recess. Auten opens door and leads them out.[4]

Format and Content of the Lesson

The *format* of a lesson refers to the learning outcomes the teacher seeks, teacher-designed activities to reach those outcomes, instructional moves the teacher makes in seguing from one activity to another, handling student behavior, time management in moving the lesson along, and overcoming distractions that take students off task. This intricate cascade of goals and activities works best when the teacher cultivates a sense of community among students. Hence, student participation in activities to reach the lesson objectives the teacher has set becomes essential.

Typically, teachers plan lessons that call for a mix of whole group instruction, small group work, and activities where students work independently. These activities often vary by the lesson objectives, content to be learned, students' behavior, and teacher beliefs about how students best learn. Student involvement in asking and answering questions and making choices also varies depending on the teacher's lesson plan.[5]

Content refers to the specific subject matter and skills the teacher wants students to learn in reading, math, science, history, and foreign language.

The format of the lesson I observed was a sequence of teacher-directed activities geared to a beginning, middle, and end of the lesson, including a mix of whole group and small group activities. The teacher timed each segment and moved students from one activity to another for the eighty-five-minute period. Momentum in completing the lesson was obvious in how Auten signaled the time left for each activity. Students were involved in the lesson in choosing topics, deciding whom to partner with, and asking questions about the different software that they were to use to prepare their presentations. They appeared to be on task throughout the lesson.

For the content, students chose a research topic, read materials, took notes, began preparing a brief presentation, and knew they had to check the rubric before they turned the assignment in to the teacher. Skills included writing a paragraph that contained three details about the topic, finding examples to support each point, practicing self-assessment through the rubric, and constructing a presentation to the class. All content and skills are consistent with the state's Common Core standards for the second grade in English and language arts.[6]

When I asked Auten whether she had changed in how she taught since adopting iPads, she said:

> Yes, my teaching has changed. I'm sure I could think of more, but here are . . . ways that immediately come to mind.

Ready access to iPads has made it much easier to differentiate/ personalize learning for my students. It is easier to find a variety of ebooks or book apps written at a variety of reading levels on a specific topic or theme than if I had to track down physical books at the school or public library. Plus, students can highlight and take notes in the book and have material read to them if the reading level is still too challenging. Similarly, math apps/software allow students additional practice or challenge as needed even if everyone is working on a single concept, such as measuring in inches. iPads also allow students to watch re-teach videos related to math lesson.

With personalization/differentiation, students are working more at their target interest and level, which means fewer students who are frustrated or bored. And this in turn equates to a happier classroom environment.

With iPads, it's easier to change lessons in midflow or earlier in the day. I don't have to rely as much on the Xerox machine for worksheets for every lesson, so if I suddenly decide students "get it" and don't need to answer ten questions on a worksheet, we can skip it and I'm not frantically thinking about how I will fill that extra time without a ditto. Or if they need extra practice, I can use digital resources without hoping a coworker has a teacher manual with more practice problems. If we are reading a book about a character in Japan and a question comes up, a student, with guidance, can look up the answer for the class. If we need to slow down or pick up the pace, it's easier to manipulate a digital lesson than one that's a hard copy . . . In hard copy, I'd be borrowing/sharing teacher material books from Scholastic with my coworkers or making weekly trips to the school and public library, hoping I could find the right book at the right reading level.

Students can be more creative on an iPad. They can use a "green screen" app, make a movie, create a comic, create a book, create a presentation, draw a picture. Before, we were limited basically to drawing pictures or acting out a skit that was gone as soon as it was finished. Students can pick the mode of expressing themselves and their understanding that best fits their needs and personality.

There is more to engage students, especially the "early finishers." I have paper books and physical pentominoes and logic games and Legos, but only so many of each. All the students can play Rush Hour [a logic game app], etc. Plus, students can practice extra math if that's their passion or play chess or code or build with a block app. Some students definitely prefer the physical manipulatives, but with iPads it's easier to give more choice and find something that inspires each student.[7]

Jennifer Auten is an example of many teachers I observed during 2016 who saw that they could mix new technologies with classroom activities they had planned for each lesson. They tried out new devices and software and figured out what did and didn't work with their students. These individual teachers believed that laptops, tablets, and other devices were not add-ons but tools like the paper and pencil, notebooks, and whiteboards that helped them teach more efficiently and engage students to learn more, faster, and better. These teachers had expanded their repertoire to include new tools, using them flexibly and at the proper time to reach the learning objectives they set out to achieve.

Could Auten have taught this lesson without the many software programs she and her second-graders used? Yes, she could. But she believed that the iPads made her teaching easier and more productive and engaged students to learn more and better.[8]

While the schools in which teachers like Auten worked provided equipment and help to support the technologies—the infrastructure—individual teachers still decided to what extent they would use the new technologies in their daily lessons. School or district administrators provided the conditions, but teachers like Auten had the classroom autonomy to determine which tools to use. Other schools I observed were similar; they were also hospitable to new technologies and encouraged teachers to use them, but the decisions as to how much of the devices and software to use, in what activities, and with which content was left to the teacher who directed the lesson.

TEACHING *THE PEARL* TO THIRTEEN-YEAR-OLDS

Now look into John DiCosmo's seventh grade English classroom at Terman Middle School in Palo Alto (CA).[9]

Energetic, constantly moving around, jabbing, joshing, and dozens of other behaviors are natural for these young teenagers. Teaching a forty-five-minute lesson on John Steinbeck's *The Pearl*, then, is no easy task. And that is what faces John DiCosmo this October morning when I observe this lesson. DiCosmo describes this particular class as "boisterous."

DiCosmo, an experienced teacher in his mid-thirties who has taught for nearly a decade and is in his second year at Terman Middle School. He is a member of the seventh-grade team of teachers who plan lessons together. He wears a brown sport coat over a checked red and white shirt with a slate-blue tie and dark slacks. He, too, is in constant motion as he works through a series of activities with his twenty-five students. An instructional aide in the room works with about a half-dozen special education students going through the different activities that DiCosmo has planned.

As students enter the large room, they put their backpacks on tables, then take copies of *The Pearl* from bins in the back of the room and go to a cart to grab a Macbook laptop. On the interactive whiteboard (IWB), there is a Warm Up question that directs students' attention toward: "What would you do if you found a treasure of millions in cash, free and clear? How would your life change?"

The bell sounds and the period begins.

Students type in their answers to the warm up question, and their answers appear on the IWB (no names are attached to their answers). As DiCosmo scrolls through student responses—they are using Padlet software—he asks: "What's the pattern here in the class's answers?" Some students raise hands, and others yell out. He calls on students. He jots down on the whiteboard student responses: "Buying lots of things"; "Giving to charity."[10]

Then DiCosmo asks: "Why are we asking this question?" Some students guess that the book will be about finding a treasure. After listening to student responses, DiCosmo says that he has produced a video trailer summarizing and highlighting points in the story. He tells me later that one of the requirements he set for the unit on *The Pearl* is for students to produce their own video trailers for books they have selected, and he wanted students to see what a trailer could look like.

DiCosmo shows the brief video in which he has enlisted other teachers on his seventh-grade team to play the parts of the main characters, who live in a poor Mexican seaside village where the men dive for pearls and sell them to support their families. Students laugh loudly when they recognize their teachers.

After the trailer is finished, teacher asks the class: "What questions do you have about the book's early chapters?" Students' typed-in questions appear on the IWB. DiCosmo notes the rising noise as some students talk loudly to tablemates. He says, "If you are goofing around, I will kick your comment off the screen." Some students shush the others; class quiets down noticeably.

DiCosmo goes over student questions on the IWB. He then directs the class to look at the worksheet he has prepared about the characters introduced in the first chapter and asks the class to put in key quotes from the text. They will be hearing the first chapter read by a professional narrator. He asks students to follow the narrator and to take notes and raise questions. He hands out sticky notes so students can write notes that can be pasted to a book page and later transferred to the worksheet. DiCosmo then turns on the audio.

I scan the class. All the students have their books open and appear to be reading along as the narrator reads text. A few take notes on their sticky notes. The reader mentions "songs," and DiCosmo pauses the audio and asks: "What are the songs here?" He calls on students whether they have their hand up or not. To a few answers, he says, "Good." He tells the class that "the song of evil" will return. The audio resumes and students listen to the section where the scorpion stings the infant Coyotito and Kino and Juana fear that their child will die. Not a murmur in the rapt class.

Kino and Juana take Coyotito to the village doctor. After they knock on the heavy wooden door, the doctor's servant sees who is there and tells the doctor that a peasant and his wife are asking for help for their baby. The doctor tells the servant that since they do not have any money, to tell him that he is away. In anger, Kino smashes his fist into the door, splitting his knuckles and bloodying himself. Chapter 1 ends.

DiCosmo stops the audio and asks students to write down one reaction they have to the end of the chapter. I look around and see students writing on sticky notes and tapping away on their devices.

The wall phone in classroom rings. DiCosmo takes the call, says a few words, and hangs up. He then asks if students have posted their reaction to end of chapter 1. Many, but not all, are nodding their heads.

DiCosmo then segues to final activity of the lesson, a vocabulary drill using the game-based software Kahoot!. DiCosmo gets students to enter the PIN (projected on a slide) to access the game. The point of this game is to review word roots, including prefixes and suffixes, for a quiz next week. Students open their devices to the program and click to the slide on their screen that is exactly like the one shown on the screen in front of the room. This is a timed exercise with twenty-one questions. DiCosmo reminds students that they need to log in before they can record their answer to each question.[11]

A bouncy tune starts, and students go over a root or prefix/suffix (e.g., *chrono-, geo-, hydra-*), with four choices listed for each. Students have played this game often, and they are excited. A number are moving their bodies to and fro in time with the snappy melody. Each wants to be the fastest to answer and win. Eight of the thirteen-year-olds can't sit still; they go to the back of the room and stand next to an empty table ready and eager to punch a key for the correct answer. A countdown of how many seconds are left to complete each question shows on screen. As students tap in their answers, the number of students who submitted answers shows up on the IWB until nearly all the students have submitted their answers.

DiCosmo clicks a key, and a bar chart of the students' responses appears on the front screen (with no names) showing how many students have picked the correct answer and how many erred. Then he displays a scoreboard showing the top five students (with first names) who were the fastest and most accurate in choosing answers. Students applaud when the scoreboard reveals who is in the lead or whether the lead has changed with each question.

After finishing the competitive game, DiCosmo gives raffle tickets to the five winners; every Friday, he raffles off prizes (e.g., candy, the chance to move your seat elsewhere in the class).

With only a few minutes left in the period, DiCosmo asks students to log off and return their devices to the cart. He reminds them about homework due next class and tells them to post one "meaningful comment, question, or reply to chapter 1."

The buzzer sounds and students leave.

Format and Content of the Lesson

As in Jennifer Auten's second-grade class, these seventh-graders were as intimately conversant with the devices and software as they were with notebooks, pen, and paper. The lesson John DiCosmo taught was aligned to California Common Core standards.[12]

The forty-five-minute lesson format used whole group, small group, and independent activities in a fast-moving sequence, each seldom lasting more than ten to fifteen minutes each. As the lesson unfolded, DiCosmo segued from whole group discussions on the book and preparation of a video trailer to listening to a reading of the first chapter of *The Pearl* to students independently taking notes to a competitive, rousing vocabulary game. Students easily shifted from jotting down notes to looking up words on their tablets. Even with the interruption of the phone call, the lesson moved smoothly from one activity to another. The back-and-forth between old and new technologies appeared seamless to me. DiCosmo admonished the class once during the opening of the lesson; otherwise, these thirteen-year-olds were on task as the activities frequently shifted over the forty-five-minute lesson. Students easily participated in answering teacher questions, asked some of their own about assignments, inquired about characters in *The Pearl*, and, of course, in the final lesson segment, enthusiastically took part in the contest on prefixes and suffixes.

DiCosmo had students use devices (including the IWB) and software mixed with familiar classroom tasks to convey both content and skills. There were no bumps in the lesson; it ran smoothly.

When I asked DiCosmo whether he had changed the way he taught since using technology, he said:

> As a digital native, I have always used computers in my lessons, but each year, my teaching changes a little more to put students at the center of the lessons. I have used technology to engage my middle schoolers from the first day I stepped into the classroom, but I am increasingly "flipping" lessons to support student access to materials and to differentiate my instruction. What has changed over the course of ten years is the integration and consistent access to tech resources such as laptops . . . Tools like Google Drive and learning management systems (such as Schoology) enable me to engage twenty-first-century learners and collaborate with colleagues in an unprecedented way.[13]

Like Jennifer Auten, John DiCosmo is an example of those teachers who mixed new technologies into the classroom activities they plan and enact to reach the content and skill goals they sought. These teachers had expanded their familiar array of teaching tools to include the available hard- and software, knowing when and where to use these tools to achieve their lesson objectives.

Could DiCosmo have taught this English lesson without the technology the middle school students used? Yes, he could. But he felt that the devices and software helped him manage the teaching more efficiently than he could before and opened up possibilities for students—vocabulary drill as a software game and making a film trailer for *The Pearl*—that made possible, in his opinion, better teaching and learning.[14]

A HIGH SCHOOL SPANISH LESSON

Move now to a high school Spanish lesson of a teacher whom a district technology coordinator identified as a skilled user regularly using new technologies to teach a foreign language.[15]

Nicole Elenz-Martin teaches at Aragon High School. An eleven-year veteran, she teaches Spanish at levels 3 through 6 (including Advanced Placement). Elenz-Martin is also an instructional coach in the district and an instructor in the Stanford World Language Project.[16] On February 2016, I observed Elenz-Martin's eight-five-minute lesson for her Spanish 3 class.

Thirty-three students are present at 8 a.m. The classroom has six rows of six desks, each facing the IWB that defines the front of the room. The teacher's desk is in the rear the classroom. Student work, photos, and sayings in Spanish are posted on the walls. I sit in the rear to better scan the class and watch the activities unfold over the next eighty-five minutes.

Students have taken Chromebooks from an in-classroom cart. Many also have pens and paper out. A note on the whiteboard directs students to click on a link and see the "Daily Agenda." On the day I am there, the agenda lists what will occur and objectives for the lesson. The entire time is to be spent on learning new vocabulary, with a focus on verbs and how to use them with indirect object pronouns to "express opinions in a culturally accurate/appropriate way."

Except for occasional teacher ad libs and explanations, the class I saw was conducted entirely in Spanish. Elenz-Martin pursued a sequence of activities in the lesson, first introducing different verb infinitives (e.g., *gustar, encantar, interestar, disgustar*) in worksheets, slides on the IWB, and a constant patter of questions-and-answers with students. Then she had prepared tasks that required students to practice the different verb forms with one another, using examples from pop culture, sports, food, clothes, and other familiar topics. This abbreviated description of the lesson suggests the degree of planning that she had to do in moving the class through these fast-paced tasks, the frequent and intense student participation, and the covering of grammar.

In one example, Elenz-Martin flashes *gustar* ("to like") on the whiteboard and asks students to use it in sentence. She gives examples of Oprah Winfrey, tacos from local restaurants, chocolate pastry, Netflix, and Starbucks. She calls on individual students to explain why they like (or don't like) various celebrities, food, films, and coffee. She often responds, "Excelente!" She then asks students to talk to their neighbors and create sentences using the verb. Music plays in the background. When it stops, the students get up and move to another desk to talk to another neighbor about another verb. This goes on for about ten minutes, with students pairing up with different students whenever the music stops.

Elenz-Martin passes out a worksheet with incomplete sentences; students have to fill in direct and indirect objects for verbs. The drill is also on their tablet screens. Students begin work on filling in sentences, and Elenz-Martin walks up and down aisles checking what they are entering on screen and answering questions. After about ten minutes, students have completed filling in the sentences on their tablets. She quickly scans what students have entered and then moves onto the next activity.

She clicks her laptop and the phrase "Á los Warriors" (a reference to the NBA championship basketball team, the Golden State Warriors) appears on the IWB. She asks students to pair up and use verbs with indirect object pronouns. She then calls on students for their sentences. This goes on for a few minutes before Elenz-Martin begins to flash other verbs and examples:

- Me encanta Instagram.
- No me interesa Facebook.
- Me encanta vivir en San Mateo.

Students vote on their Chromebooks and Elenz-Martin gets instant results of students' preferences as she also calls on students (or they volunteer) their answers. She offers many "Muy biens."

She then asks students to give thumbs up/thumbs down as to whether they understand the concept of using the verb, direct object, etc.

Elenz-Martin segues quickly to a review of verbs by flashing a series of photos that she has prepared. Photos flit rapidly across the screen with accompanying infinitives. For example, she shows a dog with a water bottle on its head accompanying the verb *doler* ("to ache"). Then another of a slice of pizza with the verb *quedar* ("to remain"), followed swiftly by yet another picture of dollars and the word *sobrar* ("to be more than enough"). Elenz-Martin calls on students to say what each verb means and to make up a sentence with it for each photo, and students respond chorally in Spanish, with much laughter.

For the final activity, Elenz-Martin passes out another worksheet, asking the class to fill in the blanks in seven sentences using verbs and indirect objects. She walks up and down rows, checking work and answering questions. She brings this activity to a close by calling on individual students to tell what verb they used to fill in blanks.

Finally, she asks students to log out and return the Chromebooks to the cart. As the buzzer sounds, this swift minute-by-minute lesson comes to an end.

At the end of the lesson I observed, we talked about what I had seen, and she quoted Abe Lincoln's thought about the importance of preparation before the real work begins: "If I had six hours to chop down the tree, I would spend the first four hours sharpening the axe." The quote captures much of the unseen planning, especially the setting of lesson goals and linked activities, that goes into Elenz-Martin's classes.

Format and Content of the Lesson

The lesson Elenz-Martin taught was aligned to California Common Core standards. The eighty-five-minute lesson format mixed whole group, small group, and independent activities in a sequence that seldom lasted more than five to fifteen minutes each. The bulk of the activities were whole group guided recitation and discussion, with interludes of pairs of students working together and individual students completing exercises on handouts. I did observe a sense of solidarity among students in their frequent laughter, easy participation in answering teacher questions, willingness to move smartly from one activity to another, and sharing the visible enjoyment Elenz-Martin displayed in teaching a class on grammar.

Elenz-Martin had students use devices (including the IWB) and software mixed with familiar classroom tasks: question-answer recitation had high participation rates from students; constant application of words to real-world people and events triggered interest and laughter; showing humorous photos of the verbs in action on the IWB connected the word to life experiences; students often took notes by hand; whole class choral responses of verbs frequently wrapped up an activity. Activities where students used their devices flowed quickly as they listened and took notes on the screen and in their notebooks. The use of technology was in the background rather than foreground.

I asked Elenz-Martin whether her practice of teaching had changed as a result of using these technologies. She answered:

My teaching—in terms of pedagogical strategy and philosophical beliefs about World Language instruction—has not changed because of my regular use of technology; however, the regular use of Chromebooks in my classroom has dramatically changed my access to student learning, monitoring of their proficiency development, and my ability to cover more material over the course of a school year.

She gave examples:

My students are required to be much more engaged and participatory in their learning because of their interaction with my lessons through technology. When covering material in class, every student can interact with the presentation on my SmartBoard to share answers, respond to polls, or ask questions (Pear Deck, Nearpod, Google Forms, etc.). This has informed my instruction immensely and has allowed me to change my lesson on the fly to ensure understanding before moving on.

Students practice new vocabulary and/or comprehension questions with Quizlet, for example, and I can see their results and areas of challenge in real time. It allows me to change my path of instruction if necessary, as stated above, and it also allows me to personalize the learning for each student's level and need.

Students have built classroom community and have strengthened camaraderie with review games (Quizlet Live, Socrative Space

Race, and Kahoot!). Not only has light "gaming" sparked excitement and interest for the students in learning the material, but it has allowed me to formatively assess each student's understanding and learning on a daily basis. The comfort level and "fun" among classmates has allowed them to be better risk-takers and communicators with one another, and this is critical for a language class where students really need to feel confident and safe around their classmates.

Students have had individual access to more authentic materials from around the world, which is of course extremely important for culture and language learning. Their interaction with videos, texts, and audio can be documented in EDpuzzle, Go Formative, and Google Classroom. I can see their engagement with the material in a way that I was never able to assess before, and I can respond to students both individually and as a group much more efficiently and effectively. I can see what they are learning about a culture and I can motivate them to respond more critically to what they are seeing and comparing to their own culture.

Students are also able to show communicative proficiency development in ways that they were never able to before. Through digital portfolios with Seesaw, Google Classroom, and even simple voice recordings on a smartphone, students can record their voices and video to create an entire library of progress over time; there is evidence of growth that both they and I can applaud or question.

With regards to efficiency, having a "hyper doc" of all my lesson materials in one place makes transitions between media, internet sites, lectures, and partner/group interactions seamless. Students' ability to transfer to and from different sites on the computer during a class period is quick and seemingly effortless. Long transition times and "waiting for teacher" times are almost nonexistent, and the participation percentage is much higher than it was before access to technology.

Then Elenz-Martin continued to answer my question by pointing out how her use of technology had not altered the core of how she teaches:

Certain parts of teaching can never be replaced, enhanced, or changed by technology. The very most critical aspect of my teaching is the relationship that I create with each and every one of my students. Without having a strong, trusting, solid, and respectful relationship with each student, he or she is lost in my classroom and will be unable to learn from my teaching. Because I speak almost exclusively in Spanish, the oral communication in my classroom and the relationships with my students are the very cornerstones of my teaching.

Therefore, technology has not replaced the way I speak or communicate with my students, and since I am a Spanish teacher, they are still listening and responding to me and to each other through oral communication much more than with the technology. The amount that I expect them to speak with me and communicate with one another is the same as it has always been, even before technology access . . .

I passionately believe in the importance of "student talk" and participation for learning, especially when it comes to working with partners and small groups on a communicative and/or complex task. Technology is almost nonexistent in my classroom when students are working on an assignment that involves learning through talking with one another. Without going into too much detail, technology hardly has changed the way I engage students in partner and group work.

Most of my teaching strategies that are specific to World Language Instruction (comprehensible input strategies and comprehension checks, for example) have not been changed by our use of technology, and these are key components of my teaching practice. While the use of PowerPoint/Google Slides and a Smart-Board may supplement what it used to be (magazine clippings or pictures shown on an overhead projector transparency), it is essentially the same teaching activity.

Like Jennifer Auten and John DiCosmo, Nicole Elenz-Martin is an example of those teachers who had stretched their usual toolkit of ways to plan and teach a lesson to include new technologies, applying them when and where easily and smoothly to reach their lesson objectives.

Could Elenz-Martin have taught this Spanish lesson without the technology her high school students used? Yes, she could. She pointed out to me how much planning it took—that Abe Lincoln quote again—and were she not to have had access to the Internet for the photos for examples of verbs in use, she would have eventually found them and used the overhead projector instead. In her answers to my questions, Elenz-Martin told me that she found the technologies helpful in moving the grammar lesson along at a fast and manageable pace, covering more content than she usually does, and having remarkable access to resources both for her and her students. And as with the other teachers, these students used the tablets as naturally as breathing. Here again, the teacher use of the new technologies was clearly in the background of the lesson.[17]

PUTTING THESE TEACHERS IN CONTEXT

Two questions arise when considering how these teachers identified as exemplary used technology in their classrooms:

- What do these Silicon Valley teachers have in common?
- How alike and unlike are these teachers to peers across the country?

What Do These Silicon Valley Teachers Have in Common?

In answering the first question, it is clear that each of the districts and schools in which these elementary and secondary teachers taught had created favorable conditions for access to and use of new technologies, including directing ample resources to that end. The three districts in which these teachers taught were low-poverty (between 2 and 21 percent of students identified as eligible for free and reduced-price lunch). Nearly all students—including low-income ones—were geared to graduating high school and entering college.[18]

District decisions to make computers and software available to teachers, along with ubiquitous cable and wireless connections, made it possible for all teachers in the school to, at a minimum, experiment with integrating computers into their lessons.

Access to devices was far easier than for an earlier generation of teachers (of the 1980s and 1990s) who wanted to use the new technologies. Classroom use, however, depended on the individual teacher's decision. None of the schools or districts required teachers to employ laptops or tablets. Each district in which the teachers worked had a technology coordinator who brokered connections between technology-motivated teachers, encouraged cross-school collaboration among teachers, held workshops on use of the devices for lessons, and helped individual teachers. Surely, pro-technology principals also brought additional resources and suggestions to their teachers in these schools. Yet no mandate that teachers had to use the new technologies existed within the three districts.

These teachers determined whether they would ask for help from the coordinator, attend workshops, and meet with like-minded teachers. In a school, teachers would seek out other teachers who had already launched into integrating, say, tablet software into their daily practice or find a colleague who also wanted to begin using technology in the classroom. Because these teachers voluntarily took the initiative, integration of computers into lessons varied a great deal among their colleagues in schools where Jennifer Auten, John DiCosmo, and Nicole Elenz-Martin taught.

Teachers who did seek out ways of integrating technology into their lessons—often consulting with trusted colleagues and working with like-minded teachers in and out of the district—looked at their lessons to see how software could help them do what they intended to do faster and better than they had before. They wanted these devices and software to be in the background, not the foreground, of teaching. They constructed lessons that used new technologies as routinely as notebooks, paper, and pencils have been (and continue to be) used in classrooms. They exercised their autonomy in creating classes that peers called "exemplary."

These three teachers' beliefs in how best to teach and how best students learn, their expertise in teaching content and skills, their professional engagement with technology-minded educators, plus the school and district's establishing of promising conditions can account, in part, for their regular use of new technologies in the ways I described their lessons.

They also expressed the strong belief that using the new technologies regularly in their lessons had made securing resources for students easier, opened up arenas for higher rates of student participation, reduced distractions, and more efficient managing of the lessons they taught.

So these professionally engaged teachers identified as exemplary worked in districts where favorable conditions permitted both teacher and student access and use to new technologies. District help, not mandates, however, made it possible for these teachers to choose how, when, and under what conditions to use devices and software in their classrooms. That autonomy was crucial for them to experiment in their lessons with software to increase their efficiency in managing content and skills and engage classes in ways that resonated with students.

How Alike and Unlike Are These Teachers to Peers Across the Country?

Periodic teacher surveys and occasional case studies suggest that these three teachers (and the others I observed) are, indeed, standouts among teachers in mingling technology into their lessons since the late 1990s.[19]

In a highly regarded 1998 survey, educational researcher Henry Becker found that most elementary teachers used school computer labs for their students over the course of a day at least once a week. In secondary school academic subjects, fewer than one out of four English teachers used computers once a week. Among other academic teachers, one out of six science teachers, one out of eight social studies teachers and one of nine math teachers had used computers at least once a week. Use diverged noticeably between teachers in low- and high-poverty schools. The "digital divide" both in access and use was clearly evident.

Becker's survey revealed that most elementary and secondary teachers were occasional, not frequent, users (then defined as once weekly). The most common use of the desktop computers either in classrooms or labs was word processing, followed by reference materials on CD-ROMS, and games.[20]

Since then, teacher use of computers has increased across grade levels, in frequency, and with varied instructional and administrative software. Another survey administered by the National Center for Education Statistics in 2008 documents a substantial uptick in different uses of devices by more teachers.

The 2008 survey of a random sample of forty-one hundred–plus teachers across all states found that the number of students with limited access to desktop and handheld devices dropped dramatically—from double-digits a decade earlier to just over five students per computer. Nearly 70 percent of teachers reported that they used computers "often" in their classroom or labs. Software was mainly used for word processing (96 percent), Internet (91 percent), spreadsheets and graphing programs (61 percent), and making presentations (63 percent). The difference between high- and low-poverty schools continued but had narrowed somewhat.[21]

Finally, a 2013 Pew study done with the National Writing Project and the College Board combined online and face-to-face focus groups with a random sample survey of nearly twenty-two thousand Advanced Placement and National Writing Project teachers about their attitudes and use of technologies in lessons. The report named the respondents "'leading-edge teachers' who are actively involved with the College Board and/or the National Writing Project and are therefore beneficiaries of resources and training not common to all teachers." These selected secondary school teachers are reasonable national comparisons with the exemplary teachers that district technology coordinators, peers, and media identified in this study.[22]

What the teachers who responded to the online survey said about their teaching activities during a lesson sounded very close to the three teachers I described in this chapter and those I will profile in chapters 2 and 3. For example, in response to the prompt: "Tell us if you ever have your students . . . do any of the following":

- 95 percent of the teachers said that their students "research or search for information online."
- 79 percent said students "access or download assignments from an online site."
- 76 percent said students "submit assignments online."
- 36 percent said that students "edit or revise their own work using a collaborative web-based tool such as GoogleDocs."[23]

Teacher responses about their classroom activities in a national survey certainly overlap with those activities I described in my observations of Jennifer Auten, John DiCosmo's and Nicole Elenz-Martin's lessons. But how those surveyed teachers integrated activities into the beginning, middle, and end of a fifty- to ninety-minute lesson, I do not know. Overall, then, there are commonalities in the schools and districts that tie together the three exemplars whose lessons I described. Moreover, there is some overlap in lesson activities of the three teachers with their national peers.

Nonetheless, differences between these three teachers and teacher responses to national surveys do exist. Given the limited evidence— self-reports, peer recommendations, and descriptions of lessons by an outside observer—these Silicon Valley teachers fit the label "exemplary" in integrating technologies into their lessons.

But both my descriptions and national surveys of teachers document the opinions and activities of individual teachers voluntarily using technology in their lessons, not entire schools. Voluntarism, however, is limited in getting most teachers to use new technologies effortlessly in teaching lessons. Instructional policies that rely on voluntarism seldom gain most teachers' allegiance and use in classrooms. The assumption that an innovation—new tablets, reading or math software—is so good that it will spread rapidly among eager professionals trusts contagion far more than the history of school reforms could offer.[24]

There are schools in Silicon Valley that go beyond individual teachers deciding whether and how to integrate technologies into their lessons. Schools where all teachers integrate technology into their lessons because it is the instructional policy for the school and expected as part of their daily work in classrooms are uncommon but do exist. Chapter 2 describes such schools.

TWO

The School

Kristel Hsiao teaches science at Summit Prep, a charter school in Redwood City, California. She is a five-year veteran of teaching in Chicago's Solorio Academy High School, and one of its founding teachers. While there, she developed science curricula and piloted the use of iPad carts in classrooms. After moving to the Bay Area, she was hired to teach biology at Summit Prep. I observed her ninety-minute lesson in March 2016.[1]

As the mostly ninth-grade students enter the class, Hsiao greets each one with a hearty "Good morning!" and a high-five. Two or three students sit at each black-topped table facing the front of the room. There are twenty-six students in the room. Precisely at 10:40, class begins. Hsiao directs the students' attention to the Warm Up on a slide projected on the front screen:

Answer three questions:
- What did you do over the weekend?
- What are you looking forward to this week?
- What are you concerned about this week?

Students open their Chromebooks and click away. Two students are dallying, and Hsiao says, "Everyone should be working. No talking." After five minutes, she says, "Eyeballs and ears up here. Close computers." She counts down from 5, and students close the lids of their devices. She then returns to the agenda for the day:

- Warm Up
- Group Work—Step 1
- Presentations!
- Exit Slip[2]

Student presentations are the centerpiece of the lesson; students will report on an article they have read and analyzed. The student sitting next to me tells me she is nervous about her report. But Hsiao wants to cover more before students do their presentations.

She goes over key features of the new DNA barcoding project that the class will work on for next four weeks. Hsiao and other biology teachers in the charter network chose the DNA project. She describes the work they will do each week, the upcoming spring break, the two weeks away from class to do "Expeditions," and when they will finish the DNA unit. "Any questions?" she asks. Three students want to know about dates, lab reports, etc.[3]

Hsiao then asks students to turn to next task, Group Work—Step 1, on cognitive skills (she and students call them "cog skills") they will be covering for today's activities. The class knows the process, and Hsiao lists what each pair and trio is to do:[4]

- Right Partner: Read Cog Skill
- Today's cog skill is . . .
- To get an A we must . . .
- Left Partner: Read Objective
- By the end of class, students will be able to . . .
- Middle (or Right) Partner: Read Agenda
- First, we will . . . Then, we will . . . Finally, we will . . .

After five to seven minutes of this group work, Hsiao tells class that they now have to do self-assessment for the first step in their Personal Learning Plan (PLP).[5] This is the first thing students do when they begin a new project. They are familiar with process of setting goals for themselves and determining what level they wish to achieve. A rubric lays out specific behaviors for each skill. They begin reading and clicking away on their Chromebooks. A few put in earbuds, and everyone switches their seats to face the rear of the classroom.

When I asked a student why they moved their chairs, she told me that it is less distracting to face the back of room when they are setting goals and figuring out what level they should set for themselves and the grade they would seek. Students tap away and go over each part of this introduction to the DNA project. Hsiao asks student next to me to show what is on her screen and what she is doing. She does.[6]

This activity continues for about fifteen minutes as Hsiao moves around the classroom answering questions, checking individual students entries, and asking particular students why they have assessed themselves at the level they chose. As students work through this initial step, she says that if there are students who want comments on their presentation—the next activity—they should let her access their presentations now and she will look at them. She brings this activity to a close and moves to student presentations.

Before calling on the first student to come to front and present, Hsiao flashes the class norms for presentations onto the interactive whiteboard (IWB) at the front of the class:

BEFORE PRESENTING:
- ☐ Send Mrs. Hsiao a link to your presentation.
- ☐ The audience will clap politely as you walk up to the stage.

WHILE PRESENTING:
- ☐ Your peers will grade you using the Oral Presentation Scoring Guide.
- ☐ Your teacher will take these scores into consideration when she grades you.

AFTER PRESENTING:
- ☐ Audience will clap calmly and politely.
- ☐ Audience will ask up to 3 questions.
- ☐ Mrs. Hsiao will input your grade by the end of the day.

In the five presentations I hear, students answer four pre-set questions:

- What claim does author make in article?
- What is my analysis of claim? Evidence author used and what I thought of it.
- Why is claim important?
- Why did I choose this article?

In scanning the class during the presentations, I note that every student is attending to presenter. After each presentation, the student asks for questions from other members of the class. After the presenter answers the questions, Hsiao asks students to evaluate the presentation. Completed evaluations go to each student (they will see their peers' opinions later).

Rather than go over each PowerPoint presentation, I will describe one. This student analyzed an article about colorblindness entitled: "Your Color Red Could Really Be My Blue."[7] She went over each of the four questions in especially clear and concise sentences, showed a video of monkeys being injected with a virus that would change cones in the eyes to see other colors, and added information drawn from the article about colorblindness. At the end of her PowerPoint, she asked for questions, and there were a half-dozen. The class applauded vigorously, then each student, as they had done with the earlier PowerPoint talks, rated their classmate's presentation.

After last student presents, the class applauds and questions are asked, Hsiao counts down from 5 to get students' attention. After the class quiets, Hsiao compliments the presenters: "They were excellent." Then she segues to final task of lesson, which is to get students to move to Step 1 of DNA barcoding unit ("Learn Basics of DNA"). They will study the DNA of different Husky dogs and later seafood animals.[8]

Hsiao asks that students get in their teams (she had preassigned students to each team, and their names appear on a screen slide), assign roles for what each team member is to do in their teams, and use readings and video materials. To reinforce their understanding of task, she asks: "What step will we be working on?" and has students respond aloud, "Step 1." Students continue working in teams as the class ends.

Format and Content of the Lesson

Typically, teachers plan lessons that call for a mix of whole group instruction, small group work, and independent activities. That is the format. As the biology lesson unfolded, each of these activities came into play. The teacher is timekeeper, constantly aware of how many minutes are allotted to each activity and responsible for the momentum of the lesson. Student participation ran high and low during the course of these lesson segments. From individual recording of work in their PLP to making PowerPoint presentations to small group work, student involvement varied with the activity that Hsiao had put into play.

In terms of *content*—the specific subject matter and skills that Hsiao wanted to achieve in her introductory lesson for the new DNA unit—the materials that she shared with me, aligned with Common Core concepts and skills in biology.

Here was a teacher-directed lesson designed and implemented by an experienced biology teacher that reinforced class norms—what academics call *socialization*—with Hsiao simultaneously linking lesson activities to the beginning of a project (and Common Core content and skills), having students report on their analyses of articles they read, and for ninety minutes having "eyes in the back of her head" to prevent misbehavior. The sheer complexity of teaching was on full display during the lesson.

SUMMIT PUBLIC SCHOOLS

Hsiao was one of nine teachers I observed in two of the Summit charter schools. Diane Tavenner founded Summit Public Schools, a network of eight charter schools in Silicon Valley. A Stanford University graduate of a principals' program, she and a group of parents and teachers secured a charter and established Summit Prep in Redwood City, California. As of

2015, Summit Prep had nearly four hundred students, of whom 60 percent were Latino, 25 percent white, 8 percent Asian, and the rest African American and multiracial. Just over 50 percent of the students were eligible for free and reduced-price meals. Fourteen percent had disabilities and 10 percent were English language learners.[9]

Summit schools have been working and reworking an instructional design containing many moving parts—some of which are captured in my description of Kristel Hsiao's biology class—for nearly fifteen years. Over that period, they have amended, deleted, and added program features as administrators and faculty learned what worked and what didn't. Desktops and laptops had always been part of the instructional mix. The time span, the stability in staff, their awareness of context, and shifting demographics all came into play as Summit leaders and faculty figured out what to do in the years since the founding of the different schools.

A turning point for the network came around 2011 when Tavenner scanned the figures for Summit graduates who completed a four-year college degree. Nearly 100 percent of Summit graduates entered higher education, yet only 55 percent got their college degree. Even though the percentage was higher than for non-Summit high schools in the area, for Tavenner and her staff, it was a shocker that over four out of ten Summit graduates failed to get a bachelor's degree.[10]

Tavenner and Summit staff interviewed former students who completed college and those who didn't. Out of those interviews emerged a rethinking of what Summit schools could do better to prepare their students to succeed in college. The key, they felt, was to continue the strong teacher-student relationships that grounded learning for predominately minority students. Beyond that foundation, however, Summit students had to not only learn the academic content and skills embedded in the curriculum wired to Common Core standards but also learn to set personal goals, assess their progress toward those goals, and figure out what they needed to know and where to get that knowledge. In short, Summit students had to become thoughtful, independent, skill- and knowledge-smart learners who could successfully negotiate four years of college.

And here is where technologies went beyond their routine use as a word-processing, spreadsheet, and research tool. Instead, the instructional vision was to embed technology thoroughly into daily lessons so it would become as familiar as paper, pens, and notebooks to achieve those ends.[11]

Summit staff teamed up with Facebook software engineers—at no cost to the network—to create a Personalized Learning Platform harnessed to the existing features of the program: project-based learning, acquiring cognitive skills, practicing "habits of success," Expeditions, and mentoring individual and small groups of students during the school day.

By 2016, Summit's mission had remained the same, but a series of program changes had thoroughly embedded the role of technology into the daily activities of network schools. The schoolwide instructional policy now is that all Summit teachers are expected to mentor students before, during, and after the school day *and* integrate new technologies into their daily lessons. No teacher can opt out; technology is to be integrated into the format and content of every lesson—no ifs, ands, or buts.[12] Over the years that this policy was developed, the Summit network has been written about often and positively as an innovative charter network of schools using technologies in creative, integrated ways.[13]

Adam Carter arranged for me to visit two of the network schools: Summit Prep (Redwood City) and Rainier (San Jose). I observed nine teachers across different academic subjects teach ninety-minute lessons during what the schools call "project time." I also interviewed the two directors (or principals).

In all instances, the teachers I observed had integrated the software they had loaded onto students' Chromebooks, the playlists of videos and links to articles for projects teachers had chosen, and the Personalized Learning Platform. The charter network claims that through the platform, teachers can give each student individual help in class and out of class as mentors while students negotiate their ways through academic content and skills.

In the two schools, I observed students working on teacher-chosen projects in different academic subjects. Students used their Chromebooks frequently to access their playlists of sources that teachers compiled and using both the Personalized Platform and Plan on their own initiative and at the teachers' direction. For example, here is a lesson I observed at Summit Rainier. The class was held in a portable classroom on the Mount Pleasant High School campus in East San Jose.[14]

KATIE GODDARD'S WORLD STUDIES LESSON

One March morning in 2016, the young, slim teacher stands on the chair in the middle of the classroom to be heard above ninth-grade students clustered in the four corners of the portable classroom. The students are chattering about why they agree or disagree with the statement Katie Goddard, the teacher, put on the IWB: "There is no single group responsible for the crime of slavery. African rulers are equally as guilty for slavery." Depending on their answers, students have clustered into different corners labeled "Strongly agree," "Agree," "Disagree," and "Strongly disagree." Goddard asks students in each corner why they agree or disagree with statement. After a few students give their reasons, some classmates change their minds and migrate to different corners, making the classroom a swirl of movement. This activity occurred in the middle of a ninety-five-minute block in World Studies, when Goddard was introducing a new unit on imperialism.

Goddard had begun the class with a Warm Up question: "Should the U.S. pay reparations to black Americans whose families have been slaves?" After telling students to put away their cells and Chromebooks, she hands out two short op-ed pieces arguing opposite sides of the question. One argues that that the issues of who should pay and who should receive reparations for enslaving Africans are contested and confused. The other op-ed argues that the British should pay reparations to Kenyans for what they did in colonizing that African nation. Goddard asks the twenty-four ninth-graders to "read and chunk the text" for each opinion piece. She reminds the class to write a one-line summary of each op-ed paragraph and indicate whether they agree or disagree with it.

As students write in their notebooks, Goddard, holding a clipboard, walks around the classroom of thirteen tables, each seating two students facing the IWB at the front of the classroom, answering questions and checking to see what students are writing. Goddard asks students to hold up fingers indicating how many more minutes they want to finish task. Some hold up one, others two and three.

For those who have finished, she offers two options for them to do. She then asks students to share their summaries and opinions with their partners. As students start talking to one another, Goddard interrupts and says: "Remember, in working together, you need to turn to your partner, move your body to face one another, and listen carefully to what your partner says." Students resume talking.

When she sees that nearly all students have completed the task, she asks them for their summaries of the two articles and which one they agree/disagree with most. Students are initially reluctant to commit to a position but as a few offer their opinions, Goddard teases out the reasons embedded in arguments for and against reparations. This is the moment when she asks all the students to take a position on the statement "There is no single group responsible for the crime of slavery. African rulers are equally as guilty for slavery" and move to a corner of the room.

This Warm Up and debate about reparations were initial activities in the lesson introducing imperialism. After starting with the contentious contemporary question of reparations for slavery, Goddard would move to instances of European countries colonizing the Congo and India in the nineteenth and twentieth centuries and consider the human costs of these policies.

Before I describe the rest of the lesson, a few words about the teacher and the Rainier campus of Summit charter schools. Goddard is finishing her third year of teaching. A Brown University graduate, she completed a master's degree and teaching credential at a Bay Area teacher education program. When I asked, "Why cóme to Summit?" Goddard says: "I knew I wanted a place where there was an emphasis on mentoring students with on-site coaching that supports my practice and collaboration among teachers."

Goddard's enthusiasm for teaching history is written on the windows and walls. "YOU CAN DO THIS" is pasted in large capital letters across one of the two classroom windows. On a rear wall are quotations: "The Past Informs the Present"; "Case Studies Reveal Patterns in History." In the classroom, besides the familiar countdown to get students attention ("I'm counting down from 5"), Goddard also switches student seats daily. She has a stack of cards with student names and places a card on each desk every morning, thus accomplishing two things that she prizes: with much student pairing up and "tellback" exercises, she wants students to get to know each other; second, the tactic is a quick way of taking attendance since when the seat at a table is empty, she picks up the cards and knows exactly who is absent. As her quote indicates and her behavior in this lesson mirrors, Goddard likes being at Summit Rainier.

Summit Rainier high school was founded by a group of parents and Summit leaders who received a charter from the East Side Union High School district in 2011. With about 270 students (60 percent Latino, 17 Asian and Filipino, 15 white, 3 African American; and just over half eligible for free and reduced-price lunch), Rainier is located on the campus of Mt. Pleasant High School, on a former parking lot. There are seventeen portable classrooms, an office, and a faculty lounge. Summit Rainier is on a block schedule of ninety-five-minute periods, and the students have access to Mt. Pleasant High School for certain activities. One hundred percent of Rainier's first graduating class was accepted into four-year colleges.[15]

Now return to Katie Goddard's lesson. The agenda for the day, written on the whiteboard, lists the sequence of topics for the hour-and-a-half session:

- Reparations
- Slavery op-eds
- Criteria
- Imperialism op-eds
- Exit ticket

After the Warm Up and during the four-corner debate, Goddard gets deeper into the reparations question by introducing statements such as: "Slavery ended a hundred years ago, so the US government should not pay any money to African Americans now." One student points out that the US government has already paid reparations when it gave sums of money to Japanese Americans who had been forced into internment camps during World War II. Another points out that the money went to those who were still alive. Voices are raised, and the tone becomes adversarial. Goddard interrupts and says: "Remember our norms. The second your tone becomes combative, you don't listen. Our goal is to listen to one another." After a more restrained back-and-forth in which she specifically calls on students who have heretofore not entered the discussion, Goddard asks class if they want to shift corners. About one-third move to another corner.

Goddard now asks students to return to their tables and turn to the next question: "When are reparations necessary?" She asks class to open Chromebooks and come up with criteria to answer the question. She reminds the class that "There is no correct answer, just different opinions. Yet examples and facts are necessary to support opinions." She moves around the room asking and answering questions at each table.

After about ten minutes, Goddard asks students to close their tablets and says "We are going to study imperialism, and you are going to write an op-ed by the end of the unit. The question you will answer is 'Do former imperializing countries have a responsibility to give foreign aid to the countries they imperialized?'" She links the earlier discussion of reparations to the unit on imperialism and then previews the next twelve lessons on the IWB, going over each one briefly.

Goddard then puts up a slide that defines imperialism as "the process of taking over another country through diplomacy or military force." She asks students to come up with their definition of imperialism by using the playlist of sources (documents and videos) she gathered for the unit on the Congo, India, and other colonized countries. She gives the class the link to access the playlist. In coming up with their definitions, she urges students to talk to their partners. After pairs have come up with their definitions, she then asks them to brainstorm what they would need to know about imperialism to determine if reparations are necessary.[16]

With clipboard in hand, Goddard moves through the classroom checking to see which students are unclear about the task or having difficulties in answering questions. As time winds down to end the class, she summarizes what they have done, connecting discussions on reparations to new unit on imperialism.

As in many other ninth-grade classes, socializing students to classroom and school norms, covering content, stimulating student participation, and teaching cognitive skills becomes a complex dance of tasks and activities interacting with one another over ninety-five minutes.

Format and Content of the Lesson

Katie Goddard taught a teacher-directed, multipart lesson with a format that contained whole group, small group, and independent activities. As in other lessons I have described in chapter 1 and this chapter, the goals and academic content—aligned to Common Core state standards in social studies—was entwined with these activities at the beginning (reading the two op-eds), the middle (students sorting themselves in four corners of the room to indicate whether they agreed or disagreed with lesson's central question and then after further discussion being able to switch positions by walking to another corner), and the end (the content of the rest of the unit on imperialism). Sensitive to the momentum of the lesson, Goddard segued easily from one activity to another. Concerned about how students interacted in groups, the teacher reminded the class about how to talk to one another amid moving from one activity to another. Here again was an example of a teacher using technology routinely to knit together format and content as lessons unfold.

Had using technology daily at Rainier altered how Goddard, in her third year of teaching, taught?[17] Her answer:

> Unequivocally, yes. Technology is helping me tap into my core beliefs as a teacher. As a teacher, I want to make sure that I can

reach every single one of my students; I'm not comfortable with saying that "most" passed or "a lot of them" learned how to write. I want to make sure that every single one of my students grows every day, every unit, every year. Technology is helping me have real-time access to how each of my students are progressing or not along their individual learning trajectories. Instead of having to wait to grade a test or collect essays to read and understand, now I can go and look at their Google doc during and after class and ask myself the really real question: Did they understand? Did they grow? And that question keeps me honest and reflective as a teacher, because so many times the answer is not as straightforward as "Yep, they're good." By looking at how my students are doing every day, using technology, I'm getting to learn so much about how each of them learn and what each of them need. This makes me a stronger, more reflective, more honest teacher, and it forces me to confront the true needs of my students every day.

And then of course there are other simple perks of technology in the classroom—I can give students links to all the resources that we use in a lesson so that if they need more time to process or want to refer back to directions or examples, they can do so in their own time. Using technology well, and being thoughtful about organization of the materials and where we should use technology and where we don't need to, can offer more touch points for students to engage in the curriculum inside and outside the school.

BEYOND INDIVIDUAL CLASSROOMS: SCHOOL INTEGRATION OF TECHNOLOGY

The claim echoed over and over again by high-tech advocates—"It's not about technology, it's about learning"—may have become trite, but it captures what I saw in the Summit Prep and Rainier biology and World Studies lessons. Overall aims for Summit students to acquire academic content, cognitive skills, "habits of success," and the know-how allowing them to assess their own progress (PLP) involved online work before, during, and after lessons.

Clearly, the school did not have to use Chromebooks and software to reach the schools' overall goals and each students' personal ones. The technology did, however, enable the process of learning to be more efficient and timely while giving real-time feedback to students. Summit teachers regularly and easily used the technology to different degrees, depending on the project. Technology was in the background, not the foreground of a lesson.

All Summit teachers across the network, working together on project lessons within subject areas, were expected to use devices and software when they joined the faculty at a Summit school—in the organizational structure of schedules, Expeditions, project-based learning, and mentoring. They entered a culture where adherence to norms of using standards-based content and skills, student participation in classes, strong bonds between teachers and students in and out of classrooms, regular use of technologies, and workdays that extended well beyond 9 a.m. to 3 p.m. were expected behaviors.

Creating and sustaining these many features of the Summit schools is no easy task. None of the structures and cultural norms sprang fully formed from the brows of the Summit founders. It was (and is) a process that is constantly monitored, assessed, and altered by site leaders and staff.

SUMMIT-LIKE SCHOOLS ELSEWHERE IN THE UNITED STATES

As complex as it is for an individual teacher to integrate daily use of high-tech devices into routine classroom practices (as I described in chapter 1), technology integration at a school level is even more so.

Classroom teachers with twenty-five to thirty-five students can alter the structures of their lessons and create a culture of learning, achievement, and mutual respect within the four walls of the classroom. Hard as that is, it is doable, and I and many others have profiled teachers who have created such classrooms.[18]

Imagine, however, schools with thirty to one hundred classrooms. Then imagine getting all of those teachers to work together using a schoolwide infrastructure where a learning, achieving, and respectful culture exists inside and outside classrooms while integrating technology effortlessly in daily activities to achieve both individual lesson and schoolwide goals. Such instructional complexity has many moving parts, all of which are fragile and depend on strong relations and much cooperation between teachers and students, making such schools uncommon. I count the two Summit charter schools I observed belonging to that singular group.

Beyond Summit charter schools, districts have created non-charter schools that draw both white and minority students from inside and outside the district. One such school is Gunderson High School in San Jose, California. The technology magnet school of nearly eleven hundred, mostly minority, students has had a variation of 1:1 laptops for the past fifteen years.[19]

Another example is the regional (and highly selective) Thomas Jefferson High School for Science and Technology founded by a coalition of business, civic, and educational leaders. Located in Fairfax County, Virginia, this school of about eighteen hundred students (nearly 70 percent minority with 2 percent falling into the poverty category) selects its students from six adjacent school districts. *U.S. News and World Report* ranked the school fifth in the nation (out of over twenty-one thousand high schools) in 2016.[20] And the predominately poor and minority Robert Taft Information Technology High School in Cincinnati, Ohio, went from a failing neighborhood school to a highly touted technology school in a new building with open enrollment drawing students from inside and outside of district boundaries.[21]

There are also separate high schools in districts that feature technology use not only in their title but also as part of their daily classroom routines through project-based learning and many nontraditional activities. San Diego's High Tech High (HTH), for example, founded in 2000 by a coalition of business, civic, educational leaders as a charter high school, now has a network of thirteen elementary and secondary charter schools, enrolling over fifty-three hundred students in the San Diego region.[22] Like the Summit charter network, much has been written about HTH's founding principal Larry Rosenstock's progressive vision of teaching and learning through project-based units, internships, ambitious teaching, and staff that work closely with students, often tailoring the curriculum to their individual strengths and limitations. Independent observers who have studied the school have noted the various features of the program and the positive student outcomes in graduating students, college attendance, and completion rates for those who are the first in their families to attend college.[23]

In identifying these schools across the United States, I have relied on media reports and websites. I did not visit these schools, and there is only so much one can extract from documents and carefully selected videos and testimonials on websites. Whether these schools, as Summit charters have done, created a knowledgeable, skilled, and stable staff, built school structures and cultures that supported both teaching and learning and close connections between adults and youth, and constantly assessed how they are (and were) doing in achieving their goals, I cannot say for sure. Were there research studies or independent evaluations of the school—I found none—perhaps such queries could have been answered.

Obviously, reading website information, school reports, and upbeat stories of such schools are not the same as having researchers observing what occurs on a daily basis in classrooms across a school and conducting schoolwide studies. Michael Russell and colleagues, Mark Windschitl and Kurt Sahl, and Chrystalla Mouza have authored carefully done case studies of individual schools. But such studies still remain rare.[24]

Given the scarcity of the research, and the fact that the United States has nearly 100,000 schools spread over 13,000-plus districts, it should come as no surprise to readers that it is difficult to name elementary and secondary charter and non-charter schools far removed from Silicon Valley that resemble the Summit network. And out of those numbers, media mavens, scholars, and policymakers will notice only a handful. Even a cascade of examples, however, cannot hide how hard it is to create and then continue such schools over decades. They are complex organizations; brief mentions obscure the mindful and careful joining of many interacting elements (and luck) that make such schools worthy of attention.

Summit charters and similar schools from across the nation are time-consuming to build and even more demanding to sustain over time. Some are featured in media, then a decade or more later disappear from the scene. For example, a 1999 American Institute of Research Report listed twenty-four schoolwide reform models then in existence that could be federally funded if their Comprehensive School Reform application were approved. Some of those models continue operating in 2017, including: Success for All (launched in 1987), School Development Project (1968), America's Choice (1998), Core Knowledge (1989), and Paideia (1982). But many others have disappeared into the swamp of forgotten reform models or morphed into boutique offerings. Consider that Accelerated Schools (1986), ATLAS Communities (1992), Co-NECT (1992), Different Ways of Knowing (1989), Urban Learning Centers (1993), and Modern Red Schoolhouse (1993) no longer exist.[25]

For any number of reasons, these once-heralded schoolwide models of reform slip into obscurity, becoming footnotes in doctoral dissertations. Those that do last do so because the founders and their successors realize that building and sustaining such schools is not only taxing but complex, a jigsaw puzzle of multiple, interacting factors (e.g., stable funding, continuity in leadership, low staff attrition, continual self-assessment, and constant adapting to shifting environment) that few reformers can understand, much less put together over time.

SCHOOLWIDE REFORM AND RUBIK'S CUBE

When Rubik's Cube appeared in the early 1980s, I tried twisting and turning the blocks to get the colors aligned. I failed. Finding out that there are 3 billion possible ways to turn the cube's pieces to get the solution comforted me not a bit. Nor did knowing that one out of seven people on the planet (yes, the planet) have tried to solve the puzzle, especially after I read that the speed record—established in November 2015—for solving the puzzle is now under five seconds (not minutes nor hours, but *seconds*). A blindfolded participant in the China Championship (2015) solved the cube in twenty-one seconds. I gave up. And I have not tried since.[26]

Now, what does Rubik's Cube have to do with schools like Summit charters and integrating technologies into daily activities? Changing school structures and culture to improve classroom pedagogy—for that is the intent of integrating technology into daily lessons—is even more complex than solving the frustrating Rubik's Cube. There are far more moving parts to altering what teachers do in their classrooms: teachers' expertise, student strengths and limitations, school structures, culture, and interactions (many of which can not be predicted) between and among adults and children inside and outside the school. These organizational moving parts have to work in sync in order for students to benefit. When they do it is a beauty to behold. But most of the time they don't and it gets ugly.

Why is this? Because too many reformers believe that reforming a school is complicated, not complex.[27] A complicated problem is hard, but can be solved through smart planning, careful use of resources, and the right staff. Organizations are rational; problems arise, and engineered solutions resolve them. Complicated problems can be finessed by providing the right incentives to motivate children and adults, laying out clear and measurable objectives, planning the tasks to be done step-by-step, executing those tasks efficiently, measuring results, evaluating the outcomes, and correcting errors. Then the cycle can be repeated.

But reforming a school (or district) goes beyond clever design, putting the right people in the right slots, efficient execution of tasks, and measuring results. No recipe exists, no list of ingredients and instructions for mixing them. And this is why reformers often trip over the complexity of designing a school and improving teachers' daily lessons.

What makes school reform complex is that creating and sustaining a "successful" school, however measured, goes well beyond having the correct algorithms (as there are for Rubik's Cube) to get from here to there. Space travel—rockets to the moon, shuttles to a space station orbiting the earth, and preparations for an eventual mission to the planet Mars—involves enormously complicated projects that have been planned and executed (almost) flawlessly. But complicated does not equal complex. There is no Mission Control for school reform, however, in a decentralized national system of 50-plus states and territories, 13,000-plus districts, and 100,000 schools staffed by over 3 million teachers. One example of the complexity of school reform will illustrate what I mean.[28]

Take the US high school. Begun in the mid-nineteenth century, it evolved via reforms into the comprehensive high school with college prep, commercial, and vocational curricula housing fifteen hundred or more teenagers in the 1920s. Since then, the institution has been praised and attacked every single decade. Policymakers have adopted reform after reform: from many curricula in the high school to one designed for "everyone goes to college"; from conventionally organized schools with fifty-minute periods and academic departments to ones with ninety-minute block schedule for courses, subject matter departments disbanded, and team teaching; from fifteen hundred to two thousand or more students to small high schools (five hundred or fewer students); from dominant teacher-centered pedagogy to more personalized and individualized ways of teaching (e.g., project-based learning, student-centered teaching, online instruction).[29]

Some reforms stuck, but many did not. No surprise then that high schools that our parents and grandparents attended would be familiar to us even now.

Altering school structures and cultures significantly is tough to do because high schools—there are over twenty-five thousand public ones in the United States—are complex organizations situated in a mercurial, ever-shifting political, social, economic, and technologically rich environment. Surely, there have been incremental changes in school size, additions and deletions to the curriculum, use of technologies, and ways that teachers teach but these changes—actually political responses to the clamor of those who make policy, pay taxes, vote, and demand changes—preserved the essential organizational structures and governance arrangements (e.g., age-graded school, graduation requirements teachers assigned to separate classrooms, end-of-year tests, subject matter departments, hour-long periods of instruction, etc.).[30]

Nevertheless, there are exemplary schools others and I have identified that have lasted more than a decade such as the network of Summit charter schools. These schools have created new staffs, structures, and cultures that have integrated technologies into their daily routines. These schools have common features that capture the many interacting factors that make the complexity of making changes in schools apparent.

COMMON FEATURES OF SCHOOLS THAT HAVE INTEGRATED TECHNOLOGIES ACROSS CLASSROOMS

In observing the two Summit charter schools and other schools in Silicon Valley (see chapter 3 for exemplars from Mountain View Los Altos High School District and Milpitas Unified School District), I saw schools that have integrated new technologies requiring teachers to teach lessons using particular hardware and software. These schools differ from one another, yet all emphasize that they personalize learning, blend instruction, and differentiate their lessons to meet the needs of different students. Invariably, they say they use project-based instruction. They have created both an infrastructure and culture that subordinates technology to the larger tasks of preparing children and youth to do well academically and socially, graduate, and go to college (and complete it) or enter a career directly.

What are the common features of such schools?

Drawing on what I have observed in Silicon Valley, documented nationally in my studies, and retrieved from the research literature on such schools elsewhere in the United States, these are eight different yet interacting moving parts that I believe characterize changes that these schools have accomplished in using technology to prepare children and youth to enter a career and/or complete college. These features are:

- Recruit and train teachers who have the subject matter knowledge and skills to work with students before, during, and after the school day.
- Recruit and train school site leaders who have the expertise and skills to lead a school and be a pillow and sandpaper simultaneously with teachers, students, and parents.
- Equip all students with the knowledge and skills not only to enter college, persist through four years, and get a bachelor's degree but also have the wherewithal to enter a career immediately.
- Provide students with access to nonacademic subjects that cultivate the mind, heart, and sensibilities.
- Organize the school day, week, and month to provide students with sufficient time in and out of class to learn the prescribed material and core cognitive skills to master a subject, acquire the essential skills of planning and assessing their progress in each course they take, receive tutorial help when their skill levels are below and above par, and allow time for them to receive mentoring from teachers they trust.
- Build a culture of safety, learning, respect, and collaboration for both youth and adults.
- Create a decision-making process that is inclusive, self-critical, and strong enough to make further changes in all of the above.
- Do all of this efficiently within available resources.

Note that I did not mention new technologies in the features I have listed. Why is that?

Schools meeting the listed criteria have administrators and teachers who figure out when to use software to achieve desired outcomes, create an infrastructure to support staff in using new technologies, and determine which new technologies efficiently advance students in reaching these goals. Computers and their software are *subordinate* to the overarching goals for students and adults in the school.[31]

Note, though, that what I have garnered from direct observation, interviews, and the literature is not a formula that can be broken apart and easily reassembled. Listing features I have identified is not an invitation to unbundle some or all of these into an algorithm for producing such schools. These schools are complex, loosely coupled organizations deeply rooted in their contexts. And context matters.

Thus, listing the essential features that mark such enterprises is not a blueprint for action; it is an after-the-fact synthesis of what I saw and not easily replicable for those who have dreams of going to scale. It is what emerged from such efforts over a long period of time and requires tender, loving care every day. These schools are fragile and easily broken by changes in leadership and staff, inattention, and declining resources.[32]

If schools are complex organizations operating in an ever-shifting environment where scores of interacting factors come into play, imagine the intricacy of having districts with many schools pledged to integrating technology systemwide. That is what chapter 3 will describe.

THREE

The District

In Silicon Valley, there are seventy-seven school districts across five counties in the San Francisco Bay Area. All are heralded as integrating high tech, and all have technology plans for their schools. These districts buy lots of hard- and software, install Wi-Fi in schools, provide classroom carts of laptops and tablets, offer teacher workshops on technology integration, and then cross their fingers that teachers will use these resources for daily lessons. Voluntary participation is the rule, which means that use of devices and software varies greatly not only in every single school within a district but across districts.[1]

Only two Silicon Valley districts—Mountain View Los Altos High School District and Milpitas Unified School District—have gone beyond having a plan, buying devices, building infrastructures, and leaving it to teachers to decide how or if to use them. Only these two districts have adopted policies that nudged (but not required) all teachers in every school to use new technologies, blend learning, and create differentiated lessons. Only these two districts have built a systemwide infrastructure of broadband and Wi-Fi, incorporated newly developed software, sponsored professional development, and provided technical assistance with the explicit expectation that all district teachers would go beyond considering use the new technologies in their daily lessons and actually incorporate the hardware and software into their forty-five- to ninety-minute lessons

None of this occurred overnight. In these two districts, as the hardware and software were deployed, as the infrastructure to help teachers grew, as teachers learned from colleagues, more and more shifted to using the new technologies until the practice hit critical mass and daily use became the norm at each school.

While pilot projects, teacher preparation, and much district help account for widespread use, top district leaders' clear talk and actions about direction mattered. Eventually, all teachers were expected to use the technologies in lessons to reach their classroom content and skill objectives. In the Mountain View Los Altos district, I went to its two high schools and observed a total of ten classroom lessons. In Milpitas, a dozen miles away, two elementary school principals invited me to observe their primary and upper-grade classrooms. I visited a total of seven classrooms and interviewed principals and teachers at each school as well as district administrators.

Knowing that each level of schooling—classroom, school, and district—contains its unique complexities and knowing that districts are not command-and-control organizations where top-down orders are put into practice, I used a trifocal lens. I sought to understand why implementing policies aimed at changing what classroom teachers do, altering how schools operate daily, and improving district performance is so hard (which is why these two districts are uncommon).

Consider, for example, all the factors and constraints teachers face putting a planned lesson into practice and then interacting with the class during that lesson. In the actual lesson, teachers make hundreds of decisions—some planned, many unplanned—anchored in the content and skills to be learned, the technologies used, the students sitting in front of them, and the relationships among students and between the teacher and students. In addition to the decisions, there is the classroom culture, the norms and rituals the teacher and students practice daily (e.g., the teacher counting down from 10 to get quiet; rhythmic clapping by teacher and students to get attention; and students listening to one another and taking turns).[2]

The deep knowledge teachers have of subject matter, cognitive and social skills, and details about their students all come to the surface in the questions teachers ask, how they determine who will be with whom in small group activities, and when to segue from one part of the lesson to another (clock watching is an occupational tic for most teachers). Keeping a lesson moving along and overcoming distractions are basic habits in a teacher. Yet the inevitable unpredictability of students' responses to a lesson often calls for instant decision making: a student unexpectedly rants or cries. snow starts falling outside and students get restless; an assistant principal enters the room to observe the lesson; an incident of bullying during recess spills into the class; and on and on. Teachers' tacit knowledge of how to handle such events forms the bedrock of the relationship with students, the heart of their learning both in and out of classrooms.[3]

As one teacher told me, "Just managing the complexity of teaching a lesson can be overwhelming." Looking at all of the above factors that come into play when a teacher improvises or goes ahead with a planned decision—while seeking to put a new technique into practice—is often what staggers a newcomer to teaching.[4]

The complexity deepens when one moves from the classroom as the unit of analysis to the school and then the district. Grasping the sheer number of factors that influence a school's organization, culture, and relationships between adults and with students is tough enough. Schools with ten to a hundred classrooms, credentialed and non-credentialed staff, diversity of students, parental involvement, the neighborhood, and dozens of other factors come into play. Then consider how complexity grows in a district of ten, fifty, or a hundred or more of those schools, as crosscutting factors from classrooms, schools, and community come into play.

Each embedded level has a structure, culture, and entwined relationships.[5] Each level affects the other as teachers go about doing what is expected in classrooms, school staffs wrestle with instruction and curriculum, and both individual teachers and school staffs connect to the district school board, superintendent, and central office administrators from whom policies and resources flow downward. Describing the move from district policy to instructional practice illustrates the intricacy of finessing all the interacting factors that come into play when policy makers look for their decisions to unfold in classrooms, schools, and districts. These three levels of schooling, then, are like those large-to-small Russian dolls, nested in one another.

There are so many moving parts in this loosely coupled system called a district. Because there is so much interaction and overlap in these intertwined communities, any hope of effective implementation of a policy or program—meaning that a critical mass of teachers in each school and the district over time put instructional policies into prac-tice—depends not only on having money and staff but also continuity in student-teacher relationships, principal-staff cooperation, and school boards and district administrators building and sustaining a culture of working together. No easy task.[6]

Moreover, districts and schools are susceptible to outside influ-ences. That list of vulnerabilities is long: state policies impinge on dis-trict actions; angry parents condemn a new curriculum; vendors lobby administrators; civic and business leaders want quick improvements in student performance; teacher unions challenge school board poli-cies; and controversies erupt over the teaching of evolution, perceived foul language in textbooks, and other similar issues. Furthermore, dis-trict and site administrators unendingly search for resources and sup-port from interior and exterior groups. Also among the many moving parts, there are internal and external groups that have their own ideas of what is a "good" teacher and what is a "good" school district. Those educational decision makers who cannot let go of their vision of com-mand-and-control organizations and wrap their minds around open, loosely coupled places established to help students (not customers) will continue to flit here and there seeking school reform, yet ever be disap-pointed in the results.

Most school leaders do understand that districts, schools, and class-rooms are indeed open systems with many parts seldom tightly coupled to one another. Such leaders often opt for the strategy of "If you build it, they will come," or indulge their belief that change, like a cold, is contagious. They believe that sufficient equipment, staff assistance, and incentives will increase the numbers of teachers who choose to integrate new technologies into lessons.

Then there are those uncommon districts whose top leaders recognize the complexity of the system, but also understand that change may not spread spontaneously. Rather than rely on teacher volunteerism, they not only create the conditions for integrating technologies into units and lessons, they also nudge novice and veteran teachers to embrace these practices because it is the way the school (and district) will move.

District work aimed at having teachers use new technologies to teach desired content and skills is not for the faint of heart or those who fail to grasp the complexity spread across three organizational levels. The path toward total integration of computing in classroom, school, and district is closer to the zigzags of a butterfly than the straight, inexorable path of a bullet fired at a target.

In this chapter, I look at two Silicon Valley districts that adopted policies and built infrastructures that would push schools and teachers to integrate technology: Mountain View Los Altos and Milpitas Unified. I will describe the policy-to-practice continuum as it goes from the superintendent's office to an English lesson about *The Adventures of Huckleberry Finn* and a physics class on launching projectiles.

FROM THE CLASSROOM—
KRISTEN KRAUSS'S AMERICAN LITERATURE CLASS

Join me for a high school American Literature lesson at Mountain View High School I observed one October morning in 2016.

Mark Twain's *Adventures of Huckleberry Finn*, written in 1885, is a classic that students have read year in and year out in high school literature classes. The language used in the book, especially when the slave Jim is involved, has become a contentious issue, to the extent that some communities have called for banning the book. Issues of racist language have arisen repeatedly. And it is an issue now as Kristen Krauss, an eighteen-year veteran of teaching introduces her eleventh-grade English class to the book. The forty-five-minute lesson covers the book's initial chapters.[7]

At 7:15 a.m., there are fourteen students present. Before the buzzer sounds to begin class, Krauss asks students to take out their tablets and laptops—the school implemented a Bring Your Own Device (BYOD) policy a few years ago—and tells them to review questions and answers they worked on the previous Friday. Five minutes later, a buzzer launches the five-part lesson.

Krauss asks the class to sit in groups of three or four and begins a Warm Up activity. She clicks on a slide displayed on the whiteboard in the front of the room that asks students about the multiple-choice questions they had been given in the previous lesson and for each student to think of a "silly anecdote about yourself as a child." Students begin interacting in their small groups. One student asks Krauss what an "anecdote" is. She bounces the question back to the class. One student says, "It is a story." Krauss then gives an example of an anecdote from her life.

Krauss segues to a series of ten questions about the story and plot of *Huck Finn's* first three chapters. She asks for volunteers to come to the front of the room and read each question that appears on the slide projected on the whiteboard, call on students, and judge the answer. All of the questions ask for students to complete the sentence and are in Actively Learn, a software program that all students have on their devices.[8]

Two students volunteer. "Bob" reads the question and "William" calls on a member of the class and then grades each answer with a "+" (nailed the answer), a "0" (missed it), and a "0–" (didn't come close). Krauss asks students at their desks to judge the answer as well. She says that none of the student answers to the sentence completion questions will count toward a grade. This is a review for an upcoming quiz.

Here are some of the questions on the slide:

1. Huck lives with . . .
2. Miss Watson is responsible for . . .
3. Early on, Tom and Huck sneak out at night and play . . .
4. Huck explains that Jim used this story to gain attention from friends by . . .

I scan the class and see everyone looking at the sentence-completion questions on the whiteboard and at Bob and William. Krauss prompts the two students occasionally.

After the two students go through the first four questions, William asks Krauss if they can do the rest. She says, "That would be lovely." The two students finish the final questions. Krauss compliments Bob and William and they take their seats.

She now asks the class to form small groups at their tables and give their opinions of the first three chapters of *Huck Finn*. She asks the class to consider what was challenging and what was enjoyable in these initial chapters.

She listens to the small groups as she moves around the classroom. Halting the small group interaction, she asks the class what they came up with that was challenging. A few students raise their hands and she calls on them and writes their responses on whiteboard. The grammar, one student says. Another says the slang used was hard to understand. Krauss elaborates and extends each of the student's answers.

Krauss then asks what was enjoyable. No students raise their hands at first. After a few moments, one student says: "I wanted to know what happens next." Another volunteers that she liked how the author spoke to the reader. And one more student liked that "Huck is really honest." Again, the teacher expands each student's answer.

At this point, Krauss moves to the final activity of the lesson. She gets into this segment by saying that in going over the next few chapters, members of the class will read sections aloud. She says that some students may get upset at the use of language—particularly the word *nigger*, which is used over two hundred times in the book. Krauss has already given some of the context for Twain's book that features slavery before the Civil War. Even with that context, the "N-word," as some call it, has been controversial since the middle of the twentieth century. So Krauss asks: "As we read aloud from the book, how are we going to handle the language describing Jim?"

Krauss then introduces a twelve-minute video excerpt from CBS's *60 Minutes* about how the N-word is handled by teachers and students across the nation.[9] In the excerpt, there is an interview with a book publisher who put out an edition of *Huck Finn* and replaced *nigger* with the word *slave*. A contrasting view comes from a university scholar who advocates the uses of the N-word. Each gives their position clearly in the segment. There are interviews with teachers about whether the word should be used in class when reading and discussing the book. The *60 Minutes* journalist also interviewed students who were the only African Americans in their classroom (of Krauss's fourteen students, one was African American).

In looking across the room while the video played, I noted students' rapt attention. At the end of the video, Krauss says: "My purpose in showing this video is simply this: What are you thinking of how to approach word in class? The word is there. What do we do with it?"

She asks students to open their devices and go to Google Classroom and "write a sentence about whether to use the N-word in class or not. We will take a vote before reading aloud this week. I want to know what we should do as a class in approaching the word."

Krauss says that only a few minutes remain in the period. "After you finish," she says, "send your sentences to me." She walks around room as students type their sentences. As they are clicking away, she announces: "I will not share your answers with the rest of the class."

In the last two minutes, Krauss calls the class's attention to a slide on the whiteboard. The top of the slide has two objectives:

- Make an informed and respectful choice about how we will approach the reading of Huck Finn.

- Place the novel in the literary historical context in which it was written.

The rest of the slide has instructions for reading chapters 4–6 and answering particular questions.

Krauss goes over these instructions and reminds students not to cut and paste paragraphs from other sources; she reminds them to use their words.

The buzzer sounds, ending the period.

Format and Content of the Lesson

Switching between large group, small group, and independent work, Kristen Krauss's lesson format had students write an embarrassing story from their childhood and discuss it in their small group. Class then segued to ten factual questions about the beginning of *The Adventures of Huckleberry Finn* led by two student volunteers and then students writing about what was challenging and enjoyable about the initial three chapters of Twain's classic book. Students discussed their responses in small groups. Finally, Krauss raised the issue of the word *nigger*, using a video excerpt from a television news program. She asked students to choose how they wanted to handle the word.

These teacher-designed activities moved easily from one to another without interruption. Activities were consistent with the explicit lesson objectives the teacher sought. And students seemed to this observer to enter into activities without any foot-dragging.

As in all other lessons teachers teach, students' reactions to the content about the novel—the language and storyline—weave in and out of this format, one that invites frequent student participation. In a forty-five-minute period, there is a clear beginning (the Warm Up), a middle (the ten questions), and an end (discussion of how to deal with a highly volatile word in the text).

After I observed the class, I asked Krauss whether using technology had changed her teaching since she arrived at Mountain View High School in 2000. Her answer was a definite yes:

I can see mid-lesson questions and polls to re-teach right away, rather than one to two days later. I can know—while we are talking—what students know and what they are able to do. Then I can try a different strategy right then and check for understanding again. It's much more efficient.

In the past, I would have to create student models of various language arts products, including thesis statements, reading comprehension responses, or text annotations. With students completing work via online reading platforms like Actively Learn, I can—in a matter of two to three minutes—use copy/paste or screen captures to select models of student work and integrate them into my lesson slides to review in real time with students before they repeat a similar task.

The options of tech tools available inspire me to teach skills and content in diverse ways than I would have in the past. Several examples: I can easily group students using polls (interest-based groups) or ability (quick look at formative assessment in Google Classroom or Actively Learn to determine who is proficient, who is almost there, and who needs enrichment). I can use Padlet for groups to report virtual posters to the class in real time on my overhead. Students can add to my lesson slides when working in small groups on material they are responsible for sharing with the entire class (which saves time because all students can add their part simultaneously in a shared file).

In short, the clunkiness is gone. The slow-downs of grouping, creating a sharable product, and conveying information have been eliminated.[10]

Kristen Krauss was clear that using new technologies had been a boon to her teaching, making possible teachable moments that would have been unavailable without the devices and software applications. Her district's BYOD policy for all students and the infrastructure the district had put into place to help teachers teach with new technologies made it possible for Krauss to teach the lesson on Twain's *Adventures of Huckleberry Finn* that I observed.

THE MOUNTAIN VIEW LOS ALTOS HIGH UNION DISTRICT

The Mountain View Los Altos High School District (MVLA) has two comprehensive high schools. A Bring Your Own Devices pilot project began at Los Altos High School in 2014, and a year later, with the MVLA Foundation and Google providing $600,000 for Chromebooks, at Mountain View High School. With school board and superintendent approval, these high schools have operated with BYOD across academic subjects. Most students bring a tablet or laptop to school; for those who lack a device, there are classroom carts with Chromebooks available.[11]

Of seventy-seven districts in Silicon Valley and adjacent parts of the Bay Area, MVLA and Milpitas Unified (I describe this district later in the chapter) were the only two that I found in 2016 that provided devices for all teachers and students and expected teachers to use tablets and laptops regularly in their classrooms.

Nearly all districts in Silicon Valley have five-year technology plans and promote use of computers in their schools and classrooms. They provide devices for those teachers who ask for them, organize professional development sessions for teachers, and supply technical assistance. But they do not require academic subject teachers to use the devices. Commonly, teachers decide whether and how to use devices in lessons. Teacher autonomy trumps any district mandate on using technology in lessons. (I described three teachers who did opt to integrate technology in the classroom in chapter 1.)

MVLA district policy, then, is that teachers and students will regularly use devices for their lessons. How teachers will use computers, when, and under what conditions remain teacher decisions.

Mountain View High School, where Kristen Krauss teaches, has just over eighteen hundred students (2015) and its demography is mostly minority (Asian, 26 percent; Latino, 21 percent; African American, 2 percent; multiracial, 2 percent; and white, 47 percent). The percentage of students eligible for free and reduced-price lunch is 18 percent. Eleven percent of students are learning disabled, and just over 10 percent of students are English language learners.[12]

Academically, 94 percent of the students graduate high school and nearly all enter higher education. The school offers thirty-five Honors and Advanced Placement (AP) courses across the curriculum. Of those students taking AP courses, 84 percent have earned a grade of 3 or higher, the benchmark for getting college credit. The school earned the distinction of California Distinguished High School in 1994 and 2003. In 2007 and 2013, MVHS received a full six-year accreditation from the Western Association of Schools and Colleges (WASC). *Newsweek* ranks MVHS among the top 1 percent of high schools nationwide. The gap in achievement between minorities and white remains large, however, and has not shrunk in recent years. The per-pupil expenditure at the high school is just under $15,000 (2014).[13]

BACK TO THE CLASSROOM— STEPHEN HINE'S PHYSICS CLASS

Another MVLA district teacher I observed in September 2016 taught an Advanced Placement physics lesson at Los Altos High School.[14]

Stephen Hine invited me into his ninety-minute AP physics class one fall morning. Hine is in his third year of teaching. He also graduated from Los Altos and, as a student, took physics courses from the teacher who has an adjacent classroom in the two-story building housing math and science classes.

The room is spacious, and the rear section is furnished with lab tables and science desks with the latest equipment for students to use. In the front half of the classroom, pods of four desks dot the space. There are twenty-four students in the classroom when Hine begins the lesson.

Hine starts the class by asking students to copy down the objective for the day, which is on a slide projected on the whiteboard in the front of the class:

Students will be able to [SWBAT] create instructional videos using white-board animations in order to demonstrate problem-solving skills and provide instructional support to peers.

At the various tables, students have notebooks and pens next to their tablets and laptops. The district mandated a BYOD program two years ago and makes Chromebooks available to students who do not have their own devices. As they write and click away, Hine takes attendance and asks about a few missing students.

Hine then points to the agenda for the day shown on the whiteboard:

1. Lab Peer Review
2. Problem-Solving Videos

Hine then asks students to review each other's lab report on the projectile launch that they had just completed. He wants class to use a rubric that he had given to students to assess the quality of their lab work and that of a partner.[15] However, accessing the rubric from the mixed set of laptops and tablets students have (Apple, PC, and Android) is cumbersome. Each machine has its own operating instructions and class sharing of documents from one device to another becomes an oft-repeated and complicated procedure.

Hine gives three sets of step-by-step directions to students with different devices to share lab reports across computers. Expressing frustration, he gives another set of directions for students using Chromebooks.

Students turn to their task and begin assessing each other's lab reports using the criteria in the rubric. I look around the room and see that all students appear to be on task. Hine moves among students' desks, checking their screens, solving technical glitches, and answering questions.

Hine tells the class that they have ten more minutes before end of this activity, and adds, "If you see anything missing on your partner's lab, tell them and help. Give constructive criticism, please."

As the activity winds down, Hine gives five- and three-minute warnings. For those who have finished, he says, "Submit your review and go ahead and read the overview on your screens about instructional videos." He then asks everyone to submit their peer review and to close the lids of their computers when they have clicked "Submit."

Now Hine segues to second and last activity of the ninety-minute lesson: pairs and trios of students making instructional videos to show how the class will solve problems about different projectiles' velocity, range, etc. Hine had assigned a different problem to each group (e.g., "A basketball referee tosses the ball straight up for the starting tip-off. At what velocity must a basketball player leave the ground to rise 1.25 m above the floor in an attempt to get the ball?"). For the next seven minutes, Hine, standing at the whiteboard, reviews with the class each of the steps in making a problem-solving video: diagram the solution; write the necessary formulas; do the story board; take photos of what they have done; where to put their names; and voiceovers.

Some students ask whether they can use paper and pen (Hine says "yes"). Other students ask about the different problems, including: "When is the video due?" Hine points out the tubs of materials on a lab table (e.g., markers for the whiteboards attached to each cluster of desks; iPods to do the filming for students whose devices lack a camera).

The directions below that Hine gives to students identifying the problems and what they are to do are available to students on each of their devices.

> **Overview:** In a pair, you will be solving one of the problems below using our perfect solution format. Once you have correctly solved the problem and confirmed the provided answer(s), you will be creating an instructional video using a whiteboard animation of the process. Once everyone has completed their video, we will have a class folder with all of the videos to help you study for the unit test.

> *Perfect Solution Requirements:*
> Please use Actively Learn for examples of solving these problems:[16]

1. Simple diagram of the scenario with important quantities or characteristics labeled.
2. List of given and known conditions. For kinematics, this should include initial and final position, initial and final velocity, acceleration, and time.
3. Initial formula used to solve the problem written entirely in symbolic form.
4. Complete algebraic solution to the problem that is written entirely in symbolic form. The final step should involve your desired quantity isolated on one side of the equation.
5. A final boxed numeric answer with correct units.

Whiteboard Animation Requirements:

1. Either a school iPod or your own smartphone can be used to film. Smartphones must only be used for this academic purpose and nothing else.
2. Whiteboard must fit entirely in the field of view of the camera and must be at a perpendicular angle to the lens's axis.
3. Partner first and last names must be written on the whiteboard either at the beginning or the end of the animation.
4. A single shot of the entire solution or single images of each animation step are acceptable. Proper video formatting must be performed, depending on which method you choose.
5. Video must be easy to follow and not sped up too quickly (check with Mr. Hine about speed concerns).
6. A voiceover must be included explaining the solution process.

Hine asks students to pick their partners. After some milling around in the room, students divide themselves into mostly pairs, with two trios. Much background noise from students ensues. Hine counts down from 15, and students quiet and begin work with their partners at different pods of desks. Hine tells them they have about an hour to solve the problem, create a diagram of their solution, write the formulas as directed, do the storyboard, film it, and record the voiceover.

As students begin work, Hine moves around the room, stamping homework and passing back a quiz students had taken earlier in week.

For the next forty minutes, student groups work at different paces, moving through the steps laid out in the assignment. There are many student questions. Mostly, they are specific queries about the diagrams they have drawn, formulas they are using, the visualization of the problem (e.g., dropping a water balloon from the two-story building they are in), and technical questions about camera shots and voiceovers. Students often raise their hands, and Hine moves from one group to another, listening carefully, asking questions of the pair, listening again, and seeing whether they are OK to move on. During these forty minutes, Hine is in perpetual motion, listening and explaining, often visually simulating what tossing a basketball in the air might look like.

From time to time, I scan the classroom and see that every student seems to be working on assigned tasks. I move around the room, querying the pairs about which problem they are working on, which step are they on, and what do they do next.

A few pairs are already setting up their storyboard with their diagrams and filming at one the lab tables in the rear of the room. As other groups create the formulas to solve the problem, they too move to the rear tables. With about fifteen minutes left, more than half of the class has drawn storyboards and taken camera shots of the boards. One pair has already completed a voiceover.

With fewer than ten minutes left, all but four pairs are at the back of the room videoing their diagram, displaying formulas, and in various stages of doing audio.

After an alert from Hine about the few remaining minutes, students return the iPods and markers to the tubs on the lab table in the front of the room.

A few students are packing up as the chime sounds. AP physics is over for the day.

Format and Content of the Lesson

To reach the lesson's objectives, Hine combined whole group instruction (going over the day's agenda and elaborating directions for solving the problem on launching projectiles) with small group activities (peer review of previous lab on projectile launch using the class rubric; creating story boards for their videos and setting up their solution to video). Independent work occurred only at the beginning of the ninety-minute class.

Most of the class time was spent on two teacher-directed activities—pairs reviewing each other's lab report and teams solving the assigned problem on projectiles. Then students began creating a video of their problem and solution. There was much student-teacher interaction (e.g., asking individual questions about problem and solution and creating video as Hine walked around the class monitoring small groups).

With one exception, the teacher-directed lesson moved seamlessly from one activity to another. The climate in the class, as I sensed it, was task-driven, and students seemed to work easily with one another and with Hine.

As expected in such lessons, content was present in all activities. What students had to consider in their final workup ("Perfect Solution") concerning velocity, angle, and range illustrates the interweaving of physics content with the activity.

The use of smartphones and Apple, PC, and Android devices (including Chromebooks) was in the background save for the few minutes Hine spent giving directions to the class on how best to align the software with varied devices to do the peer review and solve the problem he had assigned.

Stephen Hine was very knowledgeable about the different devices the students were using. He answered technical questions about switching applications and the strengths and limitations of particular softwares. After the class, I asked him whether his use of technology in the two-plus years he had been teaching had altered his lessons. He answered:

> I would say not really from a typical "change" perspective. I was trained into the technology-focused educational environment so I have been integrating tech into my classroom since my student teaching days. I have definitely developed my lessons to more smoothly utilize the various instructional tools, so you could say my teaching has changed in that way. I am always open to learning about new tools as well. An example is, halfway through last year I

began to use Actively Learn, which is an online reading assignment tool that allows for built in questions that students have to answer before continuing through the assignment. I now use it for all of my class reading homework.

I was also raised in a tech-focused culture having grown up in the Silicon Valley so I am definitely a "digital native." This has improved my teaching by allowing me to pass my knowledge on to other teachers in the district. I have facilitated a few professional development workshop sessions regarding tech.[17]

Teaching at Los Altos High School in the Mountain View Los Altos Union High School District, Stephen Hine was one of nearly 150 teachers in a Silicon Valley district whose school board and superintendent had adopted an instructional policy seeking widespread use of technologies to advance student learning in two comprehensive high schools. The other district was Milpitas Unified School District.

MILPITAS UNIFIED SCHOOL DISTRICT

Cary Matsuoka, formerly a high school science teacher in a small Northern California district, eventually moved into administration and in 2006 became superintendent of the Los Gatos-Saratoga Union School District. The district had two high schools, one of which he had taught in for thirteen years. After five years as superintendent, he was named superintendent of the larger Milpitas Unified School District (MUSD) in 2011.[18]

Milpitas then had nine elementary schools, two middle schools, and one high school. The district served about ten thousand students, and was far more diverse than the smaller mostly white Los Gatos-Saratoga Union district.

Matsuoka left MUSD in 2016 to serve the larger Santa Barbara district of twenty-two schools and over fifteen thousand students.[19] But what a five-year run in technology integration it was for Milpitas!

A year after Matsuoka arrived, district voters approved a $95 million bond proposition for new buildings and technology infrastructure.

The superintendent now had the resources and school board support to alter the direction of teaching and learning in MUSD.[20]

Taken with how contemporary designers pose problems and involve those who have to execute decisions in classrooms. Matsuoka posed this question to district staff: "If you could design a school, what would it look like?" He then established a process to answer that question. He involved staff, the school board, and teacher union in providing answers. No command-and-control decisions would come from the board or superintendent. Answers would come from those who had to execute the designs. This was a radical process: With referendum funding, district administrators asked schools to come up with new designs for their schools. Teachers and principals—implementers of policy—designing instructional policy is unusual in most districts.[21]

To answer the design question, Matsuoka and Chin Song, director of technology, took groups of teachers, administrators, and board of education members to see about fifty schools throughout California. Also, as Song explained, teachers were brought in from technology-savvy schools to share their practices: "We wanted to bring people to campus because it was easier, timing-wise. Maybe it'll be teachers from Rocketship, maybe Summit [charter schools], maybe Santa Barbara . . . we like variety."[22]

Ideas emerged slowly over the next school year, driven by what staff had learned and widely shared truths of teaching in public schools: facing classrooms with thirty-plus students, meeting district curriculum standards, doing well on state tests, tailoring instruction to meet differences between students, and individualizing learning. Negotiating these constraints, much less creating schools that leapfrog them, is very hard to do.

Matsuoka said that the models individual schools came up would be judged and a few selected to become pilots for the district. The designs had to: "(1) integrate technology, (2) use data to inform instruction, (3) be student-centered, and (4) be flexible in how they used space, time, and student grouping."[23]

District committees evaluated the designs and chose two elementary schools (Curtner and Weller) to be pilots. By the end of 2013, the direction was clear. The elementary school pilots and work at one middle school (Russell) showed that staff at a newly designed school could integrate technology into daily lessons. The district school board and superintendent adopted an instructional policy directing all district schools to have "blended learning" with open spaces set aside for newly constructed Learning Labs.[24]

By 2013, with bond proposition money, nearly five thousand Chromebooks had been purchased and distributed across the district. By 2015, six elementary schools, one middle school and the one district high school had been remodeled to include Learning Labs.[25]

In the district's adopted model for primary grades, teachers rotate learning stations during a lesson within the classroom: students moved from small groups in reading, to math, and then to tablet computers to work individually. In the upper elementary grades, rotation of stations would occur within classrooms and in addition, students would go to the newly constructed Learning Lab. In middle and high schools, the newly built "Learning Labs"—open space design holding up to one hundred students—became centers for technology integration. Individual teachers and departments scheduled their classes to use the new spaces. This became the blended learning model that MUSD gradually spread through the district.[26]

This also became the district version of personalized learning. As Matsuoka put it in a letter to the *Milpitas Post* in September 2014:

> What does personalized learning look like? It begins by looking at education as both acquisition of information and application of information. Then we must create learning environments that nurture a strong relationship between the teacher and the student, and a strong sense of community within each classroom. Students should have opportunities for collaboration and learning with and from their peers. Students should have more choice about what they learn, more control over time and pacing, and use technology to create a personalized learning pathway.[27]

In the fall of 2016, I visited two of the elementary schools that had been involved in the redesign, one of which had been selected earlier as a pilot for blended learning, and spent two mornings each observing primary and upper-grade lessons and interviewing teachers.

MARSHALL POMEROY ELEMENTARY SCHOOL

Marshall Pomeroy Elementary School has 761 students, of whom 72 percent are Asian, 12 percent Hispanic, 5 percent white, 1 percent African American, and 10 percent mixed race or other. In addition, the school has 36 percent English language learners and 25 percent free or reduced-price lunch. Sheila Murphy Brewer is principal. She and an assistant principal, twenty-nine teachers, and nineteen staff members guide the school.[28]

Pomeroy was built in 1967 as an "open space" school, but within a few years, movable and permanent walls went up and teachers reclaimed their own classrooms, while still retaining common space in the primary grades. As the school's enrollment grew, portables were added and renovations in the main building occurred. The Learning Lab space is, in effect, a resurrection of "open space" in the original part of the school.

Deanna Sainten's Sixth-Grade Class

The recently built Learning Lab at Pomeroy is a large room with colorful chairs, cubbies for students to sit in, and tables where students can work together. On the morning of October 21, 2016, the lab is filled with twenty-eight sixth-graders working on different tasks. Teacher Deanna Sainten tells me, "We are doing blended learning to the max."[29]

After asking the veteran teacher, who has spent ten years at Pomeroy, a number of questions, I walk around the large, multicolored space and speak to students sitting in pairs, trios, and alone. Three students tell me that they are reading a *Scholastic News* article called "Vote for Me," about the Clinton/Trump presidential campaign. They are moving back and forth from the text to a worksheet with questions about the article. Another boy is writing in his notebook as he paged through his math text.

Two other sixth-graders are working on their Personal Learning Plan (PLP; developed at a Base Camp held in partnership with Summit schools; see below), checking which items they have mastered, (these show up in green on their screens) and ones that they had yet to complete (these show up in red). I ask them whether they have set personal goals—the PLP helps students acquire skills of self-assessment—and one shows me a screenshot of his goal "Going to College." The other boy is at sea in figuring out how to use that part of the PLP.[30]

Elsewhere in the Learning Lab, I see a line of about five students waiting to see Sainten, who is sitting at a small desk in the center of the space. The students want her to check their work or ask questions about the task they are working on.

I walk over to other students to see what they were doing. One boy is writing out answers on a worksheet about Ron Jones's *Acorn People* and then entering the answers into his Chromebook. When I ask him why he is doing that, he says: "It's neater." Two girls are working on the *Scholastic News* article on the presidential campaign and Googling on their tablets for information to answer questions. A boy and girl at a table are working on the class's unit on the Paleolithic era on their Chromebooks. Both are typing notes on their tablets from the readings on screen. They tell me that after they finish with the notes, they will have to submit them for Ms. Sainten's approval before they can move to the PLP on-screen assessment that determines how much they learned on this part of the unit.

As I scan the room every trio, pair, and individual appears to be at work on different academic tasks.

At the 12′ × 12′ whiteboard, under a huge banner spanning the Learning Lab ("The Mind Is Not a Vessel To Be Filled But a Fire To Be Ignited"), a boy and girl are working out a math problem called "opposites of numbers." They are talking to one another and jotting down notes to be sent to the teacher after they are finished.

Sainten informs class that they have five minutes left to complete their work before returning to their room. Four students wait in line to see her. She looks around the learning lab and says aloud to the group, "Make sure conversations are on task."

With less than a minute before the buzzer sounds, Sainten tells the class: "You have to leave the Learning Lab cleaner than you found it." Students straighten out tables and chairs and pick up scraps of paper on the floor. The buzzer sounds, and the students return to their classroom.

Sainten and her colleagues organize their daily lessons to keep activities moving while managing large groups of children. They switch students between small groups, individual work, and large group instruction, ever aware of possible distractions and limited attention spans. The teachers rotate their students through various teacher-designed activities (reading, math, independent work using Chromebooks whenever appropriate) within a forty-five-minute lesson. The Learning Lab is used once or twice weekly.

Ashima Das's Fifth-Grade Class

After leaving the Learning Lab, I walked over to visit Ashima Das's fifth-grade class. Lined up on the cement outside the classroom as I enter are student backpacks in a rainbow of colors. Inside the room housing twenty-nine students, each wall is laden with posters, students' work, and photos. The room feels crowded.

Das is seated at a table in the front of the room, working with individual students whom she calls up one at a time to meet with her. The rest of the class is at work on different activities, some reading from their Chromebook screens, others in pairs taking notes and talking to one another, and even others helping classmates with a question. Das looks across the room and says: "Eyes and ears up here," meaning that students need to stop and look at her. "You have been working in pairs, and if you need more help you can turn to others at your table," she says.

A former parent and volunteer at Pomeroy, Das eventually acquired her credentials and began teaching at Pomeroy five years ago. Like her upper-grade colleagues, she participated in Summit's Base Camp and created lessons that could be used (and shared) by other fifth-grade teachers. The Summit network of charter schools (see chapter 2) had reached out to districts seeking to use Summit's materials, especially its Personalized Learning Plan. The Pomeroy upper-grade teachers had joined the Summit Base Camp during the summer of 2015, and that school year and the following summer had learned how to have students use the PLP and, in addition, had customized playlists for their upper-grade elementary school students.[31]

After class, Das told me that she works closely with one other fifth-grade teacher, particularly on how best to manage time and cover all the content and skills that are required and find time especially for those students who need help. After her summer work with Base Camp, she says, she has shifted from "direct instruction" in content (she teaches science, language arts, math, and social studies) to using the Personal Learning Plan. Now, she says, content is available to students on their Chromebooks as they learn subject matter in different "modalities."

Das also pointed out to me that fifth-graders now learn far more and explicitly from each other. They work on their individual PLPs and know what they have finished and what they still have to work on. They know how many items they have mastered and how many items in lessons need further work. She now parlays small groups working together, pairs, whole group instruction, and individual attention—as she was doing when I entered the room—into a multilayered lesson that unfolded as I was there.

Das has decentralized her instruction by using PLPs. Moreover, she has trained members of the class to be "mentors" to other students who need help on a particular skill. On one wall is a list of students' names and the skills they have mastered. After being approved by Das, students write in their names and what content and skills they can help other fifth-graders with. When these "mentors" complete their tasks during a lesson, they are allowed to help other students who ask them for aid. Das and other upper-grade teachers also have access to Learning Lab weekly.

Vicky Ramirez's Second-Grade Class

On another day, I visited Pomeroy to see how primary grade teachers put "blended learning" into practice. As part of the school plan, these teachers did not have access to the Learning Lab. I saw two second-grade classes (with a large common space between the two rooms), where teachers taught lessons by rotating students through three activities in the classroom.

For example, in Vicky Ramirez's second-grade room, there are twenty-three boys and girls. Ramirez has been teaching at Pomeroy for over twenty years. I see eleven students sitting in the back of the room, using the i-Ready application with earphones/ear buds working on math in their Chromebooks (there is a cart of devices in the room). In a rocking chair, Ramirez reads a story with eight students sitting on rug. She asks questions and students answer. From time to time, she scans the room to see if students are on- or off-task. Elsewhere in the room, four boys are lying on rug working on clipboards listing work they have to complete.[32]

Ramirez has divided the lesson into three activities: the teacher-led reading group, independent work (above boys with clipboards), and others using i-Ready. After about fifteen or twenty minutes, Ramirez announces that the students will rotate to another activity. Students respond quickly. Some go up to her for reading, another group dons earphones/earbuds, and the rest work independently on worksheets.

Over the two morning visits to Pomeroy, I observed that "blended learning" and "personalization" operated differently in the primary and upper grades of the school. The Learning Lab catered to the upper grades as an alternative venue for individualizing instruction, while in-class rotation of stations was the order of the day in primary grades. In both instances, the use of the devices was taken for granted and slipped into the background, not the foreground, of each teacher's lessons.

JOSEPH WELLER ELEMENTARY SCHOOL

Raquel Kusunoki is principal at Joseph Weller Elementary School. As a young child, she and her family emigrated from the Philippines to the Bay Area. Kusunoki eventually became a credentialed teacher. She taught for thirteen years in San Jose Unified District. She has been the Weller principal for four years after serving as assistant principal at the school. "My umbilical cord," she told me, "is connected here."[33]

With nearly 450 students (K–6), Weller has a diverse cultural mix. Sixty percent of the students are Asian (including Filipino), 29 percent are Latino, 4 percent are African American, and 4 percent are white (2015). Of that enrollment, 44 percent are English language learners and 47 percent are eligible for free and reduced-price lunch.[34]

I spent an October morning at Weller interviewing the principal and observing two teachers' lessons.

Richard Hart's Combined-Grade Class

I first went to Richard Hart's combined fifth- and sixth-grade class. While the students have access to the Learning Lab at scheduled times, when in their classroom, Hart's class rotates activities between whole group instruction, small group, and individual work in language arts, math, and online units that Weller teachers had designed during the summer with Summit Base Camp.

It is 8:30. There are thirty-two students in class sitting at pods of four pushed-together desks scattered throughout the room. The walls have displays of students' work—hand-drawn architectural drawings of community centers, part of a recent unit. There is a Chromebook cart in the room and shelves of books along the walls. There is also a printer and TV monitor in the room.

All students are engaged in different activities. On the whiteboard is an agenda for the day's work showing that students will work on their "Myths" project and their Personalized Learning Plans. As I move about the room, I see ten students working on their PLPs. They are doing their self-assessment of what they have completed and what they still have to finish in the "Myths" unit. Others have their tablets open and are reading, taking notes, and conferring with classmates. Some students are using earbuds to listen to the videos they are watching.

Each student has a playlist (much of which has been created by Weller upper-grade teachers) readings, videos, worksheets, etc., for the "Myths" unit. They take notes, and when they have completed their playlist, they check with Hart. If he approves their work, students take the assessment (see below).

Hart walks around the room talking with individual students as they work on their PLPs and sees where they are in the project. When students want his help, they raise their hands. Hart carries his Apple laptop and sees what is on each sixth-grader's screen (he is using gScholar dashboard software to track individual student's work). Hart does question-and-answer with each student as he moves around the room. He often leans over and shows a student what he has on his screen tracking that student's work.[35]

I see some students go to a whiteboard easel and sign their names when they finish a topic. Their names and topic signal that Hart will have to review the notes each student has taken, approve what student has done, and then give permission to student to take an assessment for that part of the unit. After one quick conference with a student who has completed his task, I see Hart do a fist bump with the student. I also see one English language learner working online by herself.

As I scan the classroom close to 9 a.m., room noise is minimal with the murmuring of the teacher in conference with students or a pairs of students talking about a task. After walking through the room, I note that no students are off-task.

Juhi Sharma's Fifth-Grade Class

I then go to Juhi Sharma's combination fifth-grade class. Twenty-seven students sitting in the room in groups of three to six at tables in no particular order. Student work covers walls. Whiteboards on three sides of room contain instructions, daily agenda, and goals.

One whiteboard has instructions for her fifth-graders in the morning and sixth-graders in the afternoon:

5th PLP—activity Chap. 2 Review/test
PLT—Focus Area Math [Personal Learning Time when students can choose to work on different topics]
WorkShop: Powers of 10

6th—Complete Checkpoint 1 (PLP)
Complete 6.2 & 6.3—[refers to chapters in textbook Go Math]^{36}

On the front whiteboard, the schedule for that week is displayed.

8:00 HR/PE [home room and physical education]
9:00 Math
10:00 RTI [*Response to intervention:* Used to identify students needing academic or behavioral support]
11:00 Recess/Lunch
12:00 Math
1:00 Science
2:00 Clean Up

As I look around the room, I see ten students sitting in two rows facing another teacher, Beverly McCarter, who is teaching place value. The title of the workshop is "Powers of 10." McCarter points to a chart on the whiteboard as she explains the concept and gives examples to the whole group and then asks students to use place value as she poses questions. Sharma will do a similar math workshop with a portion of McCarter's class at another time.

As I scan the room, the rest of the class is working individually, as I saw in Richard Hart's class. Sharma walks around with laptop in hand, asking and answering questions and monitoring work (like Hart, she uses gScholar to see where the class and individual students are). I see that Sharma does a high-five with a student after he shows her that he is finished. When students have completed a topic, they write their names on a whiteboard. Once Sharma approves students' notes, they can move to assessment—in this instance, the class is working on multiplication and fractions. Looking over the shoulder of one student's PLP, I see that he has finished and passed all of topics but one. He is using his Personal Learning Time to finish up.

Noise in the room increases as the "Powers of 10" workshop finishes up and the ten students return to their tables, writing their names on whiteboard and conferring with others at their tables. Sharma says, "Voices, please." Class quiets down, and she says "Thank you."

After thirty-five minutes, I look around the class and see students working on different tasks during PLP, going from their Chromebook screen to writing in their notebook and working on assessments they can submit and then move on to next task.

Five minutes later, Sharma announces that one student has passed all of his unit tasks. There is scattered applause from students.

A buzzer sounds, ending the class.

A month later, I returned to Weller to see two primary teachers do their in-class rotation of activities in small groups, large groups, and independently, again using Chromebooks for individual and small group work on content and skills.

Jackie Dang's Third-Grade Class

Third-grade teacher Jackie Dang is in her third year teaching. As I enter her room, I see twenty-one students at seven tables, each seating two to four students. In the rear of the room, there is a circular table where Dang sits, listening to one child reading aloud. High on one wall are photos of every child in the class, large enough to see from anywhere in the room. On another wall is a set of posters about what a "mindset" is and its importance (Dang told me later that she taught five lessons on "growth mindset" at the beginning of semester). And on another wall are posters of the branches of the US government.[37]

The class has just finished a rotation of activities. One group of nine students with their Chromebooks open is taking a quiz on readings they completed. Ten students are sitting on a bright multicolored rug—red, orange, green, blue—writing in notebooks, reading on the topic of the day, and watching videos.

After Dang finishes with the individual student, she calls up another. She listens as student reads a story to her and then hands the girl a worksheet that gets at comprehension of the story. The questions on the worksheet ask student to make predictions based on what she read and then to write short sentences to summarize the story.

As I walk around the room, I see that all of the students are on task. From time to time, Dang needs to announce something. To get everyone's attention she sings: *bump-de-bump-de-bump*. Students stop what they are doing and repeat the syllables. On one of these occasions, Dang says that two worksheets were turned in that did not have names on them. Two boys come up and collect their papers from her.

Before calling up another student to read to her, Dang walks around the room checking on what each student is doing. She returns to her table and summons the next student. The girl reads to Dang, who goes over worksheet the child had turned in.

I walk over to a third-grader who is typing in her Chromebook. I ask what she is doing, and she tells me that she belongs to the "typing club" in class. I look at the screen. It displays printed sentences. The nine year-old types letters to match the words of the on-screen sentence. As she does, the screen lights up, showing the fingers of each hand as they hit the keys. The screen simultaneously shows the percentage of the letters and words that are accurate and the speed at which she is typing. After she finished, the screen flashes that she has attained 95 percent accuracy at a speed of 30 words per minute. The screen also shows that the requirement for this exercise was 80 percent accuracy at 25 words per minute; a nearby student had 100 percent accuracy at 6 words per minute.

As the activities come to an end, Dang again sings *bump-de-bump-de-bump*. Students stop what they are doing. Dang announces that class will come to the rug to begin a social studies lesson on government. After they settle in, Dang moves to a whole group discussion of the overlapping Venn circles on the whiteboard illustrating the branches of the

US government, and then moves to reviewing words they learned in the last lesson: *symbol, vote, laws, legislative,* and *judge.* Students raise hands to answer her review questions. After going over these words, Dang creates groups by counting off students 1 through 5 and then directs each numbered group of five to different parts of the room; each group is to write five sentences on cardboard strips about their assigned word.

As the small groups go to work, I speak with students near me and ask what they were doing with the Venn circles and why. They explain the task accurately to me—showing overlap between branches of government. In the next ten minutes, the noise level rises; at one point, Dang gets everyone's attention and asks them to work quietly. The noise level falls to a murmur.

Shortly afterward, the lesson ends.

Pomeroy and Weller elementary schools represent blended and personalized learning in Milpitas elementary schools. At the secondary level, the PLP and Learning Labs are in place, but there is much variation among teachers using the software and integrating new technologies into their daily lessons (save for Thomas Russell middle school, which had joined the pilot efforts years earlier).[38]

With the departure of Cary Matsuoka from Milpitas and the appointment of a veteran insider, former teacher, principal, and district administrator, Cheryl Jordan, chances are high that the program Matsuoka initiated will continue as planned—contingent, of course, on continued budget support and unforeseen events disrupting the program. Whether the instructional policy of technology integration will grab hold and stick at the secondary level as it has in elementary schools, I cannot predict.

UNCOMMON DISTRICTS?

Milpitas Unified School District and Mountain View Los Altos High School District are rare (two of seventy-seven districts in the Bay Area) in their adopting technology integration as an instructional policy and erecting an infrastructure and culture that pushes teachers to use hardware and software regularly in their daily lessons. They are unusual not only in Silicon Valley but across the nation.

Yes, there are other districts scattered across the United States that have adopted technology integration policies seeking to prod all teachers toward that outcome. These also are uncommon among the thirteen thousand–plus school districts in the nation.

In these districts, similar to MVLA and Milpitas, it is expected that teachers will integrate technologies into their classroom activities. While teacher autonomy is not restricted, the school and district incentives, support, culture, and direction make clear that, over time, all teachers are to use approved software and devices in their lessons.

How, when, and under what conditions, however, the teacher decides. The choice, of course, depends on many organizational and personal factors, including district curriculum standards; the particular content, skills, and attitudes being taught in a unit; teacher beliefs, and a collaborative culture within the school that supports teachers. Teachers make these important decisions. And these districts, like the two Silicon Valley ones described in this chapter, have established ways of helping teachers put the new technologies into practice while keeping the technology in the background, not the foreground, of lessons.

From large to small districts and affluent to low-income, district-wide programs to make integration of devices and software ubiquitous have appeared in Henrico County, Virginia, beginning in 2001; Kyrene, Arizona, in 2005; and Mooresville, North Carolina, in 2007. These initiatives have moved many, but not all, teachers in these districts to integrate technology in varied ways. Media reports and district documents record the introduction and spread through schools and classrooms.[39]

In each of these districts, a superintendent working closely with the school board initiated the program from the top—as did Cary Matsuoka in Milpitas (but not in Mountain View Los Altos Union, where the initiative started among teachers and principals at the two high schools). Top district administrators orchestrated monies to fund technology initiatives from various sources such as bond referenda, reallocation of budgeted items, vendor donations, and foundation grants. These nationally recognized districts have hosted a river of visitors wanting to see what promoters called "the future."

Nonetheless, such districts remain scarce.[40] Why is this so?

Most district leaders in the United States are more than aware that parents and taxpayers expect children and youth to become adept with contemporary technologies to enable them to enter college and get jobs after graduation. They know that the costs for wiring schools, increasing bandwidth, acquiring devices, training teachers, and providing technical assistance add up to sizable chunks of their budgets, and they know the promised returns on these investments promoted by parents and vendors (e.g., higher state and district test scores, high school graduation rates, and going to college) appeal to most voters—even when the potential goes unfulfilled.

So most school leaders ensure that their districts buy and distribute new devices and software to schools and create technical assistance for those teachers who opt to use them. They know in their gut that no contemporary school district can reject the costs of new technologies without being labeled Neanderthals. That is a political fact of life in a setting where school officials are wholly dependent on taxpayer and voter support.

Yet that fact of life does not necessarily lead to instructional policies requiring all teachers to use the new technologies in their daily lessons. Sure, nearly all districts have strategic plans for getting student access to and use of the new technologies. All of these districts with such plans and brand-new devices leave it up to individual teachers to schedule a cart of laptops for math lessons or ask for one-to-one tablets for the entire middle school—and when and where to integrate laptops into their lessons.

And many do; the growing number of teachers integrating new technologies into their the classroom is evident across many districts. Limiting teacher autonomy, however, to make instructional decisions in using new technologies is a battle that few districts lust for. Whether teacher discretion should or should not be abridged is a policy issue that only a few schools and districts (e.g., Summit charter schools and Milpitas Unified School District and Mountain View Los Altos High School District) have addressed.

Thus, even with remarkable national gains over the past decade in students having access to tablets and laptops, interactive whiteboards, and other devices and their increased use across so many classrooms, adopting and adapting these technologies for daily lessons remains voluntary for teachers in most schools, a choice that few districts override.

When it comes to the history of school reform aimed at altering how teachers teach—in this instance using new technologies—none of this is new. As with this current generation of school reformer—filled with dreams of students learning more, faster, and better using new technologies—previous generations have wrestled with the dilemma of asking teachers, whom they often see as the cause of instructional problems, to turn around and be agents in implementing new instructional policies seeking changes in the traditional ways of teaching. The common compromise was to leave implementation decisions, then and now, to teachers, which is why so few districts expect all teachers, as part of their job, to integrate devices and software into their lessons.

Will instructional policies relying on teacher discretion or those requiring teachers to integrate technologies into lessons increase student academic achievement, reduce existing achievement gap, and engage students in learning more, faster, and better? The answer is: No one knows.

FOUR

Putting "Best Cases" into the Context of Past and Present School Reforms

Classroom, school, and district exemplars of technology integration in Silicon Valley have been the focus of previous chapters. The research strategy of sampling "best cases" is to see how they were put into practice, how they operated, how teaching changed, and what common features of teachers and schools emerged that might explain why these exemplars exist. This research approach has been used often in analyzing earlier school reforms such as "effective schools," best instructional practices, and in the current rush to personalize learning.[1]

What's missing from most "best cases" analyses like this, however, is the historical context for reforms seeking to alter classroom instruction through teachers' integration of new technologies into their daily lessons.

If you were to suffer from amnesia about the history of US schools, you might think that these best cases in teachers' daily lessons, schoolwide efforts, and districts pushing teachers to use new technologies to reach content and skill objectives were exceptional—brand-new reforms without any roots in the past. Not so. For the past two centuries, different generations of reformers have sought to improve what teachers did in their classrooms, get schools to operate more efficiently and effectively, and help districts perform better than they have. Since the early 1980s, the presence of new electronic technologies in schools leaped exponentially as costs came down, computer speed increased, and interactivity between software and user accelerated. As with earlier reforms, visions of engaged students, improved lessons, and schools and districts working better at less cost than before spurred policy-makers and administrators to invest heavily in new devices, software, and infrastructure.

The pervasive social belief that technology will improve one's life has fueled the American economy, politics, and culture for centuries. Contemporary techno-enthusiasm is just another incarnation of that historic belief. Periodic school reforms pushing for instructional television and the introduction of desktop computers mirrored the larger society's dazzled belief that technology would be able to solve national and personal problems.[2] Technology integration, particularly the recent and persistent calls for "personalized learning," is part of the recurring story of well-intentioned and well-heeled crusaders seeking to improve teaching and schooling.[3]

SCHOOL REFORM SINCE THE 1900S

> **Palimpsest:** A manuscript, typically of papyrus or parchment, that has been written on more than once, with the earlier writing incompletely erased and often legible.[4]

Think "palimpsest" when the phrase "personalized learning" is used in 2018.[5] Reformers have long dreamed of tailoring knowledge and skills to an individual student—one definition of the phrase. And instructionally minded reformers put parts of that dream into practice in the early twentieth century, in the 1960s, and in the second decade of the twenty-first century.

Today, personalized learning, a subset of what many call *blended learning*, is the pinnacle of lessons that integrate digital technology. So much talk about personalized learning has obscured, but not erased, the original progressive rhetoric and actions of the past hundred years. Knowing that past progressive efforts to educate Americans might bring a sharper and more fully informed perspective to the contemporary claims that champions of personalized learning express to policymakers, parents, and teachers, I link past reforms to present ones. That resurrecting of the original and partially obscured text—the palimpsest—highlights the pedagogical and efficiency-driven wings of the progressive movement then and today.[6]

The Progressive Movement, 1890s–1940s

In these five decades, progressive education was the reigning political ideology in US schooling. There were two main ideas, anchored in the emerging "science of education" that spurred and divided US progressives. Both drew from the writings of John Dewey and his embrace of a science of education.[7]

First, there were adherents of student-centered instruction, small group, and individualized learning (sometimes called *pedagogical progressives*) and, second, advocates of "scientific management" (sometimes called *administrative progressives*) who admired what corporate leaders were doing in the private sector. They sought to prepare children and youth to fit into work and society far more efficiently than the traditional schooling of the day had done.

School boards, superintendents, and researchers of the day glommed onto scientific management. Proud to be called "educational engineers" during these years, these reformers created lists of actions that superintendents should perform to strengthen district performance and that principals could use to evaluate teachers. They measured buildings, teacher performance, and student achievement.[8]

The efficiency-driven, behaviorist wing of the reformers, spurred by the writings and research of Edward Thorndike and other academics, was victorious by the 1930s and has largely dominated school improvement initiatives since. Innovations appeared each decade trumpeting the next new thing that would make teaching and learning more productive, effective, and individualized.[9]

In the 1950s, building on the work of Ohio State psychologist Sidney Pressey three decades earlier, the term of the day was *teaching machines* (popularized by behavioral psychologist B.F. Skinner); in the 1970s, it was *mastery learning* (anchored in the work of University of Chicago psychologist Benjamin Bloom); then *competency-based learning* since the 1990s. Each of these efficiency-seeking innovations, in different guises, can be found in schools in 2018.[10]

In all instances, psychologists and school reformers broke down knowledge and skills into small, digestible parts so students could learn at their own pace through individualized lessons and teacher use of positive reinforcement. Extrinsic rewards from teachers, and later software programs, guided students along paths to acquiring requisite skills and knowledge. Promoters of these innovations claimed that such approaches were both efficient and effective for students' gaining required content and skills, graduating, entering the labor market, and becoming civically engaged adults.[11]

Since the 1920s, challenges to this dominant behavioristic approach to teaching and learning came from the student-centered, "whole child" wing of the progressives. These reformers championed project-based teaching, student choice, and collaborative learning (e.g., the Eight Year Study; the Project Method) to achieve the same ends. While these determined efforts to individualize lessons to match academic and ability differences between students and create more student agency in lessons and units rose and fell over the years incrementally increasing within more schools, the efficiency-driven whole group, teacher-directed approach prevailed.[12]

Neo-Progressive Reforms, 1960s

Progressive educational ideas revived during the 1960s amid desegregation struggles, the Vietnam War, and societal changes. Neo-progressive reformers, unknowingly borrowing from an earlier generation of administrative progressives, launched innovations such as performance contracting. Corporations took over failing schools in Texarkana, Arizona;

Gary, Indiana; and a hundred other districts, promising that their methods of teaching reading using new technologies such as programmed learning would raise test scores fast and cheaply. Partial to the corporate managerial strategies in running schools, these reformers sought accountability through agreements they signed with district school boards. By the mid-1970s, however, most school boards had dumped their contracts.[13]

Meanwhile, the pedagogical wing of the progressive movement—interested in student-centered classroom activities, democratic practices, and more interaction with the "real world"—pushed for individually guided education and open classrooms (also called *open education* and *informal education*).[14]

The story of how the British import, informal education, became the reform du jour in the mid-1970s begins with critics' heavy pounding of failing schools following World War II. Across the political spectrum, critics flailed US schools because education, they believed, could solve national problems arising from Cold War competition with the Soviet Union, caste-like treatment of black citizens, and a pervasive culture of conformity that suffocated imagination.[15]

With the struggle over school inequalities rising in the 1960s, pedagogical reformers saw hope in the open classroom. Richly amplified by the media, the open classroom, with its focus on students learning by doing in small groups and making individual choices of how and what to learn, resonated with vocal critics of creativity-crushing, factory-style classrooms. Thousands of elementary school classrooms—out of millions—became homelike settings where young children sitting on rugs moved from one attractive "learning center" for math to other stations in science, reading, writing, and art. Teams of teachers guiding multi-age groups of students working on projects created non-graded elementary schools.[16]

The progressive movement in schools—both the efficiency and pedagogical branches—took flight in the mid-1960s, but plummeted swiftly within a decade as a new generation of reformers promised a "back to basics" approach.[17]

The Onset of Personalized Learning, Early 2000s

In recent decades, efficiency-minded school reformers (many of whom are high-tech entrepreneurs), driven by unalloyed optimism about the power of new technologies, sought to transform teaching and learning through online and classroom-based lessons. These reformers have become evangelists for integrating technologies, especially the dream of shifting from traditional, whole-group instruction to personalized, student-driven independent learning. They have appropriated the language of "whole child," student-centered teaching and the aim of connecting the student to the real world from progressives a century ago.

As with the other catchphrases, *personalized learning* means different things to various breeds of reformers. What all share is a common commitment to use technologies to individualize learning as earlier generations of reformers had done through such programs as competency-based learning or mastery learning. Now, with digital tools available and a reform-driven climate hostile to what many reformers call a "factory model" of schooling, the motivation and capability to convert personalized learning into daily online schoolwork has spread rapidly across the nation's suburban and urban schools.[18]

Bursting with visions of students being prepared for a world where in a lifetime adults change jobs a half-dozen times, these efficiency-minded reformers tout schools that have tailored lessons (both online and offline) for individual students, turned teachers into coaches, and classrooms into places where students collaborate with one another, thus reflecting the changed workplace of the twenty-first century. These reformers' victorious capture of the vocabulary of personalized learning has made parsing the present-day world of programs aimed at tailoring lessons to individual students difficult, but not impossible, once those century-old progressive struggles over the whole child, efficiency, and engineering lessons are connected to the present.[19]

For example, some advocates of personalized learning believe, as a Wisconsin high school teacher who put it: "The role of the learner . . . is to determine goals based on student needs, interests, learning styles and career goals, and to develop the individual paths to reaching them."[20] Pedagogical progressives circa 1920 would applaud this view.

Yet other administrators and teachers, equally adamant about advancing personalizing learning, believe that it is the software designers working with teachers who are in the best position to customize content and skills (through playlists of readings, videos, and individualized learning plans) that students must master to complete a course, get promoted to the next grade, and eventually graduate from high school. Concerned about educational productivity and savvy about new technologies, these "neo-progressives" see their job as guiding students to success step by step along well-lit paths tailored to students' strengths and limitations. Were Edward Thorndike and other educational engineers in the early twentieth century alive today, they would give three cheers for these modern-day reformers.

Between the spotlight on learners being central to determining what they need and getting it and the spotlight on teachers as dominant in the process of personalizing learning lies the swamp of actual programs, each claiming that it is best. This dilemma of where the center of gravity should rest between the learner and the teacher in determining both the lesson format and what content and skills should be learned is old hat to those familiar with the arguments of progressives a century ago. Then, as now, it was not either/or. Advocates of teacher- or student-directed lessons negotiated compromises that yielded hybrids in public schools, with programs spread across the spectrum of personalized learning confounding any common definition.[21]

A brief look at actual classrooms billed as personalized learning venues give substance to this array of programs across the United States.

FROM THE CLASSROOM—TEACH TO ONE

Teach To One is a middle school math program that rearranges traditional classroom space and furniture, tailors daily lessons for individual students and uses different forms of teaching (*modalities* is the favored word) within a ninety-minute period. The program grew out of a pilot venture in New York City called School 4 One that got rave reviews. Two of its founders left and created a nonprofit that markets Teach To One; it is now in twenty-eight schools in eight states, teaching math to ten thousand students.[22]

On May 15, 2016, I spent an hour and a half shadowing Lupe (all names are pseudonyms), an eighth-grade student at ASCEND charter school in Oakland, where she and about a hundred seventh- and eighth-grade classmates (the sixth-graders were on a field trip the day I visited) received their daily math instruction through Teach To One. Teach To One's director, Winona Bassett, briefed me on the first-year program, answered a number of my questions, and found the student I would shadow. She explained to me the different modalities I would see during the morning.[23]

What I observed are clear instances of both teachers and students seamlessly integrating technology in a lesson on scientific notation. The math skill of scientific notation is listed on the online portal. The portal shows the playlist and the skill the student is working on for that day (it is numbered A 280: "I will solve real-world problems involving numbers in scientific notation" and is aligned to Common Core math standards). The portal also includes each student's all-important Exit Slip, which contains multiple-choice questions that the student has to answer and submit daily.[24]

The Exit Slip assesses students' grasp of the skill and their accuracy in applying it. One question, for example, asks: *"A website had approximately 300 thousand visits in 2010. The number of visits rose to 6.31×10^{10} in 2011. In scientific notation, how many more visits were there in 2011 than in 2010?"* The student chooses from among four possible answers. The central server in New York City reports daily to the local staff how well or poorly students have done on the questions—how many were missed, how many correct. Using the portal, students (and their parents) can see exactly how they are faring on each skill, how much work they have to do and whether they have "room for growth, are almost there, and great and perfect" (Teach To One calls these skill levels *foundational, core,* and *extension*). Lupe is working on a skill that is at grade level. This version of personalized learning is clearly competency based.[25]

Students' answers to the daily Exit Slip questions determines what they will work on the following day. All Exit Slips are sent electronically to New York City, graded, and in Bassett's words, "using algorithms and human judgment," the next day's Exit Slip is sent back within hours to her and the teachers of the program.[26] Students then can access the portal and know what they will work on the next day and whether or not they are progressing or regressing (or have mastered) each skill. As with all competency-based learning programs, math skills are aligned with state standards in a highly flexible physical environment unlike a traditional classroom.

The Physical Space

Taking over the charter school's library, the large space is demarcated into four separate rooms, each with a sign of a local university (e.g., San Jose State, San Francisco State). Each room has been designed with Teach To One consultants. Metal library shelves separate them from one another. The first room I am in has long tables—each movable chair clearly numbered for where up to six students are to sit. There is much noise from different segments of the larger room, since the library-shelving units that separate the spaces do not buffer noise. Students, teachers, and aides go about their business, creating the ebb and flow of sound across the divided space.

One space is used for a teacher-directed lesson (modality) on scientific notation; in another students use their Chromebooks to work on the individually designed lesson on scientific notation based on their results of work the previous day recorded on their online Exit Slip (another modality); the third space is for collaborative work between and among students and teachers. The fourth space is used for another teacher-directed lesson on circumference. Thus, there are three modalities for student learning in play (teacher-delivered, independent, and small group collaboration).

This morning, the seventh- and eighth-graders are distributed between the rooms, spending a half-hour in each space before moving on to the next modality. For each segment of the ninety-minute class, students sit at different tables with different classmates.

The Students

These seventh- and eighth-graders are mostly Latino boys and girls, aged thirteen to fourteen. They range from large to pint-sized, and are at varying stages of puberty. They are filled with energy, zest, and seriousness mixed with playfulness. As an old white man with a cane, I stand out, and when I sit at a table next to Lupe, many ask my name and what I am doing there. I tell them that I am shadowing Lupe and will write about the class on my blog. I tell them my name and one student yells out: "Larry, the Cable Guy." The name sticks as I move from one modality to another.[27]

As I observe students in each modality, I see them using their Chromebooks, reading from the screen and writing in their notebooks. There is much back-and-forth between students about the task they were working on and playful kidding with each other as they exchange information about friends, clothes, and how each looks.

The Teachers

For the fifty students there this morning, there are two credentialed teachers and two teaching assistants. I watched both teachers in their different spaces for thirty-minute periods. During the ninety-minute math period, chimes signal when students are to switch modalities (e.g., go from ten-minute Math Advisory—like a "homeroom"—to a teacher-directed lesson), when they must complete their Exit Slip, and when they must move to their next ASCEND class elsewhere in the building.

The first teacher I observe is doing what the program calls "live investigation." An experienced teacher, Julia Kerr has ten students at three tables. For thirty minutes, she conducts a recitation/whole group discussion on converting standard notation to scientific notation. She begins with a matrix of four cells on the whiteboard, each cell holding the following symbols: $+$, $-$, $\times$, $\div$. Students open their notebooks and draw the matrix. She then asks students: "What are the rules when we add decimals?" She calls on students by name.

At my table, there are two boys and two girls. They have their Chromebooks open and have taken out their notebooks and pens. As they exchange information and gossip, they move easily between Spanish and English. One of the boys is a big, nonstop talker who prods the other boy—much shorter and slighter—with jokes and comments about others in the class. The smaller boy laughs but hardly responds. The two girls say nothing to the larger boy's comments. Kerr, who scans the class constantly, sees what is happening at the table and admonishes the larger boy by name. He quiets down and returns to his Chromebook and notebook.

Kerr asks: "What do you do when you multiply (3.4×10^2) by (6.2×10^3)?" A few students raise their hands and reply. Kerr builds on their responses and gives examples to tie down the point. She then moves to subtraction part of matrix. She moves around room while talking, ensuring that everyone is on task. When one student yells out an answer to one of her questions instead of raising his hand and waiting for her to call on him, she looks directly at him and says: "You have a warning."[28]

Kerr moves through each cell of the matrix, giving examples and asking students by name to respond to her questions about how to convert standard to scientific notation. They use their calculator app on the Chromebook and move easily back and forth between paper and screen. As she walks around, students show her their screens and notes they have taken.

Chimes ring a five-minute warning. Kerr begins to sum up by asking students to "pay attention." She goes over rules students should follow in doing conversion from standard to scientific notation and asks the large boy at my table to "do it for me." He does. Then she asks students to work with a partner to review each other's work. They do. There is no back-and-forth at my table—it's all work. Kerr puts another example of conversion on the whiteboard. Chimes ring, and the ten students disperse to work in a different modality.

I ask Lupe what she got out of the class. She tells me that Ms. Kerr helped her better understand what scientific notation is. She will use her notes when she works on her Exit Slip. When I ask if she could convert standard to scientific notation, she pauses, hesitates, and murmurs something I can't hear. She smiles, and we go to the next class.

In this modality, there are twenty-four students in the room. Lupe and her classmates will work individually in their Chromebooks, consult their notebook, and ask veteran teacher Donald Percy questions about scientific notation that they are stuck on. They open their Chromebooks and notebooks. Most dig right into the task. Some are clearly stuck. Percy sees this whether they raise their hands for help or not. He moves easily around the tables, questioning a student, making suggestions, and going to the whiteboard to show what a student is stuck on and what the student needs to do. At my table, there are one boy and four girls. The boy cracks jokes, and one girl occasionally laughs. He is working from another sheet of paper and answering questions on a paper "independent practice" handout (while some students who work at independent practice use Chromebooks, some do not). I learn later from Winona Bassett that this student is having a very hard time with previous skills and the current scientific notation. The girls at my table generally ignore him and proceed to move from writing in notebooks to tapping away in their Chromebooks. At another table, Percy works with three boys who need help. He goes to the whiteboard and writes down examples, explaining how to go from standard to scientific notation. Chimes ring, signaling that it's time for everyone to transition back to ten-minute Math Advisories to complete their Exit Slip.

Those at my table begin doing so. Quiet descends in the room. Students click away on the questions they have to answer, given where they are in mastering the skill. Some consult their notebooks. Before the chimes ring, Percy praises the entire group for their diligent work and then asks students as they leave to plug in their Chromebooks to recharge them. In a few minutes, this session ends and students move to their next ASCEND class.

I met with Bassett to debrief. I was curious about the switching between paper and screen, and she explained that this was a teacher decision, not a company one, since teachers wanted a record (*evidence* was the word she used) that staff could assess and then compare what they see on paper with students' progress through the competency-based math curriculum via Exit Slips. She explained to me the rapid electronic turn-around between the New York City computer servers and math teachers at ASCEND, Teach To One accessibility to distant staff, and the ups and down of being a first-year program. I thanked her for setting up the shadowing of a student.[29]

Teach To One is an example of a teacher-directed, competency-based program tailored for each student to master the skills and content the math Common Core standards require and that will be on the state test. The format of providing different modalities in which students learn, including face-to-face, small group, large group, and independent work, differs from most self-contained math lessons on scientific notation.

Yet testing and accountability continue to bedevil those productivity-minded, contemporary reformers championing competency-based learning even as they have seized the vocabulary of "whole child," "individualized learning," and "student-centered" instruction and learning.[30] As one report put it:

> Personalized learning is rooted in the expectation that students should progress through content based on demonstrated learning instead of seat time. By contrast, standards-based accountability centers its ideas about what students should know, and when, on grade-level expectations and pacing. The result is that as personalized learning models become more widespread, practitioners are increasingly encountering tensions between personalized learning and state and federal accountability structures.[31]

Strains arise in public schools over end-of-year testing, meeting annual proficiency standards, and judging academic performance on the basis of student scores. Few policymakers and contemporary progressive reformers eager to install competency-based learning in the form of personalized learning in their schools, however, have mentioned these core conflicts embedded in the DNA of this currently popular reform.

FROM THE CLASSROOM—SUMMIT RAINIER CHARTER SCHOOL

Now consider a chemistry lesson taught in a project-based learning unit in 2016.

Just before spring in Silicon Valley, I observed Edward Lin at Summit (Rainier) teach a lesson on metals (including a lab) from 11:25 a.m. to 1:00 p.m. There are seventeen students sitting two to a table facing an interactive white board at the front of a portable classroom. A periodic table hangs from one wall of the classroom. A large sink in the back of the room is used by students to wash hands and vials, and to get water for experiments. Also at the rear of the classroom, tables hold tubs of equipment, goggles, test tubes, and other paraphernalia..

After spending six years working for pharmaceutical companies, Lin, who had tutored students while working as a chemist, decided to change careers. He went to University of California, Berkeley, and secured his state teaching credential. Attending various career fairs for teachers, Lin heard about Summit, researched the school, got an interview, and was hired as a chemistry teacher. He is in his third year of teaching at Summit Rainier.[32]

Lin has prepared a series of lesson activities, beginning with a Warm Up on the interactive whiteboard. He previews with students the activities he will segue through over the course of ninety-five minutes.

One slide lists the items today's lesson will cover:

- Project Introduction
- Molecule Selection
- Is it a metal? Lab
- Are atoms in your molecule metal or nonmetal?

The Warm Up that introduces the project asks the following questions:

- With your group, list out 5 tools (kitchen, woodwork, etc.)
- For each tool, answer the following questions:
    a. How does the tool's shape allow it to do its job?
    b. What material(s) is the tool usually made of?
    c. Why is this tool usually made from this material(s)?

Students pair up and generate examples such as knives, wrenches, pencils, etc. in response to Lin's request. Discussions seemingly engage each table as I scan the room. Lin then asks the students to answer three questions about each tool they identified: How does the tool's shape allow it to do the job? What material(s) is the tool usually made of? Why is the tool usually made from the material(s)?

A whole group discussion of these tools ensues for about ten minutes. Lin calls on students by name. Few raise their hands. As I scan the classroom, most students are listening and responding to Lin's prompts. A few are not. Those who are not listening are looking at their cell phones, which are lying on their desks, or are quietly chatting with tablemates. Lin stops talking, and motions to one of the chatterers, and she stops. He continues to guide the discussion and makes the central point that the tools students identified are made of metal and other materials containing molecules with certain properties allowing the tool to do its work. The discussion continues until Lin moves to the next task of reviewing the entire unit project.

Lin goes through a series of slides covering what students have to do (e.g., choose a molecule they want to work on; produce a 2-D or 3-D model of the chosen molecule, which can be made out of clay, drawn, crocheted, etc.; make an oral presentation, e.g., write and read an essay, present a comic book, do a PowerPoint lecture).

Lin gives many examples for each of the tasks students need to complete and then asks students at each table—usually two, and sometimes three—to take the next fifteen minutes to choose a molecule from the list that they have in a handout. Students use their Chromebooks to look up particular metal and non-metal molecules and ask Lin questions as he circulates around the class. Some of the students have quickly glommed onto the task and tell him immediately which molecules they want to do their project on. Lin takes down names and the molecules they chose. There is a flurry of activity when two different tables of students choose the same molecule. Lin negotiates agreements between tables competing for the same element.

Lin then segues to the handout labeled "Is It a Metal?" that will guide the lab (see figure 4.1, the first page of the handout).[33] He has prepared samples of elements (e.g., lead, magnesium, calcium, copper, silicon) as well as lab directions. Pairs of students are to work on samples from the array of elements lying on the tables in the front of the room, test each one at a time, and record data, making observations of what they see happening (or not happening). Each element—say, copper or aluminum—has certain properties to be observed (e.g., appearance, conductivity, brittle or flexible, reaction to acid). These properties are listed in handout. Students are to check the reaction of each element to hydrochloric acid and copper chloride. Based on the data students collect and the properties these elements have, they are to determine whether, for example, silicon, carbon, and magnesium are metals, non-metals, or metalloids. Lin sets a large stopwatch in the front of the room, timed for forty-five minutes.

Most of the students go to the rear of the portable where I am sitting and pull equipment from various tubs on the lab tables—pairs of goggles and test tubes. They return to their tables and then go up to where the elements are arrayed at the front of the room to test the properties of the one they had chosen and test them at their tables. A few students hang back and as they see others engaged begin to take part in lab. Lin walks around the room answering questions, offering hints to puzzled students, and monitoring those less engaged in the lab. Most of the students are working on the task. They carry their Chromebooks with them to record data and confer with one another in their group about what they see.

FIGURE 4.1   Handout "Is It a Metal?" (page 1) for chemistry lab at Summit
Rainier school

Name _____   Section _____

Is It Metal?

Introduction: In this lab, you will investigate several properties of multiple
elements and then decide whether each element is a metal, nonmetal, or
semimetal (aka a *metalloid*).

Procedure:

1. Obtain samples of each element and test them one at a time. Record
your data and observations in the data table on the next page.

2. **Appearance:** Record:
   - Color
   - Luster (Is it shiny?)

3. **Conductivity:** Using the conductivity tester, test each element to see if it
will conduct electricity. (Note: You need to wipe the white powder off
zinc to get a good reading).

4. **Bending:** Try to bend a sample of each element (for sulfur, try to crush it
between 2 pieces of paper). Record if it is *malleable* or *brittle*.
   - **Malleable:** It is *bendable*. It bends before it breaks.
   - **Brittle:** It breaks apart or crushes without bending.

5. **Reaction with hydrochloric acid (HCl):**
   - Place a small amount of each element in *test tubes*
   - Add about half a squirt of HCl acid
   - Observe for 2–3 minutes. Look for <u>bubbles</u>, which indicate a new
substance has formed & therefore a reaction.
   - Dump tube content into trash and rinse tube . . . "

From time to time, Lin points to the stopwatch, reminding students
how much time is left to complete filling up the sheets and recording
the data. One group of five students dips in and out of the lab work as
they do the operations chatting and laughing. Lin sits down with a few
of them to see how they are doing on the tasks. Other students have

completed the lab and ask Lin what they should do. He directs them to push ahead with other parts of the unit that he had previewed earlier in the period.

At 12:45, the stopwatch is at 0:00, and Lin tells students to clean up. Students line up at sink to wash out test tubes, dry their hands, and at their tables compare what they have found with other groups of students.

Lin then convenes the whole class—he counts down from 5 to get silence—and says: "Let's chat a bit." He asks which of the elements are metals. Students call out answers: "Copper!" Zinc!" Lin follows up and asks what are the properties of these metals. More call-outs from students (e.g., "You can bend copper" "When acid hit, bubbles came up in the test tube."). One student is puzzled over silicon and Lin notes that and elaborates on the element. He then asks class about carbon. He clicks away on his laptop and student answers about each of the elements they examined appear on the whiteboard. "Nonmetals are brittle, dark, not shiny, and barely conductive." He then points to periodic table on the back wall and asks students to look at how metals, nonmetals, and metalloids are aligned on the table. This is a mini-lecture, with a handful of minutes remaining. Restlessness rises in the room. Lin concludes the summary, and students pack up and move toward door of portable. In a few moments, Lin releases the class to go their next one.

In this lesson, where a project on metals is introduced, some whole group mixed with much small group interaction and occasional independent work. Amid distractions and ebb and flow of non-tech-related talk, the teacher moved the class through the different activities focused on the features of metals. He had created playlists of videos, readings, and exercises that all students would use during the project focusing on a molecule. These students also had access to Summit's Personalized Learning Plan, although I did not see it being used in this lesson.[34]

AMBIGUITY OF PERSONALIZED LEARNING

The language of personalized learning and project-based instruction is on full display in this Summit charter school lesson and at the Teach

To One program I described above. In the printed materials and teacher directions, personalized learning is mentioned, even highlighted. Yet what I observed at Teach To One and in Edwin Lin's chemistry class surely contained the language of personalized learning but differed greatly not only in grade level but in the format and flow of each lesson. The variation in personalized learning should surprise no one conversant with the history of reform policies aimed at individualizing instruction.

These current programs contain pieces of earlier reforms written over the underlying, old texts guiding progressive reformers a century ago. Efficiency in teaching students (faster, better, and at less cost) through teachers individualizing instruction with digital tools combine anew the two wings of the century-old progressive education movement without lessening the internal tensions that have bedeviled reformers then and now.

Within this historical context, I turn to making sense of the full array of personalized learning programs that have mushroomed in the past decade as more and more schools integrate digital technologies into their daily instruction.

In 2016, when I visited Silicon Valley classrooms, schools, and districts, many school administrators and teachers told me that they were personalizing learning. From the Summit network of charter schools to individual teachers at Los Altos and Mountain View High School, where "Bring Your Own Devices" reigned, to two Milpitas elementary schools that had upper-grade Learning Labs and rotated students through different stations in all grades, I heard the phrase often.

But I was puzzled by what I saw and heard. When I asked what teachers, principals, and district administrators meant by *personalized learning* I heard different definitions. Of course, the history of school reform is dotted with the debris of earlier instructional reforms that also had greatly varied definitions (e.g., New Math, Socratic seminars, mastery learning, competency-based teaching, individualized instruction). In the Silicon Valley classrooms I visited, no one definition of personalized learning had a monopoly on policy or practice.[35]

So personalized learning has had diverse incarnations as it perco-
lated downward from school board decisions, to superintendent directions to principals, and principals' asking teachers to put into practice
a new instructional policy. Variation in district schools and classrooms,
then and now, is the norm, not the exception.

Translated into practice in Silicon Valley and elsewhere, the concept, like a chameleon, appears in different shades according to context.
Rocketship schools, the AltSchool, and the Agora Cyber School blazon
their personalized learning (or competency-based learning) placard for
all to see, yet what it means differs in each location.[36]

THE PERSONALIZED LEARNING CONTINUUM

To make sense of what I observed in schools and what I know historically about instructionally guided reforms, I have constructed a continuum of classrooms, programs, and schools that encompasses distinct
ways that customized lessons seek the short- and long-term goals for
schooling the young. Conceptually, I anchored the continuum in how
teachers have taught over the past century. Digital technologies are just
the latest in a history of innovations advocates believe will reform traditional teaching practices.

Let me be clear: I am not placing greater value on either end (or
the middle) of the personalized learning continuum. I have stripped
away value-loaded words that could suggest some kinds of personalized
learning are better than others.

At one end of the continuum are teacher-centered lessons and programs within the traditional age-graded school. These schools and
districts, switching back and forth between programs or combining
concepts like competency-based education, mastery learning, and personalization, use new software and hardware technologies daily to help
make children into knowledgeable, skilled, and independent adults who
can successfully enter the labor market and can help their communities.
The format of these teacher-directed lessons—including the instructional moves teachers makes in seguing from one activity to another,

handling student behavior, time management, and student participation in activities to reach the lesson's objectives—typically call for a mix of whole group instruction, small group work, and activities where students work independently. The kind of activity is often determined by the lesson objectives, content to be learned, behavior of students, and teacher beliefs about how best students learn.

For contemporary examples, consider the Virtual Learning Academy Charter School in New Hampshire, USC Hybrid High School (California), and Lindsay Unified School District (California). While these examples inhabit the teacher-centered end of the continuum, they are not cookie-cutter copies; for example, USC Hybrid High School differs in organization and content from New Hampshire's Virtual Learning Academy Charter School.[37]

Yet I cluster these schools and districts at this end of the spectrum because of their overall commitment to using online lessons anchored in discrete skills and knowledge, often aligned to the Common Core standards and tailored to the abilities and performance of individual students. The materials are packaged into playlists by software designers, curated by vendors for teachers (and on occasion created by teachers during summer workshops), and brought to students. Students use applications that permit them to self-assess their mastery of the knowledge and skills embedded in discrete lessons. Some students move well ahead of their peers, others maintain steady progress, and some need help from teachers.

Even though these schools and programs often use the language of personalized instruction and student-centeredness and encourage teachers to coach individuals and not lecture to groups—even scheduling student collaboration during lessons—their teacher-crafted playlists, online lessons that vary for each student, and use of self-assessments locate them at the efficiency end of the spectrum rather than the student-centered end. Ultimately, these programs and schools, operating within traditional K–8 and 9–12 age-graded schools, are descendants of the efficiency-minded wing of the progressive reforms a century earlier.

At the other end of the continuum are student-centered classrooms, programs, and schools using multi-age groupings and asking big unit questions that combine reading, math, science, and social studies while integrating digital technologies regularly in lessons. These places cultivate student agency; that is, student ownership of the questions they ask and the knowledge and skills they learn. Teachers see children and youth as more than "brains on a stick." They seek to shape how individual students grow cognitively, psychologically, emotionally, and physically.

Moreover, these programs want learning to come out of student questions, interests, and passions. The overall goals of schooling at this student-centered end of the continuum are similar to ones at the polar opposite: children grow into adults who are creative thinkers, help their communities, succeed in careers, and become thoughtful, mindful adults. Like the other end of the spectrum, these approaches draw from the pedagogical wing of the progressives a century ago.[38]

For example, there are over sixty Big Picture Learning schools across the nation where students create their own personalized learning plans and work weekly as interns on projects that capture their passions. High Tech High in San Diego, another example, centers its instruction on project-based learning (described in chapter 2). The Mission Hill School in Boston, The Open Classroom at Lagunitas Elementary in San Geronimo, California, and the Continuous Progress Program at Highlands Elementary in Edina, Minnesota, all have multi-age groupings, project-based instruction, and focus on the whole child. And there are private schools such as San Francisco-based AltSchool, a covey of microschools located in big cities, and the Khan Lab School (Mountain View, California) that fit here as well.[39]

As with the efficiency-minded schools, lesson formats in schools at this student-centered end of the continuum commonly call for a blend of whole group instruction, small group work, and activities where students work independently. At this end of the continuum, however, these lessons bend noticeably toward small group and individual activities with occasional whole group instruction.

Many of these schools claim that they personalize learning in their daily work to create graduates who are independent thinkers, can work in any environment, and help to make their communities better places to live. There are many such schools scattered across the nation (although I found no public school in Silicon Valley that would fit here). Like the clusters of programs at the other end of the continuum, much variation exists among these.[40]

And, of course, there are hybrid programs and schools hugging the middle of the spectrum, which mix teacher-directed and student-directed lessons. Again, in this diverse middle are teachers, schools, and programs that blend whole group, small group, and independent activities in lessons. Some teachers and schools, in their quest to personalize learning, tilt toward the teacher-directed end while others lean toward the student-centered pole. But they occupy slots in the middle of the continuum. All are located in traditional age-graded schools.

These classrooms, schools, and programs also combine lessons for individual students and teacher-directed whole group discussions, and small group work such as ones taught by Mountain View High School English teacher Kristen Krauss (chapter 3), Aragon High School Spanish teacher Nicole Elenz-Martin (chapter 1), and second-grade teacher Jennifer Auten (chapter 1) at Montclaire Elementary School.

The middle school math program I observed called Teach To One, located in an Oakland K–8 charter school, has different "modalities" that place it in the center of the spectrum as well, tilting a bit toward the teacher-directed end with its competency-based collection of numbered math skills that have to be mastered before a student moves on.

I would also include the nine teachers in the two Summit charter high schools I observed (above and chapter 2), who combined project-based teaching, online readings, and self-assessments in Personalized Learning Platforms, individual coaching, and collaborative work within ninety-minute lessons. While the two Summit schools had explicitly committed to "project-based learning," the projects were largely chosen by the Summit network teachers who collaborated with one another in making these academic subject decisions; the projects were aligned to the Common Core state standards.

While students could choose their presentations, reading materials, and other assignments, major decisions on projects were in teachers' hands. That is why I placed these teachers, programs, and schools in the center of the continuum, rather than the student-centered end.

For Pomeroy and Weller Elementary Schools in Milpitas public schools, rotation of learning stations occurs in all grades, supplemented by Learning Labs available to upper-grade students. Personalized learning and project-based units hug the middle of this continuum as well.

Such schools and teachers mix competency-based, individual lessons for children with lessons that are teacher-directed and project-based activities. The format of lessons continues the inevitable mix of whole, group, small group, and independent learning with inclinations to more of one than the other, depending on lesson objectives and teacher expertise in avoiding distractions and managing groups. In no instance, however, do whole-group activities dominate consistently.

Like those at the teacher- and student-centered ends, these programs occupying the middle of the spectrum contain obvious differences. In hugging the middle, however, they also embody distinct traces of both the efficiency-driven and pedagogical wings of the century-old progressive reformers.

Yet—and this is a basic point—wherever they fall on the continuum of personalized learning with their playlists, self-assessment software, and tailored lessons, all of these classrooms, programs, schools, and districts work within traditional age-graded school structures. No public school in Silicon Valley that I visited in 2016 departed from that custom-bound school organization.

The above paragraphs explicitly address the blending of the traditional—the age-graded school—and optimism of using digital technologies to transform teaching and learning. Personalizing learning in the past decade encompasses in its language, aspirations, and implementation earlier progressive reforms in the early twentieth century, the 1960s, the 1990s, and the present. Over time, different groups of progressives have tangled with one another over their views of children, learning, and the purposes of schooling. *Administrative progressives* saw schooling children and youth as preparation for the adult workplace and community. The dominance of behaviorist psychologists in this wing meant that it saw teaching and learning content and skills in terms of stimulus, response, and positive reinforcement done efficiently and measured constantly to see whether objectives were being achieved. New tests and protocols for judging the quality of curriculum, teaching, supervision, and buildings were and are emphasized in this view.

Progressive opponents of this view of "good" teaching and learning challenged these "educational engineers." Their view of a whole child went far beyond schools delivering information to unformed minds. They saw children as holistic beings bringing from families and communities individual interests, attitudes, motivation, and already formed knowledge and skills. Curriculum, instruction, the organization of the school day and the school itself embodied this belief of how children learn best.

In the struggle over the hearts and minds of educators, civic, and business leaders, the ideology, policies, and practices of efficiency-driven reformers trumped the pedagogical progressives throughout the twentieth century. Both perspectives show up time and again, providing the ideological context for the dramatic growth of personalized learning in the early decades of the twenty-first century. The exemplary classrooms, schools, and districts integrating new technologies that I observed in Silicon Valley during 2016 are not one-offs—singular events that have no history. They can be best understood in the school reform struggles of the previous century.

Part 2 takes up the central question of the book. After these "best cases" of digital integration have been put into practice in Silicon Valley, have teaching practices changed?

Have Exemplars Made a Difference in Teaching Practice?

Have Teachers Changed
Their Classroom Practice?

Straightforward as the question sounds, it is tricky to answer. Why?

In a society geared to constant change as America is, the word *change* has far more positive than negative connotations. Fashions in clothes, car models, gadgets, and hairstyles change every year, and the buzz is all about the next new thing to acquire. From same-sex marriage to legal use of marijuana, most Americans have changed their views and supported laws that a mere decade earlier would have astounded even fiction writers. Both presidential campaigners Barack Obama in 2008 and Donald Trump in 2016, for example, promised their supporters that America would change for the better. And don't forget the constant public and private efforts, decade after decade, to reform public schools.

Social and political change is "good." Embracing the new is progress. It is a norm in which Americans revel, especially when it comes to taking on new technologies in the past (e.g., film, radio, television) and present (e.g., desktop computers, laptops, and smartphones).[1] So teachers, doctors, lawyers, CEOs, and elected officials who do not accept the next new electronic device and change their daily practice are often seen as resistant, their fondness for the "old" condemned as out of step with American values and the future. Reform-driven policymakers, deep-pocketed donors, entrepreneurs, and vendors believe a lack of change or very slow adoption of new digital tools to be a detriment to student learning, patients, clients, customers, or voters, depending on their cause. So a social and individual bias toward change, particularly technological change, is built into American society, history, institutions, and professional behavior.

Acknowledging a historical bias toward change hints at the trickiness of the question I ask. Teachers' increased use of digital tools by 2016 is strikingly evident. Yet judging whether teachers have actually altered their daily classroom practice is surprisingly hard to do. Imbued with the culture's values, teachers often say that they have changed their lessons from week to week, year to year due to new district curricula, tests, and programs. Policymakers and researchers, however, are less certain that such changes have actually been made.[2]

Consider that researchers ordinarily find out whether teachers have changed their practices by directly observing lessons before and after an identified change occurred, interviews, surveying faculty opinions, sampling principal evaluations, and soliciting student views.[3] Few researchers, however, have the access, time, or funds to tap all of these sources, so they use shortcuts and depend on one or two sources at best and snapshots of one moment in time. Occasional teacher interviews, drop-in classroom observations, and faculty surveys are often how researchers end up answering the question.

Yet even when researchers believe they have sufficient information to determine that teachers have changed how they teach lessons, that does not tell you the direction of those changes (that is, from more teacher-centered to more student-centered or vice versa), whether those changes were superficial or substantial, or whether they were a step forward or a step backward in classroom practice.

Think, for example, a low-tech device teachers used for nearly two centuries to reach students, and that has only within the past half-century been replaced by an expensive digital classroom tool. I speak of the chalkboard.

The innovative slate chalkboard, introduced in the early nineteenth century, was eventually replaced in the mid-twentieth century by greenboards and soon after, by whiteboards with erasable markers. Now interactive whiteboards (IWBs) have become pervasive (as of 2014, they are to be found in 60 percent of US K–12 classrooms).

All of these iterations have helped teachers display lesson objectives and activities and have students practice skills.[4] But does the conversion of chalkboards over time from slate to IWBs represent a minor or major change in teaching practice? And is that change an improvement directed toward deeper alterations in teaching practice or strengthening of an existing pedagogy?

Answers to these questions probe the deeper meaning of changes in what teachers do in their lessons. But that deeper meaning is often up for grabs because judging whether the changes were shallow or deep, moved the center of gravity from teacher-directed lessons to student-centered ones, or sought improved relationships with students or higher test scores depends on *who* determines that changes have occurred (e.g., the teacher, researcher, principal, policymaker, parents, or students).

Here is an example of a lesson I viewed in 2016 followed by the teacher's answers to my questions about whether she had changed her teaching over time because of using new technologies in her lessons.

A HIGH SCHOOL MATH LESSON

I observed an Algebra 2 class at Hacienda (pseudonym), a Northern California high school, in September 2016. The high school has over nineteen hundred students, mostly minority (Asian and Latino). About 20 percent are eligible for free and reduced-price lunch. Over 98 percent graduate, and a very high percentage of those graduates enter college. Less than 10 percent of students are English language learners and just over that percentage have been identified with disabilities. This is a high school that prides itself on academic and sports achievements and is recognized in the region, state, and nation as first-rate.

Beverly Young (pseudonym) is a veteran teacher of twenty-two years at Hacienda. A slim woman of average height, wearing black slacks and white blouse with a beige sweater, she has been department head and very involved in coordinating the math curriculum at the school. Since the tablet appeared, she has been using an iPad with educational apps, particularly Doceri, for her math lessons.[5]

The fifty-minute lesson on a Friday morning went swiftly as the fast-paced, organized Young taught about factoring quadratic equations. Announcements about the upcoming quiz were posted on bulletin board next to the whiteboard: "9/14–9/15, Quiz 4.1 to 4.2"–and upcoming test–"9/21–9/22, Test on 4.1 to 4.4" (the numbers refer to sections of the textbook).

There are twenty-six students in the room, sitting in five rows of three tables, all facing the IWB. Young, carrying her iPad as she walks around, uses a remote control to post slides and videos on the whiteboard during the lesson. For the first five minutes, Young shows a brief video about the Rio de Janeiro Paralympics. As students watch the video, Young records who is present and stamps homework that students had laid out on their desks. I look around; the class is intently watching as athletes with disabilities perform extraordinary feats.

Two minutes later, school announcements appear as a video on the whiteboard. These are school-made videos with student anchors making announcements. In most schools where I observe classes, audio announcements come over the public address system, and generally students ignore them as they drone on. I look around and see that all but a few of the students are watching intently.

After announcements end, Young turns to the lesson. Displayed on a slide on the whiteboard is the objective for the day: "Factoring and Solving $x^2 + bx + c = 0$." She asks if there are any questions on the homework. No hands go up. Young then passes out the handout for the day and directs students to go to Google Classroom on their devices. She then asks students to go to Socrative, a software program, and gives instructions how they should log in. She walks up and down aisles to see what is on students' screens. After all students have logged in, she clicks on a short video that explains factoring quadratic equations by using an example of jellyfish.[6]

Young explains what the key terms are, the different variables described in video and then applies it to factoring. She gives examples of binominals and asks questions as she goes along. She encourages students to talk to one another if they are stuck. With iPad in hand, she traverses the room as students answer. She then reviews binominals and moves to trinominals. "Now, look at polynominals." One student asks for clarification of terms. Young clarifies and asks, "You guys understand?" A few heads nod.

Young moves to next set of slides about x intercepts and examples of distribution. She then asks, "Why do we do factoring?" A few students answer. Young explains what the key points are and the differences between factoring and solving an equation. She asks students more questions, encouraging them to talk to one another to figure out answers.

Young segues back to a Socrative slide and to a question that she wants student to answer. She encourages students to help one another as she circulates in the room: "If you don't remember, write it down. It's OK." She checks her tablet to see what each student is doing and says aloud, "I see two guys who got it right. I am waiting for fifteen of you guys to finish. Talk to one another." A few minutes later, looking at her tablet, she says, "Most of you got it. I will give you another minute. I am waiting on eight more here."

She talks to individual students, answering questions and complimenting students as she walks the aisles.

"Looks like most of you have the idea," she says.

I scan the class. All students have their eyes on the screen, and are clicking away or whispering to neighbors what appear to be answers to the teacher's question.

"Now you guys work on the second question." She chats easily with students. "Do you have an answer here?" she asks while checking her iPad.

She then directs class to go to next question: "Do it and give me an answer for this; it's a little tricky. You are more than welcome to ask one another."

One student asks a question, and Young uses the student question to correct a misconception about solving a quadratic equation. She answers the student, referring back to jellyfish video.

As I scan the class, all the students appear engaged. Young tells them, "If you guys have an answer like this [pointing to what she wrote on the whiteboard] then you got it wrong. Here's a little hint . . . I'll give you another fifty seconds. I just want to see what you guys remember."

Again, checking her iPad, she can see each student's work and can help students in real time as she cruises through the classroom.

"Now let's go to fun stuff," Young says. After she posts a slide from her iPad on the whiteboard on how to factor trinominals, she explains each problem. She sees that some students are confused, so she starts over. She continues to work on the numbered problems appearing on the slide, explaining what she is doing at each step. Then she asks students to factor particular parts of equations. She checks her tablet and says: "I see guys having an answer already—that's great!"

"When is a 9 equal to zero or a plus-9 equal to zero? Now can you answer no. 8?" Students talk to one another as I scan the room. Young circulates and attends to different students to further explain if they are stuck.

She asks, "Are we ready?" She then walks students through how she solves problem on whiteboard, using the iPad. She then asks whether students know the difference between factoring and solving the lesson objective ($x^2 + bx + c = 0$). One student says yes. She then asks students to jot down their answers to the question—she walks around and talks with students as they click away.

Young ends the lesson a few minutes before the bell and then answers different students' questions. Other students begin packing up their things to await the bell. It rings a minute later.

In answer to my questions about whether integrating digital tools into her daily lessons had changed how she teaches, Young told me:

> I feel that the way I get information to the students has changed. I mostly focus on creative and "buy-in" lessons for my students. It has helped my classroom management and finding students who are struggling quicker and identify them better. The technology allows me to be more creative with my lessons.[7]

Making sense of this response to my question and watching a math lesson where a veteran teacher uses her iPad and apps to get instant information about how each student is doing is not easy. Determining whether technology had changed the way she teaches depends greatly on where you sit. Beverly Young's opinion was that because of the digital tools she used, her teaching had become more individualized, productive, and original. But her opinion, while credible and authentic—even true for her—is not the only possible one. There are other views including mine as a researcher that also have a chunk of truth in them.

Where one sits has a lot to do with judgments reached about the changes integrating technologies have led to in teachers' lessons, the direction of those changes, and their significance. Given these considerations, the central question in this chapter, *Have teachers changed their practice?*, needs to be unpacked further, evidence evaluated carefully, and conclusions tied to what has been observed and what is known about teaching historically. This is why the question is tricky.

HAVE TEACHERS I OBSERVED AND INTERVIEWED IN SILICON VALLEY DURING 2016 CHANGED THEIR PRACTICE?

According to what teachers told me, they have.[8] These teachers identified as being exemplary in integrating technology took attendance, recorded assignments, checked homework, assessed students, and emailed parents routinely using laptops, tablets, and other devices. They used their time more productively.

Teachers organized lessons to include whole group and small group instruction, and independent student work. Digital tools aided teachers in keeping a lesson's momentum on course and avoiding distractions. Many of the teachers I observed created individual playlists of math, science, and social studies resources for their students to use in research projects. They individualized lessons and helped students self-assess their grasp of content and skills. So these teachers have, according to their recall of how they taught previously, altered their classroom practices after using digital technologies.[9]

But just listing new and altered practices associated with the spread of electronic devices does not get at the depth of the change in classroom practice. Consider the following queries:

- Is using an interactive whiteboard instead of an overhead projector and chalkboard a substantial change or simply a modification of a habitual practice?
- Is it a shallow or deep change in classroom practice when a teacher takes attendance on her tablet instead of checking off names on a sheet of paper?
- Is it a small or large change when students submit their notes and assignments to Dropbox instead of turning in paper homework?[10]

The answers to these queries certainly reveal changes in familiar practices. The teachers I observed and interviewed would readily acknowledge that such alterations in routines have been important to them because they save time and energy. In conversations with these teachers, the word *efficient* popped up repeatedly. Using less time for administrative details and having at one's fingertips information from multiple sources for students to access was of great importance to these teachers. Such changes gave teachers an edge in racing against the clock during a lesson.

Technologically driven school reformers, however, might begrudgingly admit that these examples are "changes" but not ones that they envisioned. Entrepreneurs eager to help schools dump the "factory model" of schooling (e.g., age-graded school, traditional teaching) might categorize these changes as merely superficial or perhaps trivial compared with the kind of changes taking place in schools that convert to blended learning, combining personalized online and face-to-face lessons. They want to see teachers creating individual student playlists, students working together on projects every week, frequent use of online lessons, and similar "transformative" changes. Anything less than these kind of fundamental (sometimes called "real") changes in pedagogy, they would be disappointed.

Or researchers partial to student-centered learning, observing lessons in these teachers' classrooms, might see such changes as mere adjustments that reinforce dominant patterns of teacher-directed lessons. Yet these researchers, unlike techno-enthusiasts, know that they must be alert to their values and biases when they collect, analyze, and publish their studies.

Teachers, principals, parents, researchers, ardent reformers, and policymakers, for example, have different organizational roles and experiences. They approach data from varied viewpoints. And they are Americans socialized to see change as progress and an unalloyed good. These different viewpoints among academics and members of district and school communities have to be made explicit in making sense of what teachers say and do.

So answering the question of whether widespread student access and teacher use has "changed daily classroom practices" depends on who is the asker, who is the doer, and what actually occurs in the classroom.

In 2016, after I observed and interviewed forty-one Silicon Valley teachers in various schools and districts identified by policymakers and principals as exemplary in integrating technologies into their daily lessons, I asked these teachers the following questions: Has your teaching changed since you have begun regular use of laptops, tablets, interactive whiteboards, etc. in your lessons? If yes, in what ways? If no, why not?[11] Below are some typical responses of teachers who said "yes."

Brendan Dilloughery, a veteran teacher of nearly a decade in international schools in Ecuador, Switzerland, and elsewhere, is in his second year of teaching geometry and computer science at Mountain View High School. He says:

> The integration of technology into the classroom has definitely affected my teaching. The most notable changes are: distribution of and access to course resources, interactive activities that give immediate feedback, and facilitating collaboration.

Students can access their digital textbook as well as worked-out solutions to every homework problem on their cell phone from anywhere in the world. They can easily access class notes and homework assignments when they are absent from class.

Websites such as Khan Academy and IXL have been a game changer in my classroom.[12] In the past I struggled greatly to have students critically evaluate their homework problems ... I seemingly tried everything—giving access to worked-out solutions to every problem, shortening homework assignments, having them start in class, work in pairs ... No matter what I tried, at least half of my students were just "completing" their homework without using it as a time to really practice and hone their skills. Enter Khan Academy and IXL. [Here] if a student correctly completes their current problem, they move on to a more difficult question. If the problem is incorrect, they are shown a colorful, in-depth explanation of how to complete the problem. This immediate feedback has greatly increased my students' level of comprehension while working on assignments ...

When beginning with Khan Academy and IXL, I had students work individually. Through collaboration with peers ... I now have students working in pairs on a single whiteboard with a single laptop. I am constantly amazed at how much quality discourse happens amongst my constantly changing partnerships in class. The most unlikely pairs can be heard explaining the reasons behind steps of proofs or how they solved an equation when their partner doesn't understand. Students who would never raise their hand to ask a question will ask a partner how they got to a certain answer.[13]

Edwin Avarca has been teaching for six years. A graduate of a Bay Area teacher education program that awards a master's and teaching credential after fourteen months, Avarca's first job was at a charter school in downtown San Jose. After two years there, he joined Summit Rainier charter school and has been teaching Advanced Placement US history courses since. His answers:

My teaching has dramatically changed since I've had more access to tech. For example, in my previous school, if we wanted access to the projector, we had to sign up for it beforehand; also we had to sign up for a laptop cart in advance in order for students to have access to one-to-one computers during class. Having a projector has made teaching more efficient. I can spontaneously pull up a website, video, or other resource that students can benefit from in some way. For example, if a question came up about the economic costs of World War II, I could quickly look for the answer and show students. Prior to SmartBoards/projectors, I used an overhead projector, and the logistics of it could be frustrating.

One-to-one computers have revolutionized my classroom. Students have so much access to resources, and this gives them the opportunity to utilize the resources while we're in class. Thus, I can coach students through a research project much easier, since I can model for them and walk them through the process as well.

Classroom management has also changed. I need to be very thoughtful about how students should be held accountable while they are on their computers. I also have to monitor the room more, since students can easily be distracted by YouTube or other sites if they do not have specific structures to hold them accountable to the work they need to complete.[14]

A native of New Zealand, Sue Pound is in her eighteenth year of teaching science at Jordan Middle School in Palo Alto. She and a colleague team-teach eighth-graders in a large room furnished with a wet lab and many long tables for students to sit at when not doing lab work. She told me:

My teaching has definitely changed since computers and iPads became available in our school. In the most basic terms, I am not copying many handouts and I am able to share so much more electronically with students. I have been able to be more adventurous and creative with activities, labs, and projects and support their learning in different and, I think, better ways.

Students have more choice in the products they generate. We are also not tied to one resource for our information [the textbook], and that supports the different needs students have for learning. It is much easier to do wider-reaching group work and individual work, and have me do less old-style teaching. While I would like to get to the place of doing much more differentiated teaching, where students are truly learning at their own pace and learning is tailor-made for each one, I also know there is so much value in collaboration in the classroom.[15]

Eleven percent (N = 4) of the teachers answered both "yes" and "no" to my questions. These teachers made a distinction between how they taught lessons before they had new technologies and what they now do with devices and software. They referred to students having more information available than before and how essential aspects of their lessons could be done easier and faster than before. But they drew a distinction between the help that high-tech tools give them and the constancy of core practices that are part of their planning and interactions with students during a lesson. They saw both change and stability in their lessons as a result of integrating digital tools into their teaching.

Nicole Elenz-Martin (profiled in chapter 1) is an eleven-year veteran of teaching. She teaches Spanish level 3 through level 6 (including Advanced Placement) in the San Mateo Union High School District at Aragon High School. Her "yes and no" answer to my question:

My teaching—in terms of pedagogical strategy and philosophical beliefs about World Language instruction—has not changed because of my regular use of technology; however, the regular use of Chromebooks in my classroom has dramatically changed my access to student learning, monitoring of their proficiency development, and my ability to cover more material over the course of a school year.

Why yes?

- My students are required to be much more engaged and participatory in their learning because of their interaction with my lessons through technology. When covering material in class, every student can interact with the presentation on my SmartBoard to share answers, respond to polls, or ask questions (Peardeck, Nearpod, Google Forms, etc.) This has informed my instruction immensely and has allowed me to change my lesson on the fly to ensure understanding before moving on.

- Students practice new vocabulary and/or comprehension questions with Quizlet, for example, and I can see their results and areas of challenge in real time. It allows me to change my path of instruction if necessary, as stated above, and it also allows me to personalize the learning for each student's level and need.

- Students have built classroom community and have strengthened camaraderie with review games (Quizlet Live, Socrative Space Race, and Kahoot!). Not only has light "gaming" sparked excitement and interest for the students in learning the material, but it has allowed me to formatively assess each students' understanding and learning on a daily basis. The comfort level and "fun" among classmates has allowed them to be better risk-takers and communicators with one another, and this is critical for a language class where students really need to feel confident and safe around their classmates.

- Students have had individual access to more authentic materials from around the world, which is of course extremely important for culture and language learning. Their interaction with videos, texts, and audio can be documented in EdPuzzle, GoFormative, and Google Classroom. I can see their engagement with the material in a way that I was never able to assess before, and I can respond to students both individually and as a group much more efficiently and effectively. I can see what they are learning about a culture and I can motivate them to respond more critically to what they are seeing and comparing to their own culture . . .

Why no?

Certain parts of teaching can never be replaced, enhanced, or changed by technology. The very most critical aspect of my teaching is the relationship that I create with each and every one of my students. Without having a strong, trusting, solid, and respectful relationship with each student, he or she is lost in my classroom and will be unable to learn from my teaching. Because I speak almost exclusively in Spanish, the oral communication in my classroom and the relationships with my students are the very cornerstones of my teaching. Therefore:

- Technology has not replaced the way I speak or communicate with my students, and since I am a Spanish teacher, they are still listening and responding to me and to each other through oral communication much more than with the technology. The amount that I expect them to speak with me and communicate with one another is the same as it has always been, even before technology access.

- Complex Instruction and Group-worthy tasks: I passionately believe in the importance of "student talk" and participation for learning, especially when it comes to working with partners and small groups on a communicative and/or complex task. Technology is almost nonexistent in my classroom when students are working on an assignment that involves learning through talking with one another. Without going into too much detail, technology hardly has changed the way I engage students in partner and groupwork . . .[16]

And here is Sarah Press, who has been teaching English at Hillsdale High School in the San Mateo Union High School District since 2007. Press, like Elenz-Martin, makes similar distinctions between the deeper aspects of teaching including the structure of lessons that cannot be altered by digital tools and the features of teaching that can change:

In some ways, my teaching hasn't changed much at all. My goals are the same—to give my students opportunities to do something with the ideas I suggest to them in class, to engage with each other around those ideas and to offer lots of ways to be smart. I still have a heavy focus on literacy—sustained engagement with text and inquiry around meaning making. I continue to try to find authentic ways for students to show what they've learned and what they think, not just regurgitate what they've heard.

I also struggle with many of the same issues I always have: what to do with the huge range of skill sets in my room, how to differentiate activities and assessments to meet the needs of all learners, how to give feedback in meaningful and timely ways, how to engage all learners despite varying interests and abilities, how to create a positive socioemotional atmosphere in my classroom so students feel comfortable taking and learning from risks.

So I think it's important to remember that technology is just one of many tools I have available to me to try to meet those goals. That said, it's an incredibly powerful tool, and I do see some potent ways in which technology helps me get closer to being the teacher I hope to, someday, become.

A huge one is the amount of choice I am able to offer students, about what they learn and how they learn it . . . Another is the increased sense of collaboration in my room. While I have always striven to have students use each other as resources, to value each other's expertise . . . I have not always been successful. Because technology allows students to simultaneously have access to a group project in a shared digital space that is co-editable . . . everyone can see a developing project and no one can "mess it up." It's also easier to track exactly what each student has contributed . . .

It's a not insignificant note here that risk-taking becomes easier to encourage when erasing or changing work is as easy as "Control + Z" or "Delete . . . "

Finally, technology is powerful because it makes it so much easier and faster to collect, distribute, and respond to data. I find myself experimenting more and more with forms of assessment when I can instantaneously collect responses from every student in my class . . . All this helps me adjust, clarify, and re-teach in much tighter, shorter cycles than before.[17]

Like Elenz-Martin, Sarah Press saw both constancy and change in her lessons after adopting digital tools.

Only one of the thirty-seven teachers I asked these questions to said that his teaching had shifted from teacher-centered to student-centered. John DiCosmo, the middle school English teacher profiled in chapter 1, told me:

> As a digital native, I have always used computers in my lessons, but each year my teaching changes a little more to put students in the center of the lessons. I have used technology to engage my middle schoolers from the first day I stepped into the classroom, but I am increasingly "flipping" lessons to support student access to materials to differentiate my instruction . . . [18]

Turning to the nine "no" responses (24 percent) I received from teachers, I sorted them into two bins. Six teachers explained that using digital tools had not changed their ways of teaching because they had been using high-tech devices since they entered the profession or labeled themselves as "digital natives" even before they began teaching.

The other three teachers who said "no" gave different answers.

Lyuda Shemyakina, a biology teacher at Mountain View High School has been a teacher for six years, two of which were in Chicago. Her response was:

> Technology facilitates the gathering and disseminating of information in my classroom, but I wouldn't say it has fundamentally changed how I teach.
>
> For example, designing, scaffolding, and handing out homework and classwork are integral parts of my teaching practice. Whereas in another country or another decade I might have made paper copies or made students write these down, many/ most things now are electronic. Students can see all my presentations (directions for class); students can email me with questions, and students have fewer excuses for not knowing the homework. I literally post it in five different places, from the whiteboard in my room to a public online space. I also post links to helpful videos, worksheets, etc., to help both struggling and advanced students . . .

Ultimately, though, a teacher is still an intellectual who must design or select instruction and instructional materials, including assessments. If I don't have the skills to appropriately design and assess activities, no amount of technology can help me. For instance, during the class you saw, I chose to have students design and share analogies. These were very telling as a measure of their understanding of basic genetics. If I had asked the wrong question, like "Do you get genetics?" it wouldn't have mattered what technology I used.[19]

Summing up these results, nearly two-thirds of the Silicon Valley teachers I interviewed and observed said that digital tools had changed how they teach, with frequent mentions of increased productivity, such as in saving time doing familiar tasks and being able to individualize their work with students.

The rest of the teachers had either said "no" because they had been using high-tech devices for years before I observed them or on substantive grounds, as some stressed the deeper, persistent features of teaching that they must perform in structuring lessons, regardless of what technologies they used. These features include setting goals for the lesson, constructing activities for students, insuring that students interact with content, managing class behavior, and sustaining individual and group relationships. This distinction represents the craft knowledge of teachers in constructing activities linked to lesson goals and determining when and under what conditions to vary grouping, given the content with which students work.[20]

Even those who said "no" acknowledged the efficiencies that these high-tech devices brought to their lessons. They saw change both in the use of digital tools daily and stability in the essential features of planning and executing a lesson. Rather than only black and white, they saw gray.

Does this mean that most of these elementary and secondary schoolteachers identified as "best cases" of integrating technology in Silicon Valley have actually altered how they teach using new technologies? Almost two-thirds certainly believed so. Yet a full answer to the question requires looking at perspectives beyond the teacher's.

INSIDER VERSUS OUTSIDER: WHOSE DEFINITION OF "CHANGE" MATTERS?

As a researcher, I observed and interviewed forty-one teachers for this study. I was an outsider identified as a retired Stanford professor. The teachers were insiders telling me their stories.

Because I had not done observations of these teachers before they began using these electronic devices, I could not confirm whether their teaching had actually changed from how they had taught previously. From all indications, these teachers believed strongly that they had modified their daily practices due to the regular use of digital tools. I believe them.

However, as a researcher who has studied teaching practices between the 1890s and the present and an outsider to these schools and classrooms, I bring a different perspective. I have accumulated well-documented descriptions of the dominant trends that have typified teaching over the past century. I can, for example, compare what I saw in these lessons in 2016 in Silicon Valley to the historical continuum of varied teaching practice stretching back a century across the nation. In addition, I have conceptually defined different kinds of school and classroom change (e.g., incremental and fundamental) distinctions that most reformers, policymakers, and others—including teachers—seldom make. Such knowledge as I have acquired over decades, however, produces an internal conflict in me.[21]

What does a researcher make of the teacher, for example, who says with passionate confidence that he has shifted his teaching of English to eighth-graders from teacher-directed activities to student-centered ones? He cites as evidence the different materials and frequent use of digital tools that he uses in daily lessons, ones that the researcher has observed.[22] Yet during the lesson, the researcher sees those very same materials and practices being used in ways that strengthen the teacher-centered activities and undercut the student-centeredness that the teacher seeks. Neither the teacher nor researcher is lying. Each has constructed an authentic, plausible, and credible story. So who do you believe?[23]

I am not the first (nor last) researcher to have met teachers who described substantial changes in their lessons in response to district or state policies. Consider "A Revolution in One Classroom; The Case of Mrs. Oublier."[24]

In the mid-1980s, California policymakers adopted a new elementary math curriculum intended to give students a deep understanding of math concepts rather than memorizing rules and seeking the "right" answer. This instructional policy sought changes in how teachers traditionally taught a math concepts and skills. The state provided staff development to help elementary teachers implement the new curriculum. Then researchers started observing classroom lessons.

One researcher observed third-grade teacher Mrs. Oublier (a pseudonym and hereafter Mrs. O) to see to what degree she had embraced the innovative math teaching the state sought. Widely respected in her school as a first-rate math teacher, Mrs. O told the researcher that she had "revolutionized" her teaching. She was delighted with the new math text, used manipulatives to teach concepts, organized students' desks into clusters of four and five, and had student participate in discussions. Yet the researcher saw her use paper straws, beans, and paper clips for traditional classroom tasks. She used small groups not for students to collaborate in solving math problems, but to call on individuals to give answers to text questions. She used hand clapping and choral chants—as the text and others suggested—in traditional ways to get correct answers. To the researcher, she had grafted innovative practices onto traditional ways of math teaching and, in doing so, had missed the heart and soul of the state's instructional policy.

How can Mrs. O and teachers I have interviewed report that they have changed their teaching, yet classroom observations of these very same teachers reveals familiar patterns of teaching? The answer depends on what kind of "change" the teacher seeks and who judges—the insider or outsider—the substance of the change and its direction.

Change clearly meant one thing to Mrs. O and another to the researcher. Many teachers, like Mrs. O, had made a cascade of *incremental* changes in their daily lessons as a result of integrating devices and software into their lessons. Researchers, however, kept in mind what policymakers and reform designers intended for the state's new policy of teaching math to effect *fundamental* changes in the how those math lessons were taught.

So whose judgment about change matters most? Should researchers "consider changes in teachers' work from the perspective of new policies . . . [or intentions of policymakers]? Or should they be considered from the teacher's vantage point?"[25]

Researchers, however, publish their studies, while teachers like Mrs. O and the gracious teachers who let me observe their lessons and answered my questions seldom get to tell their side of the story to an audience outside their family and school.

Teachers' perceptions of change have to be respected and voiced because they are genuine insider accounts that explain how and why they have altered their practices. As two veteran researchers of teaching and teachers have said:

> We need to listen closely to teachers . . . and to the stories of their lives in and out of classrooms. We also need to tell our own stories as we live our own collaborative researcher/teacher lives. Our own work then becomes one of learning to tell and live a new mutually constructed account of inquiry in teaching and learning. What emerges from this mutual relationship are new stories of teachers and learners as curriculum makers, stories that hold new possibilities for both researchers and teachers and for those who read their stories.[26]

Yet researchers cannot just take what teachers say as gospel truth and dismiss what is known of the history of teaching as immaterial. Researchers are more than scribes.

The answers teachers give to researcher questions are constructed from their insider view. With a historical perspective on past ways that teachers have taught, I have constructed an outsider's view of what teachers do daily in their workplace with digital tools. Both points of view have to come into play for me to make sense—to get at the truth as best as I can—of both the teachers' answers to my questions and what I observed in classrooms.[27]

As a former high school history teacher between the 1950s and 1970s and a university researcher since 1981, I have tried to manage this dilemma of giving value to teacher stories about classroom change while honoring what I, as a researcher, have learned about teaching, past and present.

This is the dilemma that I negotiate in answering the central question in this chapter: *Have teachers altered their practice?*

SUMMARY

Keep in mind the data I had: of the thirty-seven teachers I asked questions about using digital tools, twenty-four (65 percent) said their teaching had indeed changed as a result of integrating new technologies into their daily lessons. Four (11 percent) said their teach both had and had not changed. And nine (24 percent) said their teaching had not changed.

I have assembled an answer to the central question of this chapter that draws from what the teachers said, what I observed in their lessons, and my accumulated knowledge of past teaching practices. In short, I combine two perspectives on changes in practice—teachers' and researcher's—to makes sense of contrary teacher responses. Although nearly two of three teachers in the sample said they had definitely changed how they taught as a result of integrating digital tools into their daily lessons, a large minority of teachers said that using new technologies in lessons had not changed their practice. How to reconcile these conflicting views?

I do so by first seeing both change and stability as central to the conduct of teaching over the past two centuries. Neither one nor the other—both.

Some researchers and teachers have come to recognize that change and stability are (and have been) the conjoined twins of tax-supported schooling in the United States. They cannot be separated, since organizations—I include the classroom as one—adapt to change and end up preserving stability in lesson format and content. *Dynamic conservatism* is another way of saying that change is crucial to organizational stability—that the pedagogical hybrids that teachers have developed over decades prove how teaching changes to remain the same. Stability and change in teaching is more than a passing fad; it is a permanent condition.[28]

Second, in distinguishing between fundamental and incremental changes, I return to the concept that I have used to describe the two types of common changes that have occurred in the two-century history since the one-room schoolhouse in the nineteenth century slowly gave way to the age-graded school of efforts to reform how teachers have taught.[29]

By *fundamental change*, I mean altering the basic building blocks of US schooling, such as requiring taxpayers to fund public schools and give access to all students, establishing goals for schooling (e.g., all students will be literate, discharge their civic duties, and be vocationally prepared for the labor market), and organizing curricula and instructional practices in age-graded elementary and secondary schools. These building blocks are structures that have defined public schools and influenced what occurs in classrooms for the past two centuries.

Changing them fundamentally means altering funding (e.g., vouchers, charter schools), governance (e.g., site-based management, mayoral control), organization (e.g., moving from an age-graded school to non-graded teams and entire schools), curriculum (e.g., New Math, "hands-on" science), and instruction (e.g., moving from teacher-centered to student-centered pedagogy).

Often those who champion changes in public schools talk about "real reform" or "transformation of schooling." What they refer to are fundamental changes in one or more structures of schooling, not incremental changes.

Incremental changes refer to amendments in current structures and practices, not deep changes to or removal of these core components of schooling. Examples include creating new academic courses, extending the school day or year, reducing class size, raising teacher salaries, and introducing new reading or math programs. But such changes do not alter the basic structures of public schools. They correct deficiencies and improve existing structures. They do not replace the goals, funding, organization, and governance of schools—they are add-ons. Many promoters of deep change in schools call such changes "tinkering," usually in a dismissive way, because they want "real reform" or fundamental reordering of existing structures.[30]

In most instances, reform-minded teachers, administrators, policy makers, and non-educators push for change without distinguishing between one kind or the other or acknowledging the importance of stability in the belief that what they promote will make a difference in how teachers teach and students learn. Often, as a result, what was urged as a reform that would substantially alter what occurs in classrooms turns out to be a minor modification of existing practice—a butterfly alighting on a rose—disappointing many advocates who seek a change that follows the trajectory of a bullet.

The same can be said for those who sought to shake the foundations of age-graded schools with reforms such as vouchers or online schools that then fall far short of their aspirations. These concepts of the inseparability of constancy and change in teaching and the dichotomy of changes has not only helped me make sense of the language and action of school and classroom reform but also given me a way of explaining the teacher responses to my questions.

Of the 65 percent of teachers who said they had changed their practice because of using digital tools, nearly all have implemented incremental changes in how they teach using devices and software. They believe that these changes made a difference in how they teach and helped their students learn. After observing lessons and interviewing the teachers, I see no reason to doubt what they say.

Then there were a handful of teachers who said that digital tools had been helpful but had not basically changed how they teach. The basic planning, the activity sequence during lessons, and how they interacted with students in and out of class had not shifted because of the digital technologies they used. These teachers distinguished between the *productivity* high-tech tools brought to their work and their *craft and content knowledge* in formatting and enacting a lesson.

Based on my experience as a teacher and the knowledge gleaned from historical detective work on how teachers have taught over the past century, I conclude—and the distinctions these teachers drew demonstrate—there is both change and stability in teaching. Yes, there have been changes in practice. At the same time, there has been constancy in how teachers set goals, organize, and execute lessons; these have not been replaced by digital tools.

Change and Stability in Classrooms, Schools, and Districts

Organizations are dynamically conservative, that is to say, they fight like mad to remain the same.
—Donald Schön, 1970[1]

If we want things to stay as they are, things will have to change.
—Giuseppe Tomasi di Lampedusa, *The Leopard*[2]

Based on my research into exemplars of technology integration in classrooms, schools, and districts in Silicon Valley in 2016, I concluded that the teachers and administrators I saw and interviewed have, indeed, implemented software and hardware fully, over time, into their daily routines. In these settings, digital tool use shifted by fits and starts from the foreground to the background. Using devices has become as ordinary as using pencils and paper once was. And in many instances, by the time I observed lessons, the integration was seamless—no stitches showed. In what ways are describing and analyzing "best cases" of technology integration relevant to reform-minded policies aimed at altering classroom practices? This is the "So what?" question that needs to be asked.

Recall the four basic questions reform-driven decision makers must answer for any policy aimed at improving how teachers teach and how students learn:

1. Did policies aimed at improving student performance get fully, moderately, or partially implemented?
2. When implemented fully, did they change the content and practice of teaching?
3. Did changed classroom practices account for what students learned?
4. Did what students learn meet the intended policy goals?

Too often those who make consequential school decisions ignore these questions. And that is a mistake.

In answer to the first question, my data show clearly that in the forty-one Silicon Valley classrooms I observed—spread across twelve schools and six districts—the local policy of making software and devices available to every teacher and student had been implemented fully. For these teachers identified as exemplary in integrating technology into their daily lessons, access to software-loaded tablets and laptops, a district infrastructure of technical assistance, and professional development gave them many opportunities for daily use. All of the foregoing had been put into place incrementally over time. All of these teachers had the choice of regularly using technologies in their classrooms, and they chose to do so. And I saw that use in all of the classrooms I visited.

These "best cases" portray complete implementation that altered routine teaching practices—a necessary prior condition for any instructional reform to reach students—yet do not answer the next crucial question of whether use of digital tools had indeed altered the basic lesson format and content in these exemplary classrooms.

The assumption reformers carry in their heads is that fully implemented policies aimed at improved teaching will pay off in student learning. For that payoff to occur, however, there is a far less appreciated interim step: usual classroom practices would have to change in the direction reform-minded policy makers sought, such as abandoning traditional instructional practices and adopting student-centered ones. Such changes in content and practice, reformers believe, will lead to improved student outcomes and eventually achieve district goals.

So it is imperative that the second question—of whether the content and format of teaching in these "best cases" classrooms have actually changed and in what direction—be answered. Were there little to no change in how and what teachers taught, the chances of students learning more, faster, and better would diminish. Just as important, were there to be no substantial changes in how teachers teach content and skills, then the third and fourth policy questions become moot.

Turn now to these teachers' views on change as a result of using technology. Most said that their classroom practices had changed over time, even improved. About a third said that while there were some shifts in how they taught, ones they appreciated a lot, the basics of teaching their lessons had not changed. As a researcher who sat in the forty-one classrooms, I agreed with the two-thirds of the teachers who claimed that their lessons had changed, but I reached a different conclusion about basic changes in lesson format and content. Determining the truth about changes in content and practice can be dicey, as it is not clear how much weight to give to teachers' opinions and a researcher's view of both the direction and substance of classroom change.[3]

In chapter 5, without denying that 65 percent of the teachers believed their classroom practices had changed, I offered two explanations to make sense of their opinions. First, teachers who saw changes in their teaching, for the most part identified important incremental (not fundamental) changes due to technology use in planning and implementing lessons. These changes occurred over time, adding to their productivity as teachers in completing classroom administrative tasks, providing a broad array of sources previously unavailable to their students, and being able to help students in real time. Only one of the thirty-seven teachers who responded to my questions on changes in their practices as a result of using technologies in lessons claimed that his practices had departed substantially from how he usually taught.[4]

Second, as an outside researcher, I offered a historical view of public schooling evolving as a conservative institution committed to both instilling community values and also preparing the next generation to become independent thinkers, fully engaged citizens, and productive workers. This split mission for tax-supported public schools existed for well over a century and remains the order of the day in 2018. I also drew from scholarship about century-old teaching patterns within age-graded school organizations that suggested strongly that both change and stability were systemic and embedded in daily lessons. This historical view of both the institution and classroom was also moored in my experiences of nearly four decades teaching high school and graduate students.

In answering the question of whether technology use had shifted teaching practices, given these differing views, it is clear to me from what teachers said, what I observed, and what I know, that those perceived changes had occurred not in fell swoop but gradually over time. Technology-induced changes were incremental and useful to teachers but seldom altered the goals, fundamental classroom structures embedded in the age-graded school, teacher-student relationships, basic format of lessons, or the craft of teaching that has evolved in public schools for well over a century. All of these underlying features of teaching persisted amid the classroom changes Silicon Valley teachers recognized in their lessons. Change and continuity in teaching practice have been and continue to be entwined.

None of this should surprise readers. As the epigraphs suggest, stability and change are the yin and yang that these exemplary teachers, schools, and districts illustrate and are part of a far larger way of seeing how the world works. The explanation for this persistent interaction between stability and change that I offer here is consistent with similar patterns in the larger environment within which we live, the organizations in which we work and play, and our individual lives.[5]

ENVIRONMENT, ORGANIZATIONS, AND INDIVIDUAL LIVES

Millions of years ago, Earth's polar ice caps extended into equatorial South America, Africa, and Asia. Over time, these ice-bound regions receded, and moderate to tropical climate in non-polar regions returned. Using the time scale of millions of years, there has been much continuity and change in Earth's climate.

Human organizations do not have that geological time span, but one in particular—the Roman Catholic Church—has existed for almost two thousand years. Within the church, sects have arisen and broken away (e.g., the Protestant Reformation). Other groups protesting church rules have formed and, over time, their thinking has become incorporated into the church. Over the last millennium, popes banished heretics, sponsored crusades, survived the breakaway of German and English Catholics to form Lutheran and Anglican churches in the sixteenth century. In 2018, they continue to oversee the lives of over a billion Catholics across the globe. In almost two thousand years, the church has had long periods of stability punctuated by both swift and slow motion years of change.

And in a single lifetime of seventy-plus years for individual human beings, constancy and change mark individuals' personality and character as they move from infancy through adolescence to adulthood and then into old age.

On very different time scales, continuity and change characterize the environment we live in, the organizations that influence our lives, and individual experience. From millions of years to millennia to decades, stability and change are abiding partners.

Climate Change

While there are naysayers that global climate has not changed significantly beyond the usual cyclical trends that have characterized weather patterns for millennia, physical and natural scientists have concluded that human actions such as industrialization—particularly burning fossil fuels—have increased the amount of carbon dioxide and methane in the atmosphere, ocean warming, and melting polar caps. Increased floods tornados and hurricanes, expanding arid land across continents, and rising water levels have only added fuel to what has turned into a political debate across the globe. There's no question that climate change itself has become an economic and social issue engaging both the political right and left.[6]

International climate accords to restrict fossil fuel use and increase alternative power sources in both industrialized and developing nations have been signed over the past few decades. But those international agreements (e.g., Rio Earth Summit in 1992; Kyoto Protocol in 1997; Paris Agreement, 2015) are voluntary, and enforcement shifts as government leaders come and go in the major countries (e.g., in 2017, President Donald Trump reversed the regulations put into place by President Barack Obama).[7]

Going beyond the politicization of climate change are the cycles of change and continuity in climate patterns in the past millions of years. Evidence drawn from drilled ice core samples in Greenland and Antarctica, along with samples from Devil's Hole, Nevada, reveals alternating periods of warming and cooling. At least eight glacial and interglacial ages lasting from 80,000 to 120,000 years affirm both change and constancy in global climate. Only recently (geologically speaking), in an interglacial period that has lasted thousands of years, human actions since the 1750s, when industrialization fueled by coal accelerated, have—independent of the tilt of the planet, the sun's influence, shifts in ocean currents, and other factors—accelerated melting of the polar ice caps, shrinking of glaciers, warming of the atmosphere , and rising ocean levels to create changes in weather patterns across the globe.[8]

The Roman Catholic Church

Moving from millions of years to millennia, from interactions between planet's geology, sun, oceans, and climate to manmade organizations, a similar pattern of steadiness and change appear. Take the Roman

Catholic Church. Nearly two thousand years old, this organization has also experienced periods of swift and slow change interspersed with decades, even centuries, of equilibrium. Like all manmade organizations, the church was (and is) located in a larger society in which political, social, cultural, and demographic changes spill over its organization influencing what happens within its confines.[9]

The early church's fight against Roman worship of many gods proved successful when Emperor Constantine adopted Christianity in the fourth century. From that point through the Middle Ages, the church exerted a holistic and sustained hold on the lives of kings, nobles, and common people in the Holy Roman Empire. With the Protestant Reformation and growth of nationalism throughout Europe, especially after the French Revolution and the onset of industrialization the church's influence shrank as nations shied away from too close a connection with the principal religion in Europe. Separation of church and state within nations spread in the nineteenth and twentieth centuries across the globe.

Surviving corrupt popes, explosive heresies, the Protestant Reformation, mishaps covering centuries, and two world wars, the Roman Catholic Church, an absolute monarchy overseeing a centrally controlled, hierarchal institution, has adapted to unforeseen shifts in its own and world events. Through these centuries, church authorities experienced stability and unpredictable changes, century after century, that threatened their very existence as they negotiated how to maintain basic principles and practices during both tranquil and turbulent times. If longevity is a marker for organizational success, then the survival of the church for nearly two millennia is a gold medal winner.

How do organizations constructed by human hands maintain continuity amid explosive and unexpected changes? Many do not survive major changes. Governments, businesses, and universities appear and disappear. Change overwhelms many organizations. Some, however, survive and thrive.

One common pattern among institutions like the church that have lasted for centuries is to domesticate those internal and external groups

that challenge its authority—as did once the Franciscans and Domini-
cans and groups labeled as heretics. After negotiations between popes
and their opponents, former heretics would swear allegiance to the
church and become part of it.

In effect, as resisters would adapt to the church, the leaders would
create an enclave within its institution where former opponents could
operate and become advocates of papal authority. This organizational
pattern tamed reformers seeking to alter church principles and teach-
ings while assimilating ideas and practices of former opponents; such
co-optation occurs in many other institutions as a strategy to both
adapt to change while maintaining continuity in goals and direction of
the institution.[10]

Continuity and Change in Human Behavior

The time scale in years shrinks from millions on Earth to millennia in
the Roman Catholic Church to decades in a human life, but the marriage of continuity and change holds. While researchers quarrel over
what causes individuals to be who they are and behave as they do in
infancy, childhood, adolescence, adulthood, and old age there is general
agreement, based on scores of longitudinal studies, that both change
and continuity occur within a human life span.

By five years of age, for example, physical and cognitive growth
spurts have changed toddlers and young children physically, emotionally, and cognitively. Such swift growth of infants into early childhood, researchers have established, shapes personality, behaviors, and
attitudes sufficiently that predictions—with different levels of prob-
ability—can be made, for example, about a child's height, intelligence,
personality traits, and achievement as an adult. Thus, early development
changes become stable features of youth and adulthood. While continuity becomes a pattern as an individual gets older, changes fueled by
genes, peer influence, and life events still occur, but with far less impact
on traits formed in the first five years of development. These studies confirm also that growing children's interactions between these features
and the environment (family, neighborhood, school) play an important

role in their development with peers and workplace as they move into adolescence and adulthood.[11]

Hence, developmental changes and stability in a range of human characteristics between infancy and adulthood, influenced by the settings in which children and adults live, typify the decades of an individual's life span.

Since the mid-1960s, such studies of child development have had concrete implications for schooling. Policy emphasis on early childhood education—especially for poor children of color—beginning with three- and four-year-olds, federally funded Head Start, and kindergarten through third grade have occupied researchers and civic and business leaders for decades.[12]

Continuity and change and the inevitable tensions they embody, I argue, occur on a global scale through climate change, within longstanding organizations such as the Roman Catholic Church, and individuals. But none of this is self-evident in the blink of an eye that is the human life span. Were one to take a step back and ponder the changes that have occurred in one's lifetime—I was born in 1934—the political, social, economic, and technological changes over the past eight decades seem staggering. In a culture, where change is highly prized and techno-optimism about the future is baked into the national DNA, everything appears in flux. The key words in the last two sentences are *seem* and *appears*. If one were to take a historical perspective and apply a time frame that stretches out over a century or more, then the *seem* and *appear* dissolve.

Consider walking into a frame house owned by a middle-class family in New York City in 1870. It would have a kitchen with a stove serving as both furnace and oven, bedrooms with fireplaces, a parlor to entertain guests, windows, doors, furniture—everything would be faintly familiar to our twenty-first century eyes except for the outdoor latrine that serves the entire family and the stable.

Fast-forward three generations and walk into a middle-class family's home in 1940. Flush toilets ended outhouses, washing machines replaced hand wringers, gas-fired stoves took over from wood- and coal-burning stoves, and electric lights replaced candles and gas lights.

On a table would be a rotary dial telephone to call a doctor who would come to the house, and instead of a stable of horses, the family car would be parked outside the house.[13]

Now skip ahead another three generations to the early twenty-first century. Certainly, there have been many changes since the 1940s in how we live, work, travel, communicate, and get medical treatment, but the obvious changes in communication, transportation, home appliances, and opportunities to work in 2018 have been incremental ones to the existing technologies in each of these areas. Smartphones, faster planes, safer cars, and smart homes seem so dramatically different from technology of the 1940s that it is understandable—but nonetheless inaccurate—to ignore the basic continuity of new technologies enhancing older ones, not replacing them.[14] After all, a smartphone combines in one device fast and frequent communication, quick access to information, photography, and audio/video recording. Yet all of these capabilities were available in separate devices half-century ago. Faster and more fuel-efficient jets shorten travel times, but the lumbering four engine prop planes transported passengers to the same destinations. In health care, technological advances in medical diagnosis and treatments—EKGs, MRIs, and an array of pills that would stun an earlier generation—still depend on a doctor (no longer making house calls) listening to a patient, taking a history, and figuring out what tests the patient needs and what therapies to recommend based on the test results.

Think a moment about driverless cars and trucks as the most recent manifestation of new technologies altering transportation. Before these vehicles are on the road, product liability laws will have to adapt to robotic transportation. Whose fault is it when injuries and deaths occur involving driverless cars? Who, for example, is responsible for parking and traffic tickets? But the laws carry within them continuity—manufacturers continue to be responsible for the safety of their products—and adaptations to technological changes will occur as they have when autos replaced horse-drawn transportation.[15]

These changes in communication, transportation, and medical practice are incremental bolstering underlying patterns that already had existed for decades. Mistaking a smartphone or a jet for a "revolutionary" change in our lives is common hyperbole in a consumer-driven economy and a culture where techno-optimism reigns. The inflated language misses the fact that all this technology represents a constant updating of practices that have existed for many decades.

Consider further that continuity persists in the social and economic sectors. While legal segregation of races and ethnicities has been banned since the 1950s, these separations in urban, suburban, and rural neighborhoods endure, as do racial disparities in distribution of income. Sharp inequalities in wealth and income that existed in the early twentieth century shrank during the Great Depression and World War II but have returned to those earlier levels in the past three decades. Striking losses in manufacturing and factory jobs have occurred while service and technological occupations have mushroomed, yet inequalities in wealth and income persevere.

Similarly, state and federal rules that have curbed corporate influence on public policy such as government regulation, the US tax code, and health care since the 1990s has decreased measurably in the early twenty-first century. Stability and change are constant.[16]

All of these examples of stability and change in laws governing our lives, climate change, organizations, and our individual lives can be applied to teaching and schooling in the United States The forty-one Silicon Valley teachers across twelve schools in six districts that I observed and interviewed in 2016 combined both continuity and change.

To summarize, then, did teaching practices change in these Silicon Valley classrooms? Yes, they did in incremental ways, in fits and starts, over time. Did the fundamental format and core patterns of teacher-directed lessons alter? They did not.

Did these incremental changes in teaching practice make a difference in how much and how well students learned? The data I gathered from these classrooms, schools, and districts offer no answer to this question. Such an answer awaits another study.

Did the twelve schools in six districts that I examined make incremental changes to increase teacher and student access to and use of digital tools? They surely did, building slowly extensive support mechanisms to help teachers and students use tablets and laptops in daily lessons. For example, the Mountain View Los Altos High School District slowly, in fits and starts with pilot projects, moved toward its instructional policy of students bringing their own devices to school.

But did districts' goals, funding, school board governance, and the age-graded school organization undergo change? They did not.

In distinguishing between incremental and fundamental change, I have argued that in adopting new technologies, many adaptations have taken place gradually in teachers' classrooms, schools, and districts that I identified as "best cases" in Silicon Valley. But few structural changes in the core craft of teaching, school and district governance, funding, and organization occurred. For the rest of this chapter, I want to analyze why that has been the case for these Silicon Valley teachers, schools, and districts.

THE BIG MYTH: PUBLIC SCHOOLS SELDOM CHANGE AND HAVE BEEN BROKEN FOR DECADES

To dig deeper into the apparent paradox of change amid stability in teaching, I need to confront a common belief that US schools seldom change and, in fact, are broken beyond repair.[17] This is a strongly held myth many academics, policy makers, and reformers repeat often to themselves and to the public. They further hold that, as a consequence, schools fail to keep pace with economic and social changes in the larger society. Those who believe in this myth often cite the large literature demonstrating failed innovations in schools or point to calcified bureaucracies and stubborn educators who block reform after reform.

Beginning in the late 1970s, followed by the *Nation at Risk* report (1983) and culminating in No Child Left Behind (2002), the message that *all* US schools are both unchanged and failing has become accepted truth among smart, well-intentioned policy elites, including foundation officials. Even in the face of massive evidence that there are many US schools that parents rate highly—and clamor to have their children attend—the false beliefs endure. These "truths" largely go unquestioned.[18]

Like all myths, this one has a factual basis. There have been many so-called failures to transform schooling in the United States. From open-space schools to vouchers to urban charter schools, vain attempts to fundamentally alter the direction and operation of public schooling, especially in schools located in largely poor and minority neighborhoods, have occurred time and again. Failures are chalked up to school officials' and teachers' deep reluctance to make changes in what they do daily.[19]

Such a myth is politically useful for those who beat the drum that all US schools, are broken and seldom change. Those who indulge in the rhetoric of widespread failure tar all public schools across the nation as resistant to change. But all US schools are neither failed nor perennially unchanged.

Too often ignored is the fact that the United States has a three-tiered system of schooling:

Top-tier schools: About 15 percent of all US schools—such as selective urban high schools in New York, Boston, and San Francisco and schools in mostly affluent suburbs such as New Trier High School (Illinois), Beverly Hills (California), Scarsdale (New York)—meet or exceed national and state curriculum standards. They head lists of high-scoring districts in their respective states. These schools send nearly all of their graduates to four-year colleges and universities.[20]

Second-tier schools: About 50 percent of all schools, often located in inner-ring suburbs (e.g., T.C. Williams High School [Alexandria, Virginia]; Evanston [Illinois] elementary schools, and Milpitas [California] public schools), often meet state standards and send most of their graduating classes to college. But on occasion, they slip in and out of compliance with federal and state accountability rules, get dinged, and continue on their way as second-tier schools.

Bottom-tier schools: Over one-third of schools, located in big cities such as DC, Philadelphia, Baltimore, Detroit, and Atlanta and in rural areas where largely poor and minority families live. High poverty rates, from 50–90 percent of families that send their children to these schools, are common. Crime and unemployment, particularly among males, run high. Housing is expensive and often run down. Most schools in these areas are low-performing and frequently on the brink of being closed. Occasionally, principals and staffs move a school into the second tier.[21]

There have been periodic spasms of reform in the past half-century to upgrade bottom-tier schools. Some determined efforts have produced fleeting success and some have not. So persistent failure of many high-poverty schools for children of color is a stubborn fact that continues in 2018.[22]

This three-tier system reflects the political inequalities in state and local funding of schools and social inequalities in family income and residential segregation that exist in neighborhoods and districts in which these schools are located. Yet—and this is a mighty large *yet*—on occasion, schools even in this lowest tier of schools have achieved positive intellectual, behavioral, and social change in many children and youth.[23]

What is also plain to see but is seldom mentioned by policy elites and 24/7 media is the constant conflating of failing urban and rural schools with *all* US schools. This mindless mistake—stemming from dropping student scores on international tests and the 1983 *Nation at Risk* report—propagates misinformation and sustains a "crisis" mentality that continually bashes teachers and undermines trust in public schools. Large foundations, enamored of the idea of helping gritty urban schools, have furthered the idea of a systemic crisis by imposing their own solutions and failing to distinguish between urban low-performing schools and those many schools in the top two tiers that meet parental demands, have low dropout rates, and send over 95 percent of their graduates to college.[24]

In a country with over 100,000 public schools in 13,000 districts, spread across the United States and its territories, most schools are not "broken" or "troubled." In short, there is much variation in the quality of US public schooling. Labeling all schools as "broken" or "troubled" is both inaccurate and hyperbole. But it has proven a useful hyperbole for political ends, many policy makers have found since *A Nation at Risk* was published. Exaggerating the pervasiveness of troubled schools has become the basis for building political coalitions that stoke the current deep pessimism about the incapacity of public schools to change and improve. So it is a politically useful myth.

The fact is that over the last century, US schools have changed. Such changes, both incremental and fundamental, have been adopted, adapted, implemented, and institutionalized, albeit sporadically, often in herky-jerky fashion (e.g., desegregation in the South and North after 1954). Some have even been dropped and then resurrected (e.g., teaching machines in the 1920s and programmed learning in the 1950s). In many instances, these changes diverged from what reformers in past generations wanted but they were changes nonetheless.

As I have noted, many of these changes have been incremental, that is, additions to existing structures and processes of schooling. However, a few of these changes have been fundamental, altering substantially how public schools operate. Consider the following blend of incremental and fundamental changes in US schools over time:

- Before 1850, most schools were one-room and rural, scattered across each state. Between 1850 and 1920, state and local policy makers steadily but slowly created a structure of tax-supported age-graded schools that included kindergarten, grammar schools, and comprehensive junior and senior high schools, foreshadowing the end of the one-room schoolhouse.
- In the 1920s, state and local policy makers gradually consolidated 100,000 mostly rural local school districts to just under 15,000 by 2001.[25]

- Since 1954, segregation in public schools was outlawed, and desegregation of schools in the South occurred sporadically and patchily over the next three decades. However, resegregation of black and white children in the South and North has occurred, largely because of residential segregation and income inequality.[26]
- Since the early 1970s, children with disabilities have had access to public school classrooms.
- Policy makers and donors created small schools out of large comprehensive high schools in 1960s and 1990s.
- Teacher/student classroom ratios have steadily decreased since the 1950s.
- Choices of schools, curricula, and programs available to students have proliferated.
- New subjects (environmental studies, advanced placement courses in sciences and humanities, computer coding, etc.) enlarged curriculum.
- Use of small-group and individual approaches to classroom organization and instruction increased significantly.

This partial listing of actual changes in US schools prompts me to ask: *Why has the myth about all US schools being damaged and the incapability of American schools to change become mainstream wisdom?*

This myth springs in part from the political nature of tax-supported public schooling. Consider the nature of policy making in the United States, which is to dramatize an issue—say, low test scores in urban and rural high-poverty schools—then generalize the "problem" to the failure of all US schools to make necessary changes, which then becomes the rallying cry for building a political coalition with an agenda of "solutions." The coalition then lobbies local, state, and federal decision-makers to enact the "solutions."[27] There are also reform-driven observers and participants who failed to get what they wanted first time around and try again; there are reformers who ignore past efforts or overlook how schools adapt innovations and transform them into stable routines.

Amnesia, myopia, overgeneralization, and the crisis-fueled political way of making school policy are congenital defects afflicting US reformers. Yet on occasion, because of political, social, and economic events in society (e.g., war, economic depressions, cultural shifts, the civil rights movement) fundamental changes have occurred. What happened to these structural changes once they entered schools, however, is another story.

HOW FUNDAMENTAL CHANGES BECOME INCORPORATED AS INCREMENTAL ONES

The addition of the kindergarten, and later preschool, to public schools; new math and science curricula; public funding of charter schools; and the use of computers to change traditional teaching, to cite a few examples, are instances of actual and attempted fundamental changes in the school and classroom since the turn of the twentieth century. Stemming from political action and internal debates, these elements were widely adopted, incorporated into many schools, and then, over time, morphed into incremental changes. Tax-supported institutions, paradoxically, are committed to preserving community values through socializing children, yet introduce changes to not only keep pace with shifts in the larger society but also improve how they get students to learn.

How did this occur?

A familiar example is the curricular reforms of the 1950s and 1960s, guided largely by inspired university academics and funded by the federal government. Aimed at revolutionizing teaching and learning in math, science, and social studies (spurred in part by a popular perception that Soviet education was superior to American schools, as evidenced by the launch of *Sputnik* in 1957), millions of dollars went into producing textbooks, developing classroom materials, and training teachers. Using the best instructional materials that scholars could produce, teachers taught students to understand how scientists thought and experienced the hard work and pleasures of discovery, how mathematicians solved math problems, and how historians used primary sources to understand the past. Published instructional materials, including new texts, ended up in the hands of teachers who, for the most part, had had little time to understand what was demanded by the novel materials or, for that matter, how to use them in lessons.[28]

By the end of the 1970s, education researchers were reporting that instead of finding student-driven involvement in critical thinking, problem solving, or experiencing how scientists worked, they had found the familiar teacher-centered instruction aimed at imparting knowledge from a text. There was, however, a distinct curricular residue of these federally funded efforts left in textbooks published in the 1970s. The attempt to revolutionize teaching and learning evolved, in time, into new textbook content, some of which became controversial enough to be dropped from the new curricula. Reformers were sorely disappointed at minor returns from major efforts.[29]

Another way that fundamental changes get transformed into incremental ones is organizationally shunting them from the core of schooling to the periphery of the system. For example, innovative programs that reduce class size (e.g., dropout prevention), integrate subject matter from diverse disciplines (e.g., gifted and talented programs), and structure activities that involve students in real-world learning (e.g., vocational programs) often begin as classroom experiments but, over time, either migrate to the periphery rather than the core of the system or disappear. School systems have indeed adopted and implemented programs that are different from what mainstream students receive (e.g., alternative schools for dropouts and gifted students) but these innovations move to the edges of the system, becoming quasi-segregated enclaves. So it is the outsiders—at-risk students labeled as potential dropouts and vocational, pregnant, gifted, economically disadvantaged, or disabled students—who end up participating in innovative programs. Thus, some basic changes get encapsulated like a grain of sand in an oyster; they exist within the system but are often separated from core programs.[30]

Such conversions of fundamental changes into incremental ones occur as a result of deep-seated impulses within tax-supported schools to appear modern, convincing those who politically and financially support the schools that what happens in public schools is up-to-date, responsive to the wishes of its patrons, but yet no different from what happens in the "real schools" that taxpayers remember from their youth—with homework, rows of desks in classrooms, and teachers who maintain order. Thus, potent imperatives within public schools preserve its independence to act even in the face of powerful outside political forces intent on altering what happens in schools and classrooms. Reformers seeking to "transform" schooling see such incremental changes as failure; less self-interested observers see these bite-sized changes as how tax-supported, conservative institutions adapt politically to their environment.[31]

So, to sum up:

- Schools are conservative institutions dedicated to transmitting community and family values and socializing the young into dominant societal norms—the stability side of the equation— while preparing the next generation for an ever-shifting society— the change side of the equation. This dilemma of tax-supported schools maintaining what is while preparing problem-solvers, independent thinkers, and graduates to make social, political, and economic change is in the DNA of US tax-supported public schools.

- There have been many changes in governance, organization, curriculum, and classroom instruction over the past century and a half.

- Most of these changes have been incremental; only a few have been fundamental.

- None of the changes followed a straight path from a policy idea to classroom practice. The trajectory of the changes bent and zigzagged as they moved slowly from school boards to classrooms. Many of these changes were adopted, slowly implemented, and then became gradually institutionalized.

Some fundamental changes were incorporated into the core of the mainstream districts as innovations, but many others became permanently lodged as enclaves in the system.

- Over time, these changes in schools ended up preserving and strengthening continuity in school goals, structures, and classroom practices.

Change amid constancy can be puzzling. The above analysis shows that certain kinds of change in public schools—mostly incremental and slow-moving—have occurred continuously over the past century. That such changes have been severely criticized as too little or insubstantial by ardent reformers seeking wholesale renovation of, say, urban districts has been a common refrain over the decades.

Reformers who too often overlooked that schools and districts have been changing have continually tussled over which school changes have been helpful (and should be kept) and which have been harmful (and discarded). Nonetheless, many changes have occurred and accumulated over time, resulting in` maintaining and occasionally modifying familiar school structures and classroom practices. That is the story of US public schools over time. But is that true for teaching?[32]

Yes, it is.

WHY REFORMS AIMED AT ALTERING HOW TEACHERS USUALLY TEACH SELDOM SUCCEED

In previous writings, I have suggested various explanations for reform-driven policies, decade after decade, seeking to transform teaching practices into student-centered lessons, yet after some changes occurred, classroom lessons remained predominately teacher-directed.[33]

Three explanations in particular make the most sense to me in light of the study I conducted for this book. The first explanation is the quiet, continuous, and substantial influence of the age-graded school in explaining why teachers teach as they do. Second, prevailing social and individual beliefs about what are "good" schools, "good" teaching, and "good" learning influence what happens in classrooms. Finally, contemporary and previous reforms not only depend on the abiding age-graded structure for success but also end up preserving it.

The Age-Graded School

The age-graded school, a nineteenth-century innovation, has become an unquestioned mainstay of school organization (e.g., K–5, K–8, 6–8, 9–12) in the twenty-first century. Because the age-graded school is so taken for granted, it is easy to forget how this commonplace institution replaced rural one-room schoolhouses and has influenced how and what teachers teach and what and how students learn for over a century and a half.

Today, most taxpayers and voters have gone to kindergarten at age five, studied Egyptian mummies in the sixth grade, taken algebra in the eighth or ninth grade and then exited twelfth grade with a high school diploma.

If any school reform—in the sense of making fundamental changes in organization, curriculum, and instruction—can be considered a success, it is the age-graded school. This abiding structure has accommodated hundreds of millions of native- and foreign-born children since the late-nineteenth century and remains the dominant organizational instrument for public (and private) schooling in the United States.

The first age-graded building appeared in Quincy, Massachusetts, in the late 1840s. It housed children of roughly the same age in each of its eight grades. Over subsequent decades, in rural and urban districts, these so-called *grammar schools* replaced one-room schoolhouses in which a teacher would instruct a student population ranging from very young children to teenagers in all of the academic subjects for a few hours a day. In 1910, there were 200,000 one-room schoolhouses in the United States; a half-century later, there were 20,000, and by 2000, there were only 400. Over decades, rural consolidation of school districts and growing suburban and urban systems made the age-graded school the organizational norm for schooling all children and youth.[34]

The age-graded school organizes students by their ages into separate classrooms. Embedded in this arrangement is the assumption that students learn roughly at the same rate, and teachers—through direct observation and periodic quizzes and end-of-year tests—will determine which students have achieved sufficiently to be promoted to the next grade. Report cards tell students and parents where they fall in the normal distribution of achievement. Intermittent parent-teacher conferences cover the progress or regress for each student.

Annual promotion from grade to grade in the early twentieth century became the common benchmark of the age-graded school, culminating with graduation from the eighth grade of what was then called *grammar school*. Later in the 1920s, the innovative junior high school, comprising grades seven through nine, became the next step in the ladder of schooling from which to graduate (most but not all elementary schools by that time had begun adding kindergarten and ended with the sixth grade). At about the same time, the small academic high school of earlier decades expanded into the much larger comprehensive high school offering multiple curricula and an array of afterschool activities for all students. By 1940, most US students went to a six-grade elementary school, a three-grade junior high school, and a four-grade comprehensive high school. Those who completed the twelfth grade satisfactorily received a high school diploma.[35]

For teachers, the age-graded structure sends them into separate, self-contained classrooms furnished with students desks, a wall clock, a flag, blackboards, and, in the front of the room, a large teacher's desk. There is a prescribed curriculum for each grade, carved up into chunks for students, covering the content they are to learn and skills they are to acquire during the school year. A teacher in one grade is expected to have taught the prescribed content and skills so that the teacher in the next grade can begin where the other ended. Teachers test each student to determine whether content has been learned and skills acquired, recording marks on report cards. Nearly all students pass and get promoted to the next grade. Those students who fail the tests are held back and repeat the grade in elementary school or academic subject in secondary school. This is the system that has governed US schooling for a century and a half.

The age-graded school is also an institution that has plans for those who work within its confines. From the Roman Catholic Church to the US Marines to the San Francisco Police Department to Fox News to Uber, organizational structures and cultures shape behavior of those who work and live within them. And so it is for the typical age-graded elementary and secondary public school.[36]

Age-graded schools, for example, isolate and insulate teachers in their self-contained classrooms. Solo teaching and self-reliance is the norm. Relationships are with "my" children in "my" classroom. These students are the audience to which teachers attend closely, not those outside of their room. Collaboration is sporadic and seldom occurs. Efforts to team-teach in a grade or academic subject require complicated scheduling adjustments. Most teachers work alone and have learned to be self-sufficient in securing materials and aid; most know little of how their colleagues teach.[37]

Student behavior and attitudes are also shaped by the age-graded school structure and culture. What is considered "normal" behavior in a school is impressed on students early. How to walk in halls when passing from one class to another and obeying teacher directions become second nature for most students. Because the structure expects nearly all students to progress from grade to grade, those students who depart from the norm are outliers in their grade. They become an organizational problem.

Over decades, policy makers and administrators have "solved" the "problem" by promoting every child to the next grade and generating labels and distinct programs for those students who skip ahead or lag behind. It is now common to have special classes to accommodate those who deviate from the norm: "gifted and talented learners," "slow learners," "disadvantaged," "at-risk children and youth," "English language learners," "learning disabled," etc. Both adults and children accept these organizational labels and the connotations that accompany them as accurate descriptors of those in special classes.[38]

The age-graded setting, then, shapes perceptions, attitudes, and behaviors of those adults and children who live in them six or more hours a day. It is the sea in which nearly all US teachers, students, principals, and parents swim. It is so familiar to generations of students and their parents that few contemporary reformers have questioned the water in which they paddle.[39]

Why have most school reformers and educational entrepreneurs been reluctant to examine an organization that now influences daily behavior of nearly 4 million adults and well over 50 million children?[40]

Dominant Social Beliefs About Schooling, Teaching, and Learning

Prevailing social beliefs of parents and educators about what constitutes a "real school" have colored educational policies for decades. The idea is anchored in the age-graded structure. It is a school where teachers teach children to read, write, and do math in the lower grades and complete advanced academic work in upper grades; where teachers maintain discipline in their classrooms; and students receive report cards, do homework, have textbooks, and get promoted annually after meeting grade-level standards.

For the most part, these deep-rooted social beliefs endorse the purposes for public schools to prepare children and youth to succeed in society through getting decent-paying jobs, going to college, contributing to the community, and leading an upstanding life. Existing age-graded elementary and secondary schools are seen as successful vehicles for achieving those ends. Between 1999 and 2016, when parents have been asked if they are satisfied with their local school, between 76 percent and 83 percent have said they are.[41]

Strong beliefs in these "real schools" spill over innovative schools established to deviate from the norm. For example, when charter school applicants propose a new school, the chances of receiving official approval and parental acceptance increase if it is a familiar age-graded one, not one where most teachers team teach, or multi-age groups of children (ages 5–8 and 9–11, for example) learn together, and there are no rooms designated as first- through sixth-grades. Charter management organizations such as Aspire (forty schools nationally), KIPP (two hundred schools nationally), Success Academy (forty-one in New York City), and other networks are age-graded. Such widely shared beliefs about the importance of the age-graded structure preserve traditional ways of schooling familiar to parents, grandparents, and great-grandparents.[42]

Personal beliefs also intersect with social beliefs when it comes to individual parents' views about childrearing and schooling. Depending on income, ethnicity and race, and type of family (e.g., single parent, blended family, two-parents), parents vary in how they approach raising their children when it comes to teaching responsibility, disciplining errant behavior, children making choices, watching television and using smartphones, freedom of movement in and out the home, and dozens of other childrearing decisions.[43]

Experts have also differed in their advice to parents over the past century. Traditional and modern ways of raising children have gone through phases that both meshed and conflicted with individual parental beliefs, and parents had to decide whether to follow family traditions, the advice of experts, their hearts, or some combination of these.[44]

Individual parents range from demanding to undemanding, intrusive to distant, and varied combinations in raising their children; they bring those views to how schools should treat, care for, and teach their sons and daughters. Regardless of whether parents find themselves at the traditional end, in the middle, or at the progressive end in a spectrum of child-rearing practices, nearly all parents expect schools to be age-graded.[45]

Likewise, many parents are teachers, and they hold these social beliefs as well. Also note that all teachers have been students for sixteen or more years in age-graded schools and were socialized to the familiar structure as the only "real" way to school the next generation. Even though individual teachers have different ideas about how best to teach and motivate students to learn, and what schools should be about. That variation shrinks to a general agreement on the importance of the age-graded structure.

On occasion, reformers, including teachers, have deviated from the norm of age-graded schools to create non-graded schools, multi-age groupings in primary grades, and other experimental forms that offer alternative structures for students and teachers. But such examples are outliers, sitting on the periphery of districts in which they exist. In part, then, what keeps these age-graded schools dominant is a network of pervasive and historic social and individual beliefs among parents, teachers, and taxpayers about what schooling is (and should be).[46]

School Governance and Previous Reforms Keep Age-Graded Structures in Place

Decentralized governance of schools, state and federal regulations, and earlier efforts to improve schooling also constrict reformers' maneuverability in trying other organizational forms. The thirteen thousand–plus school districts in the United States, each with its own elected school board making policy for its principals and teachers, have kept the mid-nineteenth-century innovation of the age-graded school as their defining structure for maintaining student behavior, curriculum, and instruction. Although school authority for funding, graduation requirements, curriculum standards, testing, and accountability has shifted from local boards to cities with mayoral control over schools (e.g., New York City, Cleveland, and Washington, DC) to states (e.g., California, New York State, Texas, and Florida) and to the federal government since the early 2000s, no federal or state law has yet directed these local districts as to how they should organize their schools or told teachers how to teach. This decentralized governance (critics call it "fragmented") and its accompanying feature of teacher decision making has insured that the traditional age-graded school remains preeminent.[47]

State-mandated curriculum standards, tests, accountability rules, college entrance requirements, and No Child Left Behind (now Every Child Succeeds) regulations that call, for example, testing in third to eighth grade are all wedded to the age-graded structure. Even when innovations like charter schools—now over a quarter-century old—enter the portfolios of reformers, nearly all retain the age-graded structure.

The unintended (and ironic) consequence of frequent and earnest calls for radical change in preparing teachers and school leaders, school governance, curriculum, and instruction through nontraditional teachers and administrators, nifty reading and math programs, iPads for kindergartners, blended and personalized learning, pay for performance, and other reforms end up coping with thousands of local school boards that have preserved the age-graded school in amber, thereby perpetuating ongoing classroom patterns of solo teaching, sparse collaboration among teachers, and few cross-grade groupings that so many reformers and entrepreneurs want to alter. Decentralized governance and teachers' discretionary decision making in classrooms go hand-in-hand in US schools. Past and present school reforms become a case study of dynamic conservatism in schooling.

Of course, the age-graded organization does have some flexibility; it can bend to transform instructional reforms into familiar classroom activities. Every reform aimed at moving classroom practice from teacher- to student-centered has ended up with teachers borrowing pieces of the innovation to make a blend of the old and new in their lessons to fit each grade level taught. The list of such examples extends from progressive efforts to mount project-based instruction in the 1920s, new science and math curricula in the 1950s, open classrooms in the 1960s, mastery learning in the 1970s, "authentic assessment" from the 1990s, and in the past decade an influx of digital tools to personalize learning. All of these instructional reforms—and others as well—have found a home within the age-graded school, ending up just barely recognizable years later.

Thus my explanations for the constancy of teaching practices are located in the age-graded school structure, deep-seated and pervasive social and individual beliefs about child-rearing and "good" schooling, and the effects of decentralized governance and teacher choice interacting with past instructional reforms. These explanations lay the foundation for answering the second question driving this study arises: *Has putting these technologies into practice made a difference in teaching practice?*

Yes and no.

Most of the Silicon Valley exemplary teachers I interviewed who have fully integrated new technologies into their daily routines over years of practice answered yes to the question. But some teachers said that while using these new devices and software has surely enhanced their productivity in managing their classes, core aspects of planning and enacting lessons, relationships with students, and the craft of teaching had largely remained stable.

As some of the teachers had, I, too, answered the question about change in practice as a result of using digital tools regularly with a yes and no. Making distinctions between incremental and fundamental changes made it easy for me to agree with the two-thirds of the teachers who said yes, they had actually altered how they taught over time and had become more productive in planning and enacting lessons.

The "no" comes from those teachers who answered my questions and concentrated on the ongoing, deep parts of their craft, their knowledge of subject matter, and commitment to building strong relationships with students as they embraced new technologies. To these teachers and myself, the abiding craft of teaching was less subject to change because, comfortable as they had become in using digital tools, new technologies played a minor part in planning the objectives of a lesson; creating activities that moved the lesson along from beginning to end using a mix of whole class discussion, small-group work, and individual tasks; and students participating in all of these activities.

The "no," then, means that familiar teacher-directed lessons remained a constant amid the productivity gains teachers saw in managing their classes using digital tools. Is this a wishy-washy conclusion to this study followed by a plea for more research to be done? No, it is not.

I answered both yes and no to whether teachers had indeed altered how they teach and probed more deeply at what I see as the underlying stability and change, the yin and yang that mark the environment in which we live, organizations in which we work, and the individual lives that unfold as we age.

Does my yes-and-no answer to the question mean that students learned more or less as a result of using new technologies? I do not know, since I focused on what teachers did during a lesson and not what students learned. For those readers who want answers to this straightforward and fair question, other researchers will have to enter classrooms and find answers.

If I cannot answer this question, of what use is such a study to practitioners, policy makers, wannabe reformers, and researchers? This is the answer to the all important "So what?" question, one that asks about the worth of investigating exemplars of technology integration in classrooms, schools, and districts in Silicon Valley.

CONCLUSIONS: FLUTTERING BUTTERFLIES OR SPEEDING BULLETS?

My study does raise anew the question of whether reform-driven policies meant to change how teachers teach actually result in altered classroom practices. Can policies assuming that traditional teaching harms twenty-first-century students direct teachers who teach that way to reconfigure their lessons into student-centered instruction? That is the historic dilemma wrapped in all policies seeking basic changes in how teachers teach.

Early twentieth-century progressives were eager to get teachers to use the Project Method, just as mid-twentieth-century reformers sought to move teachers from the Old Math to the New Math. Similarly, two generations later, many decision makers who wanted "teaching for understanding" and "ambitious instruction" saw new technologies of desktop computers, interactive whiteboards, and tablets revamping the practice of teaching by upending the old technologies of blackboards, taking notes, and textbooks. Cohorts of reformers for the past century have dreamed of instructional policies overhauling traditional teaching practices and wrestled with the conundrum of asking the very people thought to be causing the problem to carry out the changes. The literature documenting the paths instructional policies have taken to revise what teachers do daily in their classrooms over the past century is, at best, mixed and, at worst, discouraging.[48]

Thus, in completing this study, I have avoided the bimodal literature on technological success and failure of digital tools in classrooms
(see the introduction). If they land anywhere on the spectrum from success to failure, my findings alight like a colorful butterfly at the center of
the continuum. In doing so, however, there are few clear-cut conclusions
that readers can take away.

Although my yes-and-no answer falls in the center of that success-
failure continuum and offers few directives that policy makers and practitioners can use immediately, there are a few implications that flow
from that answer to the questions of whether teachers had altered how
they teach as a result of using digital tools.

First, school reforms seeking to alter traditional ways of teaching
follow the erratic path of a butterfly flitting from flower to flower rather
than a bullet streaking toward its target. The history of school reforms
over the past century pushing uses of new technologies to get teachers
to teach differently and students to learn more, faster, and better has
been well documented. From the teaching machines of the 1920s to programmed learning devices in the 1950s and 1960s to mastery learning
in the 1970s and 1980s to personalized learning in the past two decades,
the press to use machines to individualize both teaching and learning
has been both hyperbolic and unrelenting.[49]

In each instance then and now, the path of school and classroom
reform has been erratic and fluttering, occasionally taking over teachers' classrooms but eventually diminishing over time. Yet generation
after generation of teachers have learned to take reforms aimed at altering how they teach and adapted pieces of the reform and tailored them
to fit their students and the contours of classrooms locked into age-
graded schools.

Consider the Summit charter school network, which went through
a crisis of purpose nearly a decade after the founding of the first charter
high school when it discovered in a follow-up study of that nearly half
of its graduates who entered college failed to get a degree (see chapter
2). Network leaders and the entire school faculty analyzed the data and
to figure out why so many of their graduates did poorly in college. What

they decided on in 2011 led to a shift in overall goals, overhauling the school schedule, adopting a schoolwide technology strategy, and other adjustments in the organization and operation of network schools. The shift in direction was neither expected nor linear. The past decade and a half of this network reveals that it progressed not like a wind-up toy going in one direction but in a herky-jerky, irregular path of continuous improvement in bite-sized increments.

Second, teacher expertise and capabilities are crucial to any full-bore district or school effort to have teachers use digital tools daily. Researchers have documented repeatedly that for deep changes in classroom practice to occur, multiple tools and resources for aiding teachers have to come into play. There is no one-off professional development day or week that will do the job.

Teachers need continuing support in applying curriculum standards to their lessons. They need help in using new instructional materials. They need aid in assessing student work during a lesson and at the end of a unit and providing multiple opportunities for teachers to learn from one another and experts. Classroom change is hard and steady work. And sustained support to enhance teachers' expertise and expand their capabilities, at the minimum, is essential.[50]

Third, school and district policies directing teachers to use new technologies in daily lessons—such as in Summit charter high schools, Mountain View Los Altos and Milpitas districts (except for the one district high school)—have expanded classroom use significantly. The clear expectation that each teacher has to use digital tools (while receiving ample school assistance in doing so) strips away the usual voluntarism in most districts, where teachers decide whether and how to use devices for lessons. Students have generous access to devices and software, and school leaders require teachers to regularly use the available digital tools.

And in those schools, while there was much variation, teachers did use available technologies in every single instance I observed. As the vignettes in chapters 1–4 show, schools and districts that require their teachers to use new technologies (e.g., the biology lesson at Summit Prep, described in chapter 2, and the chemistry lesson at Summit

Rainier, depicted in chapter 4), how teachers use technologies and which ones vary a great deal. The press to use the digital tools is clear and ever-present in these classrooms; nonetheless, teachers decide which devices and software to use and when in a particular lesson.

Voluntary use of devices by teachers (as described in chapter 1) or required use (chapters 2 and 3) are choices school and district decision makers must decide in policies directed at altering classroom practices. Which of these directions is better than one another in students learning more, faster, and better remains unknown.

Fourth, by concentrating on exemplars in classrooms, schools, and districts, these "best cases" reveal the gradual implementation of digital tools used for daily lessons. There is no question that the teachers and schools I described fully put into practice the integration of new technologies. And it was clear to me that it took time, was done in increments, and zigzagged considerably, according to the teachers and district leaders.

That implementation, however, has to be separated from the predictable ambiguity of determining whether, as a result of implementation of technology into lessons, teaching practices have indeed changed in the direction reformers sought. Recall the crucial policy questions I asked in the introduction about reforms intended to rework classroom practice: *When implemented fully, did they change the content and practice of teaching? Did changed classroom practices account for what students learned?*

Gains in classroom efficiency did occur as a result of using digital tools, teachers declared. And just as surely, evidence of stable patterns in planning and enacting forty-five- to ninety-minute lessons persisted within those teacher-perceived increases in productivity. Thus, it is unclear whether the changes and stability that did unfold in the classrooms and schools will have had a pronounced or diminished effect on student learning. Studies of student responses and learning outcomes would have to establish whether such changes have had the desired impact on students. That is for another study of classroom reforms.

Finally, my yes-and-no answer to the question of whether daily practices changed in the classrooms of exemplary teachers recognizes the complexity of teaching, and how reform-driven attempts in the past and present to alter what occurs in daily lessons travel an erratic path closer to the flight of a butterfly than the path of a bullet. Such darting and juking on the journey of a reform from school board policy to classroom practice end up producing teaching hybrids rather than reformers' intended outcome of a bullet hitting the target. On the zigzag path classroom improvements take, reformers can utter no full-throated hurrahs or point angry fingers. Neither uncorking champagne to celebrate or blaming teachers for maintaining traditional lessons is a realistic response to the spasmodic pattern that instructional policies take before and after entering classrooms each day a teacher starts and ends a lesson.[51]

> *There is nothing so stable as change.*
> —BOB DYLAN, 1963[52]

APPENDIX

Design and Methodology

The design of this qualitative study is a series of case studies of individual classrooms, schools, and districts located in Northern California that have integrated technology into teaching and learning. Two questions guide the design:

1. Have classroom, school, and district exemplars of technology integration been fully implemented and put into classroom practice?
2. Have these exemplars altered teaching practices?

The advantages and disadvantages of case study design have been thoroughly discussed in the research design and methodology literature.[1]

For this study, the advantages of examining a select group of cases in the different contexts at different levels of schooling and socioeconomic setting makes clear the importance of both the phenomenon—integrating digital technology—and its embeddedness in the local context. Detailed cases describing teacher, school, and district behaviors inevitably generate questions about teaching, learning, and uses of technologies that seldom arise from a survey or experimental design. Furthermore, analyzing classroom, school, and district exemplars can disclose the interactions between context and technology and how difficult it is to scale up classroom exemplars to schools and then to districts—a concern that occupies policymakers and donors who want exemplars to grow in number.

I judged that these advantages outweigh the disadvantages of case studies in their nonrepresentative samples, the impossibility of establishing cause-effect connections, and feebleness in generalizing.

Survey designs that tap teachers', students', and administrators' views seldom capture the inexorable entanglement of the setting and the phenomenon. Nor can the behaviors of the participants be manipulated through an experimental design. So a case study design using multiple units of analysis (classroom, school, and district) is a choice I have made. Yet such a design contains disadvantages. For example, while randomized samples can be used for surveys and experimental designs, my sampling of "best cases" in one geographic region is opportunistic. I relied on contacts I had in the San Francisco Bay area to tap a variety of classrooms, schools, and districts that met criteria of technology integration (see below). Moreover, using multiple units of analysis across selected districts in Silicon Valley makes it difficult to aggregate findings and generalize across the entire array of districts in the region, much less the state or nation.

Methods: Advantages and Disadvantages

I drew up a list of teachers, schools, and districts in Silicon Valley that had been mentioned in the media as exemplars of technology integration. Names also came from contacts in various districts (e.g., technology coordinators, administrators, teachers) who pointed out individual teachers and schools that were "best cases" of technology integration. At the district level, I used articles and books on Silicon Valley schools to identify two districts out of seventy-seven in the area that had system-wide policies mandating technology integration across schools and were helping their classroom teachers put it into practice (see below for definitions of *technology integration* and criteria I used to identify sites).

At no point in this early stage of identifying teachers, schools, and districts did I use the word *effective*. In current educational talk, *effective* refers most often to student outcomes such as test scores, high school graduation rates, and college attendance. In conversations with teachers, coordinators, and superintendents, I stressed the phrase *technology integration* and not whether the teacher, school, or district was successful in raising student test scores or other common metrics.

I wrote letters to district superintendents and heads of charter management organizations explaining why I was writing about instances of technology integration in their schools. At no point did these administrators ask me to define *technology integration* or even ask about the phrase; all seemed to know what I meant. In nearly all instances, the superintendent, school site administrator, technology coordinator, and CMO head invited me into the district. Administrators and technology coordinators supplied me with lists of principals and teachers to contact. Again, neither my contacts nor I defined the phrase *technology integration* in conversations; they already had a sense of what the phrase meant. I assumed that there would be variation across respondents in defining the phrase.

In fall 2015, I contacted individual teachers on the list, explaining how I got their names and what I was doing, and asked for their participation in the project. More than half agreed and invited me into their classrooms and schools. Because of health issues, I did not start the project until January 2016. For four months, I visited schools and classrooms, observed lessons, and interviewed staff. I resumed observations and interviews in two other Silicon Valley districts in the fall and completed all observations and interviews by December 2016.

I interviewed teachers before and after the lessons I observed in their classrooms. During the observation, I took notes every few minutes about what both the teacher and students were doing. I followed a protocol that permitted me to describe activities in the class while commenting separately about what both teacher and students were doing. I had used this observation protocol in previous studies. The point of the description and commentary was to capture what happened in the classroom, not determine the degree of teacher effectiveness or what students learned. I avoided evaluative judgments about the teacher activities or the worth of the lesson.

The major advantage of this approach is describing the range of "best cases" and documenting what actually exists in practice. Seeing what can be done in actual classrooms, schools, and districts gives rich detail to researchers and reformers about what the phenomenon is and can be.[2] This is especially true for classroom sites, places not commonly examined by researchers. Being in the room and picking up nonverbal and verbal asides of what is going on every few minutes as well as noting classroom conditions that often go unnoticed, I captured details that are often overlooked. As an experienced teacher familiar with schooling historically and the common moves that occur in lessons, I could also assess the relationship between the teacher and students that other observers using different protocols or videos may miss or exclude. And I was not compelled to judge the teacher's performance.

There are two major disadvantages in this research strategy. First, there is the subjectivity and many biases that I bring to documenting lessons and describing schools and districts. I thus worked hard at separating what I saw from what I interpreted. I describe objectively classroom conditions from student and teacher desk arrangements through what is on bulletin boards, photos and pictures on walls, and whiteboards and which, if any, electronic devices are available in the room. I describe teacher and student behaviors without judging. But biases, as in other approaches to researching classroom life, remain.[3]

The second disadvantage to this research strategy is what academics would call *sampling on the dependent variable*. I was investigating cases where the aim of the reform was to substantially alter how teaching was done. These were the "best cases." They were deemed "success stories." The point of this kind of sampling is to extract from multiple cases the common features (e.g., a collaborative school culture, extensive preparation of teachers) of these ventures and inform policy makers and practitioners what needs to be done should they seek to replicate the exemplars. Unfortunately, when you do this kind of research, there is no variation in the sample.

The dangers in synthesizing common features of successes become evident when you take a step back, since without variation in the sample—no control group, no comparison cases—the "wisdom" gained from looking at "best cases" may bear little relationship to the "wisdom" gained from looking at failures or those instances in the middle of the distribution. The common features of failure or success extracted from exemplars to explain why the initiatives nose-dived or soared often fall apart after a few years.[4] (See, for example, in the education literature the research on Effective Schools in the 1980s and 1990s. Schools profiled as successes in one year turn out to have sunk into failure a few years later. Also see a companion literature in business demonstrating the same pattern.[5])

By looking only at instances of digital technology use in schools where participants believed teaching had changed, I overlooked cases of where participants believed that use of digital technologies had failed to alter classroom practice. To sample on the dependent variable, then, is a bias built into the research design.

In writing this book, however, I have pulled together what I have learned from both the "failures" I have studied since the 1980s and the "best cases" I have identified in 2016. I have been able to compare both cases of those classrooms and schools that nose-dived and those that soared in integrating devices into lessons.

These two disadvantages to the research strategy I used are, again, similar to other research designs that contain similar strengths and limitations.

What I Did in Classrooms and Schools Identified as Exemplary

After observing teachers do their lessons, I sat down and had half-hour to forty-five-minute interviews at times convenient to the teachers. After jotting down their history in the district and the school and other experiences, I turned to the lessons and asked a series of questions about what happened during the period. I asked what their goals were and whether they believed those goals were reached. I then asked about the different activities I observed during the lesson. One key question was whether the lesson I observed was representative—or not—of how the teacher usually taught.

In answering these questions, teachers gave me the reasons they did (or did not do) something in lessons. In most instances, individual teachers told me reasons for doing what they did, thus communicating a map of their beliefs and assumptions about teaching, learning, and the content they taught. In all of the give-and-take of these discussions with teachers, I made no judgment about the success or failure of different activities or the lesson itself. I then drafted a description of the lesson and sent it to the teacher to correct any factual errors I made in describing the lesson. The teacher returned the draft with corrections.[6]

For schools and districts, I observed individual classrooms and interviewed teachers, administrators, and technology coordinators. I collected documents and used school and teacher websites to describe what occurred within each school and district in integrating digital devices and software into teachers' daily lessons.

Defining the concept of technology integration, however, was elusive and required much work. Even though when I used the phrase it triggered nods from teachers and administrators as if we all shared the same meaning, I still had to come up with a working definition of the concept that would permit me to capture more precisely what I saw in classrooms, schools, and districts.

Definitions of "Technology Integration"

Current definitions of technology integration are a conceptual swamp. Some definitions focus on the technology itself and student access to the devices and software. Some concentrate on the technologies as tools to help teachers and students reach curricular and instructional goals. Some mix a definition with what constitutes success or effective use of devices and software. Some include the various stages of technology integration, from simple to complex. And some include in their definitions a "one best way" of integrating technology to advance an instructional method such as student-centered learning. Thus, a conceptual swamp sucks in unknowing enthusiasts and fervent true believers into endless arguing over exactly what *technology integration* is.[7]

To avoid the confusion and the semantic arguments in identifying teachers and schools where a high degree integrated devices in daily practices had occurred, I relied on informal definitions frequently used by practitioners. From exchanges with practitioners when identifying "best cases" of technology integration, I distilled the following criteria:

- **District had provided wide access to digital devices and established infrastructure for use.** System administrators had fought insistently for student access to hardware (e.g., tablets, laptops, interactive whiteboards) and software (e.g., the latest programs in language arts, math, history, and science) through 1:1 programs for the entire schools, mobile carts, etc.
- **District had both a clear vision and established structures for how schools can improve learning and reach desired outcomes through technology.** The district established formal ways for monitoring academic student progress, created teacher-initiated professional development, initiated on-site coaching of teachers and daily mentoring of students, and provided easily accessible assistance when glitches in devices or technological infrastructure occurred.
- **Particular schools and teachers had repeatedly requested personal devices and classroom computers for their students.** Evidence of requests came from sign-up lists for computer carts, volunteering to have pilot 1:1 computer projects in their classrooms, and purchase orders for specific teachers and departments.
- **Certain teachers and principals came regularly to professional development workshops on computer use in lessons.** Voluntary attendance at one or more of these sessions indicated motivation and growing expertise.
- **Students had used devices frequently in lessons.** Evidence of use came from teacher self-reports, principal observations, student comments to teachers and administrators, and word-of-mouth from teachers and administrators in a school and district.

In speaking with district and site administrators and teachers, I learned that these varied indicators came into play when I asked different practitioners for exemplars of technology integration. These indicators merged into a de facto definition of technology integration.

I stress again that in all of these conversations, no district administrator, principal, or teacher ever asked me what I meant by *technology integration*. Some or all of the above criteria and indicators repeatedly came up in our discussions. I leaned heavily on the above signs of use and less on a formal definition in identifying candidates to study.

Formal definitions in that swampy bog of literature on digital devices in schools and classrooms, however, were another story. Of the scores of formal definitions in the literature I have sorted through, I looked for one that would be clear and make sense to experts, professionals, parents, and taxpayers. Only a few met that standard.[8] I did fashion one that avoided the conceptual morass of defining technology integration and matched the "best cases" that superintendents, technology coordinators, and teachers had selected for me to observe:[9]

> *Technology integration is the routine and transparent classroom use of computers, smartphones and tablets, digital cameras, social media platforms, networks, software applications, and the internet in daily lessons aimed at helping students reach the school's and teacher's curricular and instructional goals.*

This definition puts technology in the background, not the foreground, and best captures my sense of what I thought prior to this study and the range of tacit meanings I heard from teachers, administrators, and policy makers in the schools and districts then I visited. The next step was to move to assessing how successful (or not) technology integration has been in changing classroom practices.

Determining Success of Technology Integration in Altering How Teachers Teach

That all-important question after the technology has been fully implemented remains: *Have teachers altered their classroom practices as a consequence of the new technology?* Too little research has been done in answering this question. So in this book, I also focused on the process of change and *not* how much and to what degree students learned from these lessons. The issue of teacher, school, and district change in this study is crucial, yet most difficult to capture. Because I did not observe teachers, schools, and districts before I appeared in classrooms and schools, I did not know what were routine actions *before* I observed and documented what I saw. To correct somewhat for this weakness in the design, I asked teachers, principals, technology coordinators, and district administrators what they had done earlier with technology integration. Their answers helped sketch a picture of prior conditions. I cross-checked their accounts with whatever district and historical documents I could unearth. I asked every teacher whether using computers regularly had changed how he or she taught. Their answers communicated perceptions of how they taught before and after hardware and software appeared in their schools. In principal interviews, I asked what the situation was like in their school when they became principal insofar as technology integration was concerned.

Obviously, I would have preferred doing longitudinal studies of before and after an intervention occurred such as the introduction of laptops and tablets. So I did the best I could by entering at one point in time and taking a snapshot of technology integration in classrooms, schools, and districts.

Finally, I note again that what is often forgotten in the literature on technology in schools is that describing exemplars of technology integration is not synonymous with exemplars of "success" in student learning. That would be another book.

Notes

INTRODUCTION

1. In my writings on computers over the decades, I have used the words *technology* and *computers* interchangeably. A more precise phrase would be *digital technologies* to distinguish desktop computers, laptops, tablets, and interactive whiteboards from use of nondigital technologies such as paper, pen, notebooks, overhead projector, and the like. Both old and new technologies exist side by side in US classrooms in 2018. While I do use the phrase *digital technologies* periodically, I do not use it all of the time. Readers can grasp easily the context of the paragraph to determine whether I speak of old or new technologies being integrated into daily lessons.

2. I began writing my blog in 2009.

3. Academics would say that my research strategy was *sampling on the dependent variable* (see appendix).

   Unfortunately, when you do this kind of research, there is no variation in the sample. The dangers in synthesizing common features of failures (as well as successes) become evident when you take a step back since, without variation in the sample the "wisdom" gained from looking at failures may bear little relationship to the "wisdom" gained from looking at successes. The common features of failure or success extracted from exemplars of each to explain why the initiatives nose-dived or soared often fall apart after a few years. See, for example, in the education literature, the research on Effective Schools in the 1980s and 1990s (e.g., Ron Edmonds, "Effective Schools for the Urban Poor," *Educational Leadership* 37, no. 1 (1979): 15–24; Lawrence Lezotte and Kathleen Snyder, *What Effective Schools Do* [Bloomington, IN: Solution Tree, 2010]). Schools profiled as successes in one year turn out to have sunk into failure a few years later. A companion literature in business has suffered similarly (e.g., Tom Peters and Robert Waterman, *In Search of Excellence: Lessons from America's Best Run Companies* [New York: Harper Collins, 2006] and Jim Collins, *Good to Great: Why Some Companies Make the Leap and Others Don't* [New York: Harper Business, 2011]).

   In other words, without knowing about those cases where teachers did change how they taught when using new technologies, the barriers I identified in "failures" may just as well have been accurate as inaccurate without having

197

any comparisons to make. To sample on the dependent variable, then, is a bias built into the research design.

So for 2016, I have been looking at cases of technology integration "successes." I am sampling on the dependent variable again, but I am fully aware of the bias built into this year's study. In writing this book, however, I will pull together what I have learned from both "failures" I have studied over the decades and "successes" I have found recently.

With myriad examples of claims for "revolutionary" change in classroom practice, I cite one that captures top policy makers' belief in the power of new technologies to "transform" teaching and learning: the US Department of Education's 2016 report *Future Ready Education: Reimagining the Role of Technology in Education* (http://tech.ed.gov/files/2015/12/NETP16.pdf).

4. See, for example, chapter 1, "Restructuring Las Montanas and Technology, 1976–2010," in Larry Cuban, *Inside the Black Box of Classroom Practice* (Cambridge, MA: Harvard Education Press, 2013). In looking at these few cases, I was inadvertently beginning to sample on the dependent variable by describing instances where the introduction of hardware and software into classrooms did, indeed, influence how teachers traditionally taught. I was unknowingly creating a comparison and contrast group of cases.

5. For more on normal distribution and *bimodal distribution*, see *Wikipedia*, s.v. "Multimodal Distribution," last modified June 28, 2017, https://en.wikipedia.org/wiki/Multimodal_distribution; *Wikipedia*, s.v. "Normal Distribution," last modified August 2, 2017, https://en.wikipedia.org/wiki/Normal_distribution.

After reading and analyzing much of this work on technology in schools for the past three decades, I am confident that these reports and studies cluster at both the "success" and "failure" ends of a spectrum. However, I have not done an actual count of all articles, books, reports, and documents written about computers in schools between the early 1980s and the present. When I Googled "computers in schools, 1980–2010" on January 19, 2017, I got 280,000 results, including research reports. I sampled from these hits and came up with the twin peaks distribution in the literature on computers in schools.

6. Some examples from the "success" peak on the spectrum would be the following: For a white paper produced by a vendor, see one published by Motorola, "How Technology Is Changing How Students Learn and How Teachers Teach," 2010, http://www.motorolasolutions.com/content/dam/msi/docs/business/solutions/industry_solutions/education/document/_staticfile/wp_edu_ro-22-105.pdf. For typical "success" research studies, see Linda Darling-Hammond et al., *Using Technology to Support At-Risk Students' Learning*, 2014, https://edpolicy.stanford.edu/sites/default/files/scope-pub-using-technology-report.pdf; Jeremy Roschelle et al., "Changing How and What Children Learn in School with Computer-Based Technologies," *The Future of Children* 10, no. 2 (Fall/Winter 2001): 76-101; Sharon Judge, "The Impact of Computer Technology on Academic

Achievement of Young African American Children," *Journal of Research in Childhood Education* 20, no. 2 (2005): 91–101.

Examples from the "failure" peak on the spectrum would include Jane Healy, *Failure to Connect* (New York: Simon & Schuster, 1998); Larry Cuban, *Oversold and Underused: Computers in the Classroom* (Cambridge, MA: Harvard University Press, 2001); Francesco Avvisati, *Students, Computers, and Learning: Making the Connection* (Paris: OECD, 2015); Robert Fairlie and Jonathan Robinson, "Experimental Evidence on the Effects of Home Computers on Academic Achievement among Schoolchildren," Discussion Paper 7211, 2013, Institute for the Study of Labor (IZA), Bonn, Germany.

For a teacher's account of her disappointments with tablets, see Launa Hall, "I Gave My Students iPads—Then Wished I Could Take Them Back," *Washington Post*, December 2, 2015, https://www.washingtonpost.com/opinions/i-gave-my-students-ipads—then-wished-i-could-take-them-back/2015/12/02/a1bc8272-818f-11e5-a7ca-6ab6ec20f839_story.html.

7. In the middle of this continuum are studies that sample both success and failure on the dependent variable through comparing and contrasting both. See, for example, Chen-Lin Kulik and James Kulik, "Effectiveness of Computer-Based Instruction: An Updated Analysis," *Computers in Human Behavior* 7 (1991): 75–94; Binbin Zheng et al., "Learning in One-to-One Laptop Environments: A Meta-analysis and Research Synthesis." *Review of Educational Research* (in press); Mark Windschitl and Karl Sahl, "Tracing Teachers' Use of Technology in a Laptop Computer School: The Interplay of Teacher Beliefs, Social Dynamics, and Institutional Culture," *American Educational Research Journal* 39 1(2002): 165–205.

8. Gary Sykes and Suzanne Wilson, "Can Policy (Re)form Instruction?" in Drew Gitomer and Courtney Bell, *Handbook of Research on Teaching*, 5th edition (Washington, DC, American Educational Research Association, 2016): 854–862; David Cohen and Susan Moffitt, *The Ordeal of Equality: Did Federal Regulation Fix the Schools?* (Cambridge, MA: Harvard University Press, 2009).

I use the words *teaching* and *instruction* interchangeably because I refer to both as an interaction among and between teachers and students over specific content and skills in a particular setting. The triangle of teacher/student/content is the nexus of the concept of teaching and instruction. See David Cohen et al., "Resources, Instruction, and Research," *Educational Evaluation and Policy Analysis* 25, no. 2 (2003): 119–142.

9. The idea of using new technologies to *personalize learning* has accelerated greatly in the past decade. The history of efforts to tailor individual lessons within the traditional age-graded structure to the strengths and limits of individual K–12 students in math, language arts, and other academic subjects goes back to the 1920s. See Frank Grittner, "Individualized Instruction: An Historical Perspective," *Modern Language Journal* 59, no. 7 (1975): 323–333; Carol Tomlinson, "Mapping a Route to Differentiated Instruction," *Educational Leadership* 57, no.1

(1999): 12–16; for use of teaching machines beginning in the 1920s and running through the 1960s, see Audrey Watters, "The Rise of Programmed Instruction," February 10, 2015, http://hackeducation.com/2015/02/10/skinners-box.

No agreement on precisely what *personalized learning* or its cousin *blended learning* means now exists. For the range of definitions and the ambiguity of the phrases, see Sean Cavanagh, "'Personalized Learning' Eludes Easy Definitions," *Education Week,* October 22, 2014.

10. John Dewey used the metaphor of teaching as selling and learning as buying (*How We Think* [Boston: D.C. Heath and Co., 1910], 35–36). For millennia, policy makers, educators, parents, and voters have accepted and proclaimed the idea that teaching implies learning. But *learning* is both a noun and a verb. As a noun, it implies that outcomes (e.g., grammar rules, algorithms for adding and subtracting, the results of World War II) have been learned. As a verb, however, it means a series of activities (e.g., doing a work sheet, solving math word problems, conjugating Spanish verbs, studying the US Constitution, doing experiments to understand gravity) how learning (noun) occurred. The noun, then, is the "what" and the verb is the "how" of education. This distinction becomes important when inquiring into those technologies that vendors and techno-enthusiasts claim will "transform" learning, such as personalized learning. Do they mean both the "what" and the "how" of learning? And what about all the habits, attitudes, knowledge, and skills students pick up inside and outside the classroom beyond curriculum standards, syllabi, and lessons? This *collateral learning* occurs regardless of what the teacher is selling (see John Dewey, *Experience and Education* [1938; West Lafayette, IN: Kappa Delta Pi, 1998], p. 48). Without such distinctions, talk by either champions of new hardware and software or decision makers dissolves into empty generalities and vague claims. See Gert Biesta, "ICT and Education Beyond Learning," in *Digital Expectations and Experiences in Education*, ed. Eyvind Elstad (Boston: Sense Publishers, 2016), 29–43.

11. Donald Schön invented the concept of *dynamic conservatism*, or the actions within organizations that carry the language and resources to alter how the organization does its business but is really aimed sustaining institutional equilibrium. See Donald Schön, *Beyond the Stable State* (New York: Norton, 1973). I return to this concept later in the book.

12. Defining the geographical spread of Silicon Valley in the Bay Area varies among agencies, media, and occasional commission reports. I have included four counties because the hype, culture, and media influence of Silicon Valley extend beyond the original stretch of land between San Jose and Palo Alto to adjacent counties. The 2016 Silicon Valley Index, for example, also includes part of Santa Cruz County; see https://www.jointventure.org/images/stories/pdf/index2016.pdf. The statistics for Silicon Valley come from the 2016 Silicon Valley Index: 6,8. The number of districts and schools in these counties come from http://www.sccoe.org/schooldirectory/Pages/School-Facts.aspx; http://www.sfusd.edu/;

http://www.publicschoolreview.com/california/alameda-county; and http://www
.publicschoolreview.com/california/san-mateo-county. While I have visited
classrooms, schools, and districts in all four counties, my sample is very small
but, I believe, representative of the larger Silicon Valley.

13. A *unicorn* is a venture capitalist term referring to a start-up company that
becomes worth at least a billion dollars (e.g., Uber and Pinterest); see *Wikipedia*, s.v. "Unicorn (finance)," last modified June 25, 2017, https://en
.wikipedia.org/wiki/Unicorn_(finance); "Think Different" was Apple's ad campaign that began in the late-1990s; see Rob Siltanen, "The Real Story Behind
Apple's 'Think Different" Campaign," (*CMO Network* blog), *Forbes*, http://www
.forbes.com/sites/onmarketing/2011/12/14/the-real-story-behind-apples-think-
different-campaign/#1b92ce1f55c2.

14. For a sampling of history, sociology, economics—including venture capital bro-
kers, and the culture of start-up companies, see Michael Lewis, *The New New
Thing* (New York: Norton, 1999); Walter Isaacson, *Steve Jobs* (New York: Simon
& Schuster, 2011), Dan Lyons, *Disrupted* (New York: Hachette Press, 2016); Om
Malik, "In Silicon Valley Now, It's Almost Always Winner Takes All," *New Yorker*,
December 30, 2015; Andrew Marantz, "How 'Silicon Valley' Nails Silicon Valley,"
New Yorker June 9, 2016.

15. Other recent entries into descriptions of Silicon Valley companies and their
impact on the four county area, see: George Avalos, "Poverty Rates Near Record
Levels Despite Hot Economy," *San Jose Mercury News*, April 1, 2015, http://www
.mercurynews.com/business/ci_27830698/poverty-rates-near-record-levels-bay-
area-despite; for life in start-ups and established technology companies, see
Antonio Martinez, *Chaos Monkeys: Obscene Fortune and Random Failure* (New York:
Harper, 2016); for gentrification of poor neighborhoods and impact on cities
in Silicon Valley, see Eric Rodenbeck, "Mapping Silicon Valley's Gentrification
Problem Through Corporate Shuttle Routes," *Wired*, September 6, 2013, http://
www.wired.com/2013/09/mapping-silicon-valleys-corporate-shuttle-problem/.

   "Killer app" and " Make the world a better place" have become clichés, and
in an ever-changing argot, such phrases are seldom used by those who see
themselves as Silicon Valley insiders; see *Wikipedia*, s.v. "Killer Application,"
last modified June 24, 2017, https://en.wikipedia.org/wiki/Killer_application;
and Nicholas Carlson, "Google CEO Larry Page Is Taking a Lot of Heat over a
Silly, Clichéd Thing He Said About Competition," *Business Insider,* May 16, 2013,
http://www.businessinsider.com/google-ceo-larry-page-is-taking-a-lot-of-heat-
over-a-silly-clichd-thing-he-said-about-competition-2013-5.

16. Education Summits held in various venues in Silicon Valley bring together
CEOs, academics, entrepreneurs, and others to discuss various issues about
schools and job preparation, workforce diversity, and the intersection between
schools and the high-tech world; see https://www.edsurge.com/e/summits/
silicon-valley-tech-for-schools-summit-2013/recap; and http://www.microsoft

bayarea.com/2014/09/16/microsoft-hosts-education-summit-in-silicon-valley-expands-teals-program-in-california/.

In one example of such funding, Mark Zuckerberg, founder of Facebook, gave $100 million to the Newark, New Jersey, schools in 2010 (see Dale Russakoff, *The Prize* [New York: Houghton Mifflin Harcourt, 2015]); he and his wife, Priscilla Chan, started a new foundation to create schools that focus on personalized learning (see Terry Dolan, "Zuckerberg Explains Why the Chan Zuckerberg Initiative Isn't a Charitable Foundation," *Forbes*, December 4, 2015, http://www.forbes.com/sites/kerryadolan/2015/12/04/mark-zuckerberg-explains-why-the-chan-zuckerberg-initiative-isnt-a-charitable-foundation/#64e9 dc74394f). In 2013, entrepreneur Mark Ventilla founded a string of private schools called AltSchools (see Rebecca Mead, "Learn Different," *New Yorker*, March 7, 2016). Top donors minted in Silicon Valley, such as Marc Benioff, Reed Hastings, and Mark Zuckerberg, have funded public school initiatives such as Summit charter schools, Code.org, and innovation funds for teachers and principals to alter both schooling and classroom practice (see Natasha Singer, "The Silicon Valley Billionaires Remaking Public Schools," *New York Times*, June 6, 2017).

17. For definitions of how software firms release products to consumers, including beta versions, see *Wikipedia*, s.v. "Software Release Cycle," last modified August 4, 2017, https://en.wikipedia.org/wiki/Software_release_life_cycle. Audrey Watters describes Apple's 1984 donation of Apple II computers to over nine thousand eligible schools in California ("How Steve Jobs Brought the Apple II to the Classroom," *Hack Education*, http://hackeducation.com/2015/02/25/kids-cant-wait-apple). The Facebook poster is one of many that have come from the in-house designer Ben Barry; see http://99u.com/articles/7118/Facebooks-Ben-Barry-On-How-To-Hack-Your-Job.

18. For figures on Google funding teacher requests, see http://abc7news.com/archive/9491175/.

19. See Natasha Singer and Mike Isaac, "Facebook Helps Develop Software That Puts Students in Charge of Their Lesson Plans, *New York Times*, August 9, 2016, http://blogs.edweek.org/edweek/DigitalEducation/2016/03/facebook_summit_PLP_software.html.

20. Descriptions of Milpitas's embrace of technology, particularly "personalized learning," can be found at https://www.edsurge.com/news/2014-01-07-what-makes-milpitas-a-model-for-innovation; http://www.edweek.org/tm/articles/2015/02/18/in-calif-district-blended-learning-approach-turns-teachers.html?cmp=ENL-TU-NEWS1; and http://www.christenseninstitute.org/blended-learning-spotlight-milpitas-unified-school-district/.

21. Consider, for example, the responses to "The 32nd Annual Phi Delta Kappan/Gallup Poll of the Public's Attitude toward Public Schools" (September 2000) poll on what goals US schools should achieve. Those surveyed listed as the top five (reported on pp. 41–58):

- To prepare people to become responsible citizens
- To help people become economically sufficient
- To ensure a basic level of quality among schools
- To promote cultural unity among all Americans
- To improve social conditions for people

To reach those multiple and conflicting goals, a democratic society expects schools to produce adults who are active in their communities, enlightened employers, and hardworking employees who have acquired and practiced particular values that sustain its way of life. Those social, political, and economic values are dominant American norms pervading family, school, workplace, and community: act independently; accept personal responsibility for actions; work hard and complete a job well; and be fair. Within every age-graded school in the United States, every kindergarten, middle school algebra class, and Advanced Placement US history course, these norms show up in school rules and classroom practices. Taxpayers and voters want their public schools to conserve community values, yet they also want schools to prepare students to change themselves and their society.

The poll comes from "The 32nd Annual Phi Delta Kappan/Gallup Poll." On socialization of the young in schools, see Robert Dreeben, *On What Is Learned in School* (Reading, MA: Addison-Wesley, 1968); Steven Brint et al., "Socialization Messages in Primary Schools," *Sociology of Education* 74 (July 2001): 157–180; David Labaree,"Public Goods, Private Goods: The American Struggle over Educational Goals," *American Educational Research Journal* 1997, 34, no. 1 (1997): 39–81.

22. I do not use the word *stasis* here or elsewhere in this study since it means no change at all. I use *stability* to mean an equilibrium that is fluid and dynamic. The concept of yin and yang captures the interdependence and complementarity of stability and change.

23. Kevin Starr, *Golden Dreams: California in an Age of Abundance, 1950–1963* (New York: Oxford Press, 2009); Michelle Foster, "As California Goes, So Goes The Nation," *Journal of Negro Education* (1998): 1–6; Peter Schrag, *Paradise Lost: California's Experience, America's Future* (New York: The New Press, 1998).

24. The California statistics are for the year 2014–2015; see http://www.cde.ca.gov/ds/sd/cb/ceffingertipfacts.asp.

25. See https://edsource.org/wp-content/publications/pub-2010-09-CaliforniaRanks.pdf; https://edsource.org/2015/californias-2013-14-grad-ranking-dropped-although-rate-increased/89169; for teacher salaries, see http://www.cde.ca.gov/fg/fr/sa/cefavgsalaries.asp; for students per teacher, see NEA Research, *Rankings and Estimates: Rankings of the States 2014 and Estimates of School Statistics 2015,* March 2015, p. 36, http://www.nea.org/assets/docs/NEA_Rankings_And_Estimates-2015-03-11a.pdf.

26. Schrag, *Paradise Lost,* 139–187.

27. Ibid., 66–87; Michael Kirst and Gary Yee, "An Examination of the Evolution of California State Educational Reform," in *Ten Years of State Education Reform, 1983–1993*, ed. Diane Massell and Susan Fuhrman (New Brunswick, NJ: Consortium for Policy Research in Education, 1994).

28. In California, the schools are funded by the governor and legislature, which also establishes policies—the multivolume School Code—for over a thousand districts to follow. In addition, the governor appoints a State Board of Education that also sets rules for local districts, approves texts, and has other assorted duties. An elected State Superintendent of Schools works with the State Board of Education and has jurisdiction over the State Department of Education. Honig, who was a political independent, worked with Republican governors (who appointed loyal party members to the State Board of Education) and Democratic legislatures. The opportunities for political mischief, if not antagonism, were abundant. Honig's resignation in 1992 can be attributed in part to the political conflicts over school reform. See Ken Kelley, "The Interview: Bill Honig, Reading, Writing, and Reform," *San Francisco Focus,* June 1986, 64–68; Bill Honig, *Last Chance for Our Children: How You Can Help Save Our Schools* (Reading, MA: Addison-Wesley, 1985).

29. "Eastin Announces Statewide Plan for Education Technology: Connect, Compute, and Compete: C3" news release #96-44, California Department of Education, July 10, 1996.

30. Courtney Macavinta, "Wilson: Fast Times at Digital High," *Cnet*, August 19, 1997, http://www.news.com/News/Item/0,413538,00.html.

31. See, for example, the following articles: Joel Stein, "How Jerry Brown Scared California Straight," *Bloomberg Business Week*, April 25, 2013, http://www.bloomberg.com/news/articles/2013-04-25/how-jerry-brown-scared-california-straight; Judy Lin, "A Stanford Professor's High Stakes Plan To Save California Schools," *Los Angeles Daily News*, July 3, 2016, http://www.dailynews.com/social-affairs/20160703/a-stanford-professors-high-stakes-plan-to-save-california-schools.

CHAPTER 1

1. Technology coordinators, foundation officials, district administrators, and fellow teachers identified individual teachers as exemplars in integrating technology regularly in their lessons. I chose Jennifer Auten, John DiCosmo, and Nicole Elenz-Martin from a pool of forty-one teachers I had observed in 2016. They are typical of the "best cases" I collected over the year. See the appendix for how I went about identifying exemplary teachers.

2. A local foundation official had recommended Jennifer Auten to me as a teacher who skillfully integrates iPads and software into daily lessons. Montclaire School has just over five hundred students. Of the school enrollment, 46 percent is white, 38 percent Asian, 5 percent are Latino, and the rest include multiracial,

African American, and Filipino students. About 2 percent are categorized as poor (i.e., free and reduced-price lunch). According to Auten, many of the parents work for Google and Apple. The Apple campus (headquarters) is just over three miles away from Montclaire.

The Cupertino school district has a policy of one computer for every two students, and provides on-site tech support. For Auten to get to one iPad for each student, she became entrepreneurial. She got twelve from the district and applied for a grant to get a few more, parents contributed devices, and she corresponded with a University of Michigan professor, who acquired the rest through a program he was affiliated with.

3. http://web.seesaw.me/.

4. Committed to student choice, Jennifer Auten contributed to a district website hosted by the district Director of Technology called "Tech Integration in Cupertino Union." The website published her description of a lesson on bats; see "Choice in a Learner-Focused Classroom," December 7, 2015, https://cusdtech.wordpress.com/page/2/.

5. Jere Brophy, "Teacher Influence on Student Achievement," *American Psychologist* 41, no. 10 (1986): 1069–1077; Thomas Kane and Douglas Staiger, *Feedback for Teaching; Combining High Quality Observations with Student Surveys and Achievement Gains* (Seattle: Bill and Melinda Gates Foundation, 2012); Heather Hill et al., "Learning Lessons from Instruction" (unpublished paper, Harvard Graduate School of Education, 2016); Mary Kennedy, *Inside Teaching* (Cambridge, MA: Harvard University Press, 2006). While I focus on teachers' lesson format and content, this study does not go to the next step of correlating which formats are associated with student achievement, although the Brophy and Kane and Staiger studies do make those links. This study focuses entirely on how teachers identified as exemplary integrated technology into their lessons and to what degree and in which ways their practice had changed as a result of using new technologies. I make no judgment about which formats are linked to student achievement or which I value more or less highly.

6. See Common Core standards, pp. 11–12, at http://www.cde.ca.gov/be/st/ss/documents/finalelaccssstandards.pdf.

7. Jennifer Auten, email, April 25, 2016. In author's possession.

8. Interview with Jennifer Auten, April 19, 2016.

9. Terman Middle School enrolls just over seven hundred sixth- through eighth-graders (2015). Of that total, 61 percent are minority (the largest group is Asian, at 38 percent) with 11 percent classified as poor. Just over 4 percent are English language learners and 9 percent have disabilities. See School Accountability Report Card (2014–2015), https://www.pausd.org/sites/default/files/pdf-school/sarc/SARC_Terman.pdf.

10. Padlet is software that permits students to collaborate and teachers and students to communicate during a lesson; see https://padlet.com/.

11. For a description of the gaming software, see https://getkahoot.com/.

12. I had asked the Palo Alto district coordinator of technology, Emily Garrison, for the names of teachers who actively integrated new technologies into their lessons. DiCosmo was on the list, and he invited me to observe his class.

13. John DiCosmo, email, October 16, 2016. In author's possession.

14. Interview with John DiCosmo , October 11, 2016.

15. Dominic Bigue, technology coordinator for San Mateo Union High School District, identified fifteen teachers who had participated in technology workshops, had asked for carts of tablets for their classes, or he had recruited to teach other district teachers about using different technologies. He felt that these teachers, whom he had also observed, had integrated technology easily and well into their lessons.

16. "Aragon is a traditional comprehensive high school offering a broad range of academic and elective subjects. In fall 2015, the school enrolled 1504 students of whom 28% are Asian, 26% are Hispanic/Latino, 7% are Filipino, 4% are Pacific Islander, 2% are African-American, and 38% are Caucasian. The number of students eligible for free and reduced lunch in 2008 (5%) has increased to . . . 15% in 2015. Five percent of Aragon students are LTELs (Long Term English Learners)" (2015 School Accountability Report, p. 4), http://aragon.schoolloop.com/file/1210530025431/1210533726630/1982952913009349723.pdf).

17. Interview with Nicole Elenz-Martin, February 10, 2016.

18. School Accountability Report Cards for Aragon High School, Terman Middle School, and Montclaire Elementary School.

19. Of course, teacher surveys are often self-reports from non-random samples; the responding numbers of teachers in the sample seldom meet the threshold standard of 60–80 percent or above acceptable to researchers. Online and telephone survey response rates are much lower, typically, below 50 percent. See http://onlinelibrary.wiley.com/doi/10.1111/j.1083-6101.2001.tb00117.x/full; and http://www.knowledgenetworks.com/ganp/docs/rdd-vs-web.pdf.

20. Henry Becker, "How Are Teachers Using Computers in Instruction?" paper presented at American Educational Research Association, April 2001, Seattle, p. 2.

21. National Center for Education Statistics, *Teachers' Use of Educational Technology in U.S. Public Schools, 2009*, NCES 2010-40 (Washington, DC: US Department of Education, 2010), 3–4.

22. Kristin Purcell et al., "How Teachers Are Using Technology at Home and in Their Classrooms," 2013, http://pewinternet.org/Reports/2013/Teachers-and-technology (quotation on p. 65). The combination of focus groups and survey made this recent study not only different than the usual teacher survey but got deeper into issues that seldom get explored in questionnaires. Response rates from the random sample of Advanced Placement and National Writing Project teachers, however, were quite low: 12 and 14 percent.

23. Ibid., 73.

24. Gary Sykes and Suzanne Wilson, "Can Policy (Re)form Instruction?" in *Handbook of Research on Teaching*, 5th edition (Washington, DC: American Educational Research Association, 2016), 869.

CHAPTER 2

1. Interview with Kristel Hsaio, March 16, 2017.
2. Exit Slips are a set of questions that students have to answer at end of a class period, either on paper or submit to teacher electronically. It is an assessment of what the student has learned from the lesson; see http://www.ascd.org/publications/educational-leadership/oct12/vol70/num02/The-Many-Uses-of-Exit-Slips.aspx.
3. In the Summit Prep calendar, over the course of the school year, students take eight weeks—two weeks at a time—away from their required courses to take electives offered through a course catalog in the arts, STEM (science, technology, engineering, and math), future planning for college and career, physical and emotional well-being, and leadership and society; see http://expedition.summitps.org/overview.
4. Cognitive skills range from textual analysis to how to do inquiry to using sources for analysis and synthesis. Summit schools have a rubric for teachers and students to assess where they are for each skill and linkages to Common Core state standards, STEM standards, etc.; see https://docs.google.com/viewer?a=v&pid=sites&srcid=c3VtbWl0cHMub3JnfHNwcy1hY2FkZW1pcY3N8Z3g6NzE5ZmFjZTBjNjIzMWM2Ng.
5. Developed in cooperation with Facebook software engineers, the Personalized Learning Platform is a tool to help students self-assess their progress in each unit they take across all subject areas, set goals and objectives for themselves, and see how far they have progressed or regressed. The platform permits students to delve into over two hundred projects they study by showing their growth in cognitive skills, and gives teachers access to each student's work, thus helping them to tailor content and skills for individual students; see http://practices.learningaccelerator.org/artifacts/summit-personalized-learning-platform-plp.
6. Students have to complete fourteen steps for this DNA project. The rubric links to cognitive skills and outlines what a student has to do to get an A or B. Student tasks were developed by a team of biology teachers across the Summit network of schools in the Bay Area; see https://docs.google.com/document/d/13zq2yJhNsFREHCOcbUp3-yz32tNq-grX8gfN0faY5kY/edit.
7. Natalie Wolchover, "Your Color Red Really Could Be My Blue," *Live Science*, June 29, 2012, http://www.livescience.com/21275-color-red-blue-scientists.html.
8. According to Hsiao, "The purpose of the activity was to build background knowledge about DNA so that students are ready for the DNA barcoding unit. In the DNA barcoding unit, students will collect samples of seafood from local restaurants and then analyze the DNA in the samples to determine if the seafood

is mislabeled. Then they will make conclusions about whether or not the sea-food sold in their communities is sustainable. Throughout the project, students will practice writing and inquiry skills, as well as apply their knowledge of food webs and DNA" (Kristel Hsiao, email, March 17, 2016. In author's possession). In the text, there is no section on Hsiao's answers to my questions about whether or not using technology had altered her teaching. I made repeated requests in March and April 2017, to no avail.

9. Summit Preparatory Charter High School, "School Accountability Report Card, 2014–2015," http://summitps.org/uploads/pdf/School%20Accountability%20Report%20Cards/Summit%20Prep%20-%202014-15%20SARC%20-%2001-29-16.pdf.

10. The history of the school comes from interviews with CEO Diane Tavenner and Chief Academic Officer Adam Carter, January 14, 2016; David Osborne, "The Schools of the Future," *U.S. News and World Report,* January 19, 2016.

11. Interview with Diane Tavenner and Adam Carter; Nicole Dobo, "Despite Its High-Tech Profile, Summit Charter Network Makes Teachers, Not Computers, the Heart of Personalized Learning," *Hechinger Report,* March 1, 2016; Benjamin Herold, "Tech 'Convert' Helps Guide Network's Transformation," *Education Week,* March 28, 2016; Arianna Prothero, "Some Charters Help Alumni Stick with College," *Education Week,* April 20, 2016.

12. Casey Newton, "Inside Facebook's Plan to Build a Better School," *The Verge,* September 3, 2015, http://www.theverge.com/2015/9/3/9252845/facebook-education-software-plp-summit. As early as 2003, the founding teachers of Summit charter schools created a Personalized Learning Plan that was circulated to each teacher and family, and aimed at fitting content and skills to each student. It was eventually relegated to folders in file cabinets. Adam Carter, a founding teacher and currently Chief Academic Officer for Summit charter schools, remembered those early years:

> In 2003, a group of five teachers and one principal sat around a table and created a MS Word document template that we titled, "The Personalized Learning Plan." The document was meant to help students set long term-goals, break those long-term goals into year-long goals, and then help translate those year-long goals into daily actions and behaviors.
>
> Every teacher acted as a mentor for about 25 students, and we used the Personalized Learning Plan as the guiding document for our yearly Family Meetings—meetings of about ninety minutes in length in which a student, her parents, other important people in her life, and her mentor met to set goals, make plans to accomplish those goals, and commit to supporting the student in meeting those goals.
>
> We wanted these to be living documents—documents that reminded students, day by day and minute by minute, why they were doing what they were doing, and how their choices moved them towards, or further away from, their goals.
>
> In reality, after these papers were printed, each member of the Family Meeting

received a copy, each copy was signed by everyone present as a commitment to the student's plan, and then these papers made their ways into backpacks, purses, recycling bins, and official-looking manila folders, which were then placed in a filing cabinet in an office at the school. Though our intentions were good, these Personalized Learning Plans were not the living documents we hoped they would be. (Adam Carter, "Personalized Learning and Opening Doors of Opportunity," *Education Week*, July 1, 2016, http://blogs.edweek.org/edweek/learning_deeply/2016/07/personalized_learning_and_equity.html?qs=Stanford).

13. David Osborne, "School of the Future: California's Summit Public Schools," Progressive Policy Institute, January 2016, http://www.progressivepolicy.org/wp-content/uploads/2016/01/2016.01-Osborne_Schools-of-the-Future_Californias-Summit-Public-Schools.pdf; Shonaka Ellison and Gillian Locke, *Breakthroughs in Time, Talent, and Technology: Next-Generation Learning Models in Public Charter Schools* (Washington, DC: National Alliance for Public Charter Schools, 2014), 9–10; Nicole Dobo, "How This Bay Area Charter School Is Reinventing Education," *Los Angeles Times*, March 1, 2016; Abby Jackson, "Facebook's Newest Partnership Is Pushing an Innovative Approach to Learning in 120 Schools Across the Nation," *Business Insider*, August 10, 2016, http://www.business insider.com/facebook-partners-with-sillicon-valley-charter-schools-2016-8.

14. Carter, "Personalized Learning and Opening Doors of Opportunity."

15. See Rainier School Accountability Report Card (2015), summitps.org/uploads/pdf/School Accountability Report Cards/Rainier - 2014-15 SARC - 01-29-16.pdf.

16. A brief video of Katie Goddard preparing a class to write a culminating essay for a project in January 2015 is at https://www.youtube.com/watch?v=qrcNqc98D0I.

17. I asked every teacher I observed to respond to questions about whether or not the use of technology had changed how they taught. Goddard's answers are in an email I received on May 5, 2016.

18. For examples of teachers at all school levels who have integrated technology into their daily lessons, see vignettes of teachers in various chapters of this book and Karen Murphy et al., "Meaningful Connections: Using Technology in Primary Classrooms," *Beyond the Journal: Young Children on the Web* 58 no. 6 (2003): 12–18. See Darren Fix, a veteran science teacher, who blogs at: http://www.sciencefix.com/

19. *Wikipedia*, s.v. "Gunderson High School," last modified August 17, 2017, https://en.wikipedia.org/wiki/Gunderson_High_School.

20. "U.S. News and World Report Releases the 2016 Best High Schools Ranking," *U.S. News and World Report*, April 19, 2016, http://www.usnews.com/info/blogs/press-room/articles/2016-04-19/us-news-releases-the-2016-best-high-schools-rankings.

21. The story of the transformation of Robert Taft High School is described in Jessica Brown, "Ohio School Goes from Dead End to High-Tech Star," *Education Week*, December 1, 2010, http://www.edweek.org/ew/articles/2010/12/01/13taft.h30

.html; the school website is http://taftiths.cps-k12.org/.

22. http://www.hightechhigh.org/about-us/.

23. Jal Mehta and Sarah Fine, "Teaching Differently . . . Learning Deeply," *Phi Delta Kappan* 94, no 2 (2012): 31–35; Tara Behrend et al., *Gary and Jerri-Ann Jacobs High Tech High: A Case Study of an Inclusive STEM-focused High School in San Diego, California* (OSPrI Report 2014 03), https://ospri.research.gwu.edu/sites/ospri.research .gwu.edu/files/; Joshua Beauregard, "The Causal Impact of Attending High Tech High's High Schools on Postsecondary Enrollment" (doctoral dissertation, Harvard Graduate School of Education, 2015).

24. Mark Windschitl and Karl Sahl, "Tracing Teachers' Use of Technology in a Laptop School," *American Educational Research Journal* 39, no. 1 (2002): 165–205; Michael Russell, et al., "Laptop Learning: A Comparison of Teaching and Learning in Upper Elementary Classrooms Equipped with Shared Carts of Laptops and Permanent 1:1 Laptops," *Journal of Educational Computing Research* 30, no. 4 (April 2004): 313–330; Chrystalla Mouza, "Learning with Laptops: Implementation and Outcomes in an Urban, Underprivileged School," *Journal of Research on Technology Education* 40, no. 4 (2008): 447–472.

25. Data on programs in 1999 comes from American Institutes of Research, *An Educator's Guide to Schoolwide Reform* (Arlington, VA: Education Research Service, 1999). The Coalition of Essential Schools, founded by Theodore Sizer in 1984 and one of the twenty-four school reform models, had more than six hundred schools affiliated at its peak in the late 1990s; since then, however, it has cut back its national program to holding twice-yearly forums. In 2017, Coalition officials announced that it would close it doors (http://essentialschools.org/ thank-you-and-next-steps/.

26. Kyle Smith, "Nine Fun Facts About the Rubik's Cube on Its 40th Birthday," *New York Post*, May 20, 2014; *Wikipedia*, s.v. "Rubik's Cube," August 16, 2017, https:// en.wikipedia.org/wiki/Rubik%27s_Cube.

27. Larry Cuban, "The Difference Between 'Complicated' and 'Complex' Matters," *Larry Cuban on School Reform and Classroom Practice* (blog), June 8, 2010, https://larrycuban.wordpress.com/2010/06/08/the-difference-between-compli cated-and-complex-matters/.

28. National Center for Education Statistics, *Digest of Education Statistics*, 50th edition, 2014 (Washington, DC: Institute for Education Sciences, US Department of Education, 2016).

29. William Reese, *The Origins of the American High School* (New Haven, CT: Yale University Press, 1999); Jeff Mirel, "The Traditional High School," *Education Next* 6, no. 1 (2006), http://educationnext.org/the-traditional-high-school/; Jane David, "What Research Says about Small Learning Communities," *Educational Leadership* 65, no. 8 (2008): 84–85.

30. The number of public high schools comes from the US Department of Education, "High School Facts at a Glance," https://www2.ed.gov/about/offices/list/

ovae/pi/hs/hsfacts.html. Sometimes called *dynamic conservatism*, changes that maintain stability in structures and processes, are addressed in Donald Schön, *Beyond the Stable State: Public and Private Learning in a Changing Society* (New York: Norton, 1973); and Larry Cuban, *Hugging the Middle: How Teachers Teach in an Era of Testing and Accountability* (New York: Teachers College Press, 2009).

31. Some readers may ask, "Where do these features come from?" Decades of research and experience with high school reform from the "effective schools" research of the 1980s and 1990s, the federally subsidized research on "whole school reform," and both research and experience gained from the "small high schools" movement form the basis for generating these features. See *Wikipedia* entry for history and literature survey on effective schools at: *Wikipedia*, s.v. "Effective Schools, last modified December 21, 2016, https://en.wikipedia.org/wiki/Effective_schools. On whole school reform, see Georges Vernez et al., "Comprehensive School Reform Models at Scale," RAND report, 2006, http://www.aypf.org/forumbriefs/2011/documents/RandCSRstudy.pdf. For history and background of small high schools, see Thomas Toch, *High Schools on a Human Scale: How Small Schools Can Transform American Education* (Boston: Beacon Press, 2003). There is also the evidence drawn from contemporary small high school models launched and sustained within urban charter schools across the nation such as by Aspire, KIPP, Green Dot, Leadership Public Schools, and Summit Charter Schools (as of December 2017, each network has a website accessed through Google). Finally, my experience as a high school teacher for fourteen years, a superintendent of a district for seven years, a trustee for a charter school organization for three years, and a researcher observing and writing about successful and failing high schools have given me a framework for analyzing and imagining school improvement.

32. Careful readers may point out that describing "best cases" of such schools is sampling on the dependent variable, a research strategy that is vulnerable because no comparisons are made to non-exemplary schools. These features, according to this criticism, may also appear in other schools not identified as exemplary. The lack of variation is a weakness in using a design of only looking at best cases of teachers and schools integrating technology.

CHAPTER 3

1. have an expanded view of "Silicon Valley," which historically referred to the stretch of land between San Jose and San Francisco. But in 2017, the area encompasses Santa Clara, San Mateo, San Francisco, Alameda, and Contra Costa counties in the Bay Area. Other researchers could include other counties. I chose these five. From these counties, I identified seventy-seven school districts. The voluntarism of teachers in adopting devices and software for their students can be seen in a teacher survey (58 percent response rate) in Santa Clara County, the epicenter of Silicon Valley; see Pedro Hernandez-Ramos, "If Not Here, Where? Understanding Teacher Use of Technology in Silicon Valley Schools," *Journal of*

Research on Technology in Education 38, no. 1 (2005): 39–64.

2. Hilda Borko and Richard Shavelson, "Teacher Decision Making," in *Dimensions of Thinking and Cognitive Instruction*, ed. Beau Jones and Loma Idol (Hillsdale, NJ: Lawrence Erlbaum, 1990), 311–346.

3. Elementary and secondary school teachers make from twelve hundred to fifteen hundred decisions a day; Philip Jackson, *Life in Classrooms* (New York: Teachers College Press, 1990), 149.

4. Interview with middle school teacher James Earle, The Alt/School, November 7, 2016.

5. Jennifer O'Day, "Complexity, Accountability, and School Improvement," *Harvard Educational Review* 72, no. 3 (2002): 293–329; Richard Scott and John Meyer (eds.), *Institutional Environments and Organizations* (Thousand Oaks, CA: Sage Publications, 1994).

6. Douglas Orton and Karl Wieck, "Loosely Coupled Systems: A Reconceptualization," *Academy of Management Review* 15, no. 2, (1990): 203–223.

7. Esther Lombardi, "Why *The Adventures of Huckleberry Finn* Has Been Banned," *About Education*, February 17, 2017, http://classiclit.about.com/od/huckleberry finnfaqs/f/faq_huck_ban.htm.

8. Actively Learn is software that advertises getting students to participate and think deeply about what they are reading; see http://www.activelylearn.com/.

9. Byron Pitt, "'Huckleberry Finn' and the N-word," *60 Minutes*, June 12, 2011, https://www.youtube.com/watch?v=nW9-qee1m9o.

10. Kristin Krauss, email, October 13, 2016. In author's possession.

11. "School Launches BYOD Program," *The Talon* (Los Altos High School student newspaper), August 17, 2014, http://lahstalon.org/28897/news/school-launch-es-byod-program/; Tracy Newell, "Mountain View High Launches Bring Your Own Device Program," *Los Altos Town Crier*, August 26, 2015, https://www .losaltosonline.com/news/sections/schools/209-school-news/50978-.

12. A demographic and academic profile of Mountain View High School can be found at http://www.mvla.net/view/29542.pdf.

13. Ibid., and the Mountain View "School Accountability Report for 2015," at mvhs_sarc_15_16.

14. Los Altos High School is similar in demographics, program, and per-pupil expenditure to Mountain View. LAHS piloted the BYOD program in 2014 before the district superintendent and board approved it for the other high school.

15. The rubric can be found at https://docs.google.com/spreadsheets/d/1CzOW Q_e7RwFHQQHDa0o87KV9ANRud7mhZuRjWj35sNs/edit#gid=0.

16. Actively Learn permits students to take notes on readings, collaborate, do exercises, and submit their papers to the teacher; see www.activelylearn.com.

17. Stephen Hine, email, September 20, 2016. In author's possession.

18. *Milpitas Post* editorial, "Milpitas Students, Community Benefited from Departing Superintendent Carl Matuoka's Innovations," *Mercury News*, June 23, 2016,

http://www.mercurynews.com/2016/06/23/milpitas-post-editorial-milpitas-students-community-benefited-from-departing-superintendent-cary-matsuokas-innovations/.

19. Statistics on the district come from http://www.musd.org/about.html.

20. History and details of bond referendum can be found at http://www.musd.org/bond--construction.html.

21. Wylie Wong, "How Technology Enables Blended Learning," *EdTech*, April 1, 2014, http://www.edtechmagazine.com/k12/article/2014/04/how-technology-enables-blended-learning.

22. *State of EdTech 2016*, EdSurge Research Special Report (see chapter 4 " How Schools Are Changing"), https://www.edsurge.com/research/special-reports/state-of-edtech-2016/buyers_and_users. Rocketship is a charter network of nine elementary schools in the San Jose Unified District that combines individual online work every morning with conventional classrooms in the afternoon; see Sharon Noguchi, "Rocketship Schools Changes Course, Slows Expansion," *Mercury News*, June 28, 2014. Summit charter schools are described in chapter 2.

23. "EdTech 2016," *EdSurge* special report, https://www.edsurge.com/research/special-reports/state-of-edtech-2016/buyers_and_users.

24. In Milpitas, *blended learning* and *personalization* were interchangeable terms, testifying to the ambiguity attached to each phrase. For a description of blended learning in Milpitas, see Michael Lemaire, "Blended Learning Spotlight: Milpitas Unified School District," Christensen Institute, January 3, 2014, http://www.christensen institute.org/blog/blended-learning-spotlight-milpitas-unified-school-district/.

25. Cary Matsuoka, "Personalization of Education" letter to *Milpitas Post*, September 22, 2014.

26. Christina Quattrocchi, "What Makes Milpitas a Model for Innovation," *EdSurge News*, January 7, 2014; Jordan Money, "In Calif. District, Blended-Learning Approach Turns Teachers into Facilitators," *Education Week*, February 18, 2015; interview with Chin Song, Director of Technology, Milpitas Unified School District, December 15, 2016; interview with Norma Rodriguez, Assistant Superintendent of Curriculum and Instruction, November 7, 2016.

27. Cary Matsuoka, "Personalization of Education."

28. 2015 data on Marshall Pomeroy Elementary School comes from its School Accountability Report Card, https://drive.google.com/file/d/0BwrwPgPfahvlN mlYQ1FVWmFzN3JITTZyQUJNTWNzQzh1UmdB/view.

29. Quotes and description of teacher and student activities in the Learning Lab come from notes that I took on October 17, 2016.

30. The Personal Learning Plan (PLP) and individual playlists for fifth- and sixth-graders in language arts, social studies, science, and math come from Pomeroy teachers' involvement with Summit charter network's creation of a Base Camp for fifth- and sixth-grade teachers at Pomeroy and Weller elementary schools. Sixth-grade teacher Deanna Sainten attended the Summit Base

Camp. She and her colleagues had created lessons and units adapted to upper elementary grades, since the Base Camp was tilted toward secondary schools. The above description of Pomeroy students in the Learning Lab draws from this partnership with the Summit network of schools reaching out to other public schools (from interview with Pomeroy principal Sheila Murphy-Brewer, October 21, 2016).

31. Interview with Ashima Das, October 21, 2016.

32. Observation of primary classrooms occurred on October 21, 2016. For a description of i-Ready, see http://www.curriculumassociates.com/products/iready/diagnostic-instruction.aspx.

33. Interview with principal Raquel Kusunoki, October 19, 2016.

34. Data on Joseph Weller Elementary comes from its School Accountability Report card for 2015, https://drive.google.com/file/d/0BwrwPgPfahvlRWZGeUk2RGR TSE0yR25MWlFnMGNwY3NOTV9V/view.

35. gScholar has a version for classroom use where teachers can communicate with individual students; see http://www.promevo.com/gscholar.html.

36. For a vendor description of Go Math, see http://www.hmhco.com/shop/education-curriculum/math/elementary-mathematics/go-math-k-8.

37. Carol Dweck, "Carol Dweck Revisits the 'Growth Mindset,'" *Education Week*, September 22, 2015. I observed Jackie Dang's class on November 8, 2016. Description comes from my notes.

38. Interview with Chin Song, Director of Technology, Milpitas Unified School District, December 15, 2016; interview with Norma Rodriguez, Assistant Superintendent of Curriculum and Instruction, Milpitas Unified School District, November 7, 2016.

39. For descriptions of these districts, I have relied on published and unpublished documents and reports. I have not visited any of them.

   For Henrico County: Andrew Zucker et al., "A Study of One-to-One Computer Use in Mathematics and Science Instruction at the Secondary Level in Henrico County Schools," 2005, http://ateneu.xtec.cat/wikiform/wikiexport/_media/materials/jornades/jt101/bloc1/henrico_finalreport.pdf; Tom Lappas, "Laptop Program Controversial But Effective," *Henrico Citizen*, April 29, 2011; http://www.henricocitizen.com/index.php/news/article/laptop_program_controversial_but_effective_9822#.WL2zthwbofI; Lisa Plummer, "The Winning 1-to-1 Strategy," *THE Journal*, September 12, 2012 at: https://thejournal.com/Articles/2012/09/12/The-Winning-1-to-1-Strategy.aspx?Page=1.

   For Mooresville (where the Henrico County superintendent, Mark Edwards, eventually landed in 2007): Alan Schwarz, "Mooresville's Shining Example (It's Not Just About the Laptops)," *New York Times*, February 12, 2012; Elizabeth Farrell, "10 Lessons from the Best School District in the Country," *Scholastic Administrator*, Spring 2013, http://www.scholastic.com/browse/article.jsp?id=3757944.

For Kyrene district: http://www.kyrene.org/cms/lib2/AZ01001083/Centricity/ Domain/305/Technology%20Broch_ebook.pdf; Matt Richtel, "In Classroom of Future, Stagnant Scores," *New York Times*, September 3, 2011; Matthew Casey, "Broad Experience Is Key to Kyrene Chief's Focus," AZCentral.com, June 26, 2012, http://archive.azcentral.com/community/ahwatukee/20120621kyrene-school-district-chief-new-contract.html.

40. In Henrico County, Superintendent Mark Edwards convinced the school board to adopt the twenty-five thousand Apple laptops in 2001; he did the same in Mooresville in 2007. In Kyrene, David Schauer served from 2006 to 2016 and presided over district purchases and implementation of new technologies.

CHAPTER 4

1. See the appendix for analysis of strengths and weakness of this research strategy.
2. Landon Winner, *The Whale and the Reactor: A Search for Limits in an Age of High Technology* (Chicago: University of Chicago Press, 1986); Neil Postman, *Technopoly: The Surrender of Culture to Technology* (New York: Vintage Press, 1993); Evgeny Morozov, *To Save Everything, Click Here: The Folly of Technological Solutionism* (New York: Public Affairs Press, 2013).
3. In *Tinkering Toward Utopia* (Cambridge, MA: Harvard University Press, 1995), David Tyack and I argued that technological innovations were part of the story of US school reform; also see George Veletsianos and Rolin Moe, "The Rise of Educational Technology as a Sociocultural and Ideological Phenomenon," *Educause Review*, April 10, 2017, http://er.educause.edu/articles/2017/4/the-rise-of-educational-technology-as-a-sociocultural-and-ideological-phenomenon.
4. *American Heritage Dictionary of the English Language, 4th edition, s.v. "palimpsest."*
5. I put quotation marks around "personalized learning" because it is commonly used by school officials, vendors, donors, and reformers to describe a highly prized dream of individualized learning in a mass system of public education. While commonly used, it carries many meanings and remains blurred in what exactly it is, when it occurs, under what conditions, and its outcomes. I do not use quotation marks to suggest irony or sarcasm. For the rest of the chapter, for ease of reading, I drop the quotation marks. See Sean Cavanaugh, "What Is 'Personalized Learning'?" *Education Week*, October 20, 2014.
6. John Taylor et al., "Blended Learning: The Evolution of Online and Face-To-Face Education from 2008–2015," International Association of K–12 Online Learning, July 2015, http://www.inacol.org/wp-content/uploads/2015/07/iNA COL_Blended-Learning-The-Evolution-of-Online-And-Face-to-Face-Education-from-2008-2015.pdf.
7. David Tyack and Elisabeth Hansot, *Managers of Virtue: Public School Leadership in America, 1820–1880* (New York: Basic Books, 1982); David Labaree, "Progressivism, Schools, and Schools of Education: An American Romance," *Paedagogica Historia* 41, no. 1–2 (2005): 275–288.

8. Raymond Callahan, *Education and the Cult of Efficiency* (Chicago: University of Chicago Press, 1962).

9. Geraldine Clifford, *Edward L. Thorndike: The Sane Positivist* (Middletown, CT: Wesleyan University Press, 1984); Ellen Lagemann, *An Elusive Science: The Troubling History of Educational Research* (Chicago: University of Chicago Press, 2000).

10. *Wikipedia*, s.v. "Sidney Pressey," last modified May 23, 2017, https://en.wikipedia.org/wiki/Sidney_L._Pressey; B.F. Skinner, "Programmed Instruction Revisited," *Phi Delta Kappan* 68, no. 2 (1986): 103–110; James Block and Robert Burns, "Mastery Learning," *Review of Research in Education* 4 (1976): 3–49; US Department of Education, "Competency Based Learning or Personalized Learning," https://www.ed.gov/oii-news/competency-based-learning-or-personalized-learning. A national summit on competency-based education was held June 2017; see http://www.competencyworks.org/resources/national-summit-on-k-12-competency-based-education/.

11. *Wikibooks*, "Classroom Management Theorists and Theories/Burrhus Frederic Skinner," https://en.wikibooks.org/wiki/Classroom_Management_Theorists_and_Theories/Burrhus_Frederic_Skinner.

12. Ralph Tyler, "Reflecting on The Eight-Year Study," *Journal of Thought*, 21, no. 1 (1986): 15–23; also see Larry Cuban, *How Teachers Taught* (New York: Teachers College Press, 1993), chapters 2–5. For William Kilpatrick's Project Method in the 1920s, see John Pecore, "From Kilpatrick's Project Method to Project-Based Learning," in *International Handbook of Progressive Education*, ed. Mustafa Eryaman and Betram Bruce (New York: Peter Lang, 2016), pp. 155–171.

13. J.P. Stucker and G.R. Hall, "Performance Contracting Concept in Education," May 1971, RAND Report R-699, report prepared for the US Department of Health Education, and Welfare, May 1971, https://www.rand.org/pubs/papers/P4659.html.

14. Pyeong-gook Kim, "Challenging the Grammar of Schooling: Individually Guided Education, 1969–1979," *Education and Culture* 20, no. 1 (2004): 24–41.

15. Arthur Bestor, *Educational Wastelands: The Retreat from Learning in Our Public Schools* (Champaign, IL: University of Illinois Press, 1953); Albert Lynd, *Quackery in the Public Schools* (New York: Little, Brown, 1953); Rudolph Flesch, *Why Johnnie Can't Read: And What You Can Do About It* (New York: Harper and Brothers, 1955);

16. Roland Barth, *Open Education and the American School* (New York: Agathon, 1972); Charles Silberman, *Crisis in the Classroom: The Remaking of American Education* (New York: Vintage, 1971).

17. Janet Weiss, "Back to Basics Through the Years," *Chicago Reporter*, July 22, 2005, http://chicagoreporter.com/back-basics-through-years/.

18. See The Great Schools Partnership's "The Glossary of Education Reform" for a multiconcept definition of *personalized learning* at http://edglossary.org/personalized-learning/; for an example of reform-minded entrepreneurs using the phrase *factory model of schooling*, see Joel Rose, "How to Break Free of Our 19th

Century Factory-Model Education System," *The Atlantic*, May 9, 2012, https://www.theatlantic.com/business/archive/2012/05/how-to-break-free-of-our-19th-century-factory-model-education-system/256881/.

19. Rich Halverson et al., "Personalization in Practice: Observations from the Field," (WCER Working Paper 2015-8), http://www.wcer.wisc.edu/publications/working Papers/papers.php.

20. Ibid. See chapter 3 (pp. 88–89) in *How Teachers Taught*, describing tenth-graders at East High School in the 1930s who chose their own projects and the report they wrote about all of the project work they had done.

21. The range of views among current teachers about how to "personalize" learning echo what progressive educators argued about a century ago about how much the teacher should direct and how much the student should decide. See, for example, Larry Ferlazzo, "Personalized Learning Is 'Partnership with Students,'" *Education Week*, September 25, 2015.

22. Leo Doran, "Ed Tech Instruction Model Grows to 28 Schools Nationwide," *Education Week*, September 30, 2015. The program website is at http://www.new classrooms.org/.

23. ASCEND is an Oakland public charter school that opened in 2001. The charter serves 430 students in grades K–8 with twenty-four students in every class. Students are 80 percent Latino, 8 percent Asian, 6 percent African American, 5 percent multiracial, and 1 percent Filipino (2015). The poverty rate, determined by number of students eligible for free and reduced-price lunch, is 95 percent (2013).

24. For a video explaining the portal, see https://vimeo.com/143087720https://vimeo.com/143087720.

25. Cecilia Le et al., "The Past and the Promise: Today's Competency Education Movement," Students at the Center: Competency Education Research Series (Boston, MA: Jobs for the Future, 2014); Aubrey Torres et al., *Competency-Based Learning: Definitions, Policies, and Implementation* (Waltham, MA: Education Development Center, Inc., 2015).

26. The student I was shadowing showed me her Exit Slip; interview with director Winona Bassett, May 15, 2016.

27. *Wikipedia*, s.v. "Larry the Cable Guy," last modified August 22, 2017, https://en.wikipedia.org/wiki/Larry_the_Cable_Guy.

28. The classroom disciplinary policy is ASCEND's. Verbal warnings are given first. If there is another violation, the student's name is posted on the whiteboard. Next time a check mark is added next to the student's name. After two check marks, the student gets detention, and with three check marks, the student goes to principal. I learned this from the student I shadowed and classmates. None of the students knew of anyone who had been ejected from their math class.

29. Interview with Winona Bassett.

30. Sarah Garland, "Can Personalized Learning Flourish within a Traditional System," *Mind/Shift*, January 25, 2017, https://ww2.kqed.org/mindshift/2017/

01/25/can-personalized-learning-flourish-within-a-traditional-system/; Wyatt Kash, "As Personalized Learning Expands, Edtech 'Plumbing' Is as Important as Ever," *Edscoop*, March 10, 2017 at http://edscoop.com/personalized-learning-depends-on-holistic-edtech-strategy.

31. Anne Hyslop and Sarah Mead, *A Path to the Future: Creating Accountability for Personalized Learning* (Washington, DC): Bellwether Partners, May 2015), 3.

32. Interview with Edward Lin, March 16, 2016.

33. The handout for the lab on metals is specific in its questions. For the complete handout, see https://docs.google.com/document/d/1WjxHjwThwNDVjl-1JBUOcDWPM06oz6aawQHdBk6I3NUU/edit.

34. Lin does have students fill out parts of the Personalized Learning Plan on different days during a unit so that students can assess where they are on goals they set for the project and what they have completed and still have yet to do. Interview with Edward Lin, March 16, 2016.

35. In the glossary of educational terms, the "personalized learning" entry describes a full array of meanings for the phrase. One of the longer entries in the glossary, personalized learning includes programs, instructional applications, and academic strategies; see http://edglossary.org/personalized-learning/.

36. Each of the programs named claim that they have personalized learning. See their websites for descriptions of what each does.

   Rocketship: http://www.rsed.org/

   Alt/School: https://www.altschool.com/

   Agora Cyber School: http://www.agora.org/home

37. New Hampshire's Virtual Learning Academy's website describes its format and content (http://nhva.k12.com/); on the school's creation and operation, see Julia Fisher, "New Hampshire's Journey toward Competency-Based Education," *Education Next*, February 1, 2015.

   USC Hybrid High School's website: http://www.ednovate.org/about-usc/#image1-1; also see Mike Syzmanski, "USC Hybrid High School Graduates Its First Class, with All 84 Heading to College," *LA School Report*, June 13, 2016.

   For Lindsay Unified School District, see Christina Quattrocchi, "How Lindsay Unified Redesigned Itself from the Ground Up," *EdSurge*, June 17, 2014.

38. See Cuban, *How Teachers Taught*, chapters 2–5, for an overview of student-centered reforms in the 1920s and 1930s.

39. Descriptions of Big Picture Learning schools can be found at: Katrina Schwartz, "Can Truly Student-Centered Education Be Available To All?" *KQED News*, December 8, 2015, https://ww2.kqed.org/mindshift/2015/12/08/is-the-public-system-scared-to-put-students-at-the-center-of-education/; Stephen Ceasar, "For Students at L.A.'s Big Picture Charter School, Downtown Is Their Classroom," *Los Angeles Times*, December 28, 2014; for a YouTube description that includes interview with one of the cofounders of Big Picture Learning, see https://www.youtube.com/watch?v=VT716pobd2o.

For Mission Hill School, see http://www.missionhillschool.org/; Open Class-room at Lagunitas can be found at http://lagunitas.org/open/; Edina's Contin-uous Progress elementary school option is at http://webapps.edinaschools.org/sw/cp/newcpinfo.html; Private micro-schools called AltSchool can be found at https://www.altschool.com/; The Khan Lab School, a private school, is at: http://khanlabschool.org/.

40. For Avalon School, see http://www.avalonschool.org/pbl; Mission Hill School's website is http://www.missionhillschool.org/; Lagunitas Open Classroom's his-tory and offerings are at http://lagunitas.org/open/history/; Continuous Prog-ress School in Edina (MN) has a description of its program at http://webapps.edinaschools.org/sw/cp/newcpinfo.html.

On the AltSchool, see Rebecca Mead, "Learn Different," *New Yorker*, March 7, 2016; for the Khan Lab School, see Jason Tanz, "The Tech Elite's Quest to Reinvent School in Its Own Image," *Wired*, October 26, 2015, https://www.wired.com/2015/10/salman-khan-academy-lab-school-reinventing-classrooms/.

CHAPTER 5

1. Alex Tribou and Keith Collins, "This Is How Fast America Changes Its Mind," *Bloomberg*, June 26, 2015, https://www.bloomberg.com/graphics/2015-pace-of-social-change/; William Reese, "Why Americans Love to Reform Public Schools," *Educational Horizons* 85, no. 4 (2007): 217–231.

2. Evidence of increased access and use of computer devices and software appears in Lucinda Gray et al., *Teachers' Use of Educational Technology in U.S. Schools, 2009*, NCES 2010-040 (Washington, DC: US Department of Education, 2010); Diane Stark Rentner et al., *Listen to Us: Teacher Views and Voices* (Washington, DC: Center for Education Policy, George Washington University, 2016).

3. Judith Sandholtz, Cathy Ringstaff, and David Dwyer, *Teaching with Technology: Creating Student-Centered Classrooms* (New York: Teachers College Press, 1997); Henry Becker and Jason Ravitz, "The Influence of Computer and Internet Use on Teachers' Pedagogical Practices and Perceptions," *Journal of Research on Com-puting in Education* 31, no. 4 (1999): 356–385; Mark Windschitl and Karl Sahl, "Tracing Teachers' Use of Technology in a Laptop Computer School," *American Educational Research Journal* 39, no. 1 (2002):165–205; Cuban, *Inside the Black Box*; Kristin Purcell, et al., *How Teachers Are Using Computers at Home and in Their Class-rooms*, Pew Research Center report, February 28, 2013,

4. Kim Kankiewicz, "There's No Erasing the Chalkboard," *The Atlantic*, October 13, 2016, https://www.theatlantic.com/technology/archive/2016/10/theres-no-erasing-the-chalkboard/503975/.

5. Doceri is an application for iPads that allows the teacher to view students' work as they do it; see https://doceri.com/solutions_presentations.php.

6. Socrative is an application that permits the teacher to show videos on the IWB, give a pop quiz, and ask questions of students to see if they understand a point

and get instant feedback from them; see https://www.socrative.com/.

7. Beverly Young (pseudonym), email, September 9, 2016. In author's possession.

8. To determine whether second-grade teacher Jennifer Auten at Montclaire Elementary School (described in chapter 1), had changed how she taught by integrating new technologies, I would have had to observe and interview her before she had been given and used these devices and software routinely. That did not happen. I observed Auten only after she had been using new technologies. I thus had to depend on Auten's perceptions of how and why she changed her teaching.

   Relying on teacher reports of their changes in classroom practice, as I do in this study, is common among researchers but open to the above criticism. To reduce such criticism, I will cite other studies of teacher change where researchers examined classroom practice before and after technology use and studies that used the same strategy as I did.

   While my research strategy is open to criticism, the strengths of direct observation of lessons, immediate interviews with teachers, and capturing their perceptions of changes in practice after extensive technology use remain unvarnished assets. So readers need to keep the pluses and minuses of this approach in mind in assessing the evidence I offer on whether teachers did change how they taught when using new technologies.

9. I can compare these teachers historically to teachers and schools in Silicon Valley that I observed decades ago—not the same schools or teachers, however. Most of those teachers and schools were just beginning to integrate desktops, laptops, and computer labs into their daily routines while many of their colleagues continued to teach without the new devices and software. So I have observed Silicon Valley teachers changing over time as they incorporated new technologies into their repertoires. See Larry Cuban, *Teachers and Machines* (New York: Teachers College Press, 1986); *Oversold and Underused: Computers in the Classroom* (Cambridge, MA: Harvard University Press, 2001); *Inside The Black Box of Classroom Practice* (Cambridge, MA: Harvard Education Press, 2013).

10. Robert Marzano, "The Art and Science of Teaching/Teaching with Interactive Whiteboards," *Educational Leadership* 67, no. 3 (2009): 80–82; Dropbox is a storage and file-sharing tool used by many K–12 teachers; see Jennifer Carey, "Dropbox: A Superb Classroom Tool," *The How of 21st Century Teaching* (blog), August 10, 2012, http://plpnetwork.com/2012/08/10/dropbox-a-superb-classroom-tool/.

11. The levels and subjects taught by the teachers I observed were as follows: elementary—10; middle school—6; high school—25. Academic subjects in secondary schools: English—4; math—4; science—7; social studies—8; foreign language—2. Of the forty-one teachers I observed, thirty-seven (90 percent), spread across all levels and academic subjects, answered my questions. Four teachers did not respond to my follow-up email requests.

12. IXL is a subscription-based program offering games and customized lessons; see http://tinyurl.com/yan5jadf; Khan Academy offers teachers free online math

lessons; see https://www.google.com/#q=Khan+Academy&*.

13. Brendan Dilloughery, email, October 7, 2016. In author's possession. A description of Dilloughery's geometry class can be found at https://larry cuban.wordpress.com/2016/11/08/teaching-geometry-at-mountain-view-high-school-technology-integration/.

14. Edwin Avarca, email, May 4, 2016. In author's possession. A description of Avarca's Advanced Placement US history class can be found at https://larrycuban .wordpress.com/2016/04/06/part-7-summit-rainier-teachers-integrating-technol ogy-advanced-placement-u-s-history/.

15. Sue Pound, email, October 19, 2016. In author's possession. A description of Pound's science class can be found at https://larrycuban.wordpress.com/2016/11/ 05/teaching-science-at-jordan-middle-school-joint-planning-and-technology-integration/.

16. Nicole Elenz-Martin, email, May 8, 2016. In author's possession. A description of the lesson I observed can be found at https://larrycuban.wordpress .com/2016/02/27/part-2-from-the-classroom-teachers-integrating-technology/.

17. Sarah Press, email, May 12, 2016. In author's possession. A description of the lesson I observed can be found at: https://larrycuban.wordpress.com/2016/02/24/ from-the-classroom-teachers-integrating-technology-part-1/.

18. John DiCosmo, email, October 16, 2016. In author's possession.

19. Lyuda Shemyakina, email, October 13, 2016. In author's possession. A description of the lesson I observed can be found at https://larrycuban.wordpress .com/2016/10/23/teaching-biology-at-mountain-view-high-school-technology-integration/.

20. Gaea Leinhardt, "Craft Knowledge in Teaching," *Educational Researcher* 19, no. 2 (1990): 18–25.

21. Larry Cuban, *How Teachers Taught: Constancy and Change in American Classrooms, 1890–1990* (New York: Teachers College Press, 1993); Larry Cuban, *Hugging the Middle: How Teachers Teach in an Era of Testing and Accountability* (New York: Teachers College, Columbia University, 2009).

22. John DiCosmo, email, October 16, 2016.

23. For differences in stories told to researchers, see D.C. Philips, "Telling the Truth About Stories," *Teaching and Teacher Education* 13, no. 1 (1997): 101–109.

24. David Cohen, "A Revolution in One Classroom: The Case of Mrs. Oublier," *Educational Evaluation and Policy Analysis* 12, no. 3 (1990): 311–329; Suzanne Wilson, "A Conflict of Interests: The Case of Mark Black," *Educational Evaluation and Policy Analysis* 12, no. 3 (1990): 293–310; Ruth Heaton, "Who Is Minding the Mathematics? A Case Study of a Fifth-Grade Teacher," *Elementary School Journal* 93, no. 2 (1992) 153–162; Deborah Ball, "Reflections and Deflections of Policy: The Case of Carol Turner," *Educational Evaluation and Policy Analysis* 12, no. 3 (1990): 263–275.

25. Cohen, "A Revolution in One Classroom."

26. Michael Connelly and Jean Clandinin, "Stories of Experience and Narrative Inquiry," *Educational Researcher* 19, no. 5 (1990): 2–14.

27. Philips, "Telling the Truth About Stories."

28. Cuban, *Hugging the Middle*. On *dynamic conservatism*, see Donald Schön, *Beyond the Stable State:* (New York: Norton, 1973).

29. To be clear, I do not value one kind of change over the other. Both are important, and I highly prize each. What matters for each kind of change is context. In some settings, a small change can have significant repercussions (e.g., legislating public funding of charter schools); in other settings, a planned fundamental change geared to altering how schools are organized (e.g., going from K–12 to non-graded) can barely get off the ground. Or a teacher shifts from a routine of homework, large-group discussions, and text-bound information to project-based learning where students participate in choosing projects that cut across different academic subjects over the course of nine months in small bite-size changes. She knows where she wants to end up at the end of the school year and knows that such a fundamental change in her practice will have to be done slowly and carefully.

30. Many intended fundamental changes (e.g., shifting routine curriculum and instruction lessons in math and science to project-based learning) often get incrementalized and become pale shadows of what reformers wanted; see Cohen, "A Revolution in One Classroom." Similarly, some leaders come up with a series of incremental changes geared toward an end that will, over time, accumulate into a fundamental shift in schooling (e.g., Union City, New Jersey, as described by David Kirp, *Improbable Scholars* [New York: Oxford University Press, 2015]).

CHAPTER 6

1. Donald Schön,"Dynamic Conservatism," Reith Lectures (part 2), 1970, https://larrycuban.files.wordpress.com/2013/07/1970_reith2-1.pdf.

2. Giuseppe Tomasi di Lampedusa, *The Leopard* (1958; London: Fontana, 1963), 29.

3. As described in the previous chapter, thirty-seven of the forty-one teachers I observed responded to my questions about change in their classrooms. The ratios and percentages detailed in these paragraphs refer to these thirty-seven teachers.

   I need to be clear about the word *content*. I refer to the subject matter and skills that elementary and secondary teachers offer to students in daily lessons. With California formally adopting Core Curriculum standards in 2010 and serious teacher implementation of the standards beginning in 2014, the Silicon Valley teachers I visited in different districts had already aligned their lessons to the Common Core standards. See http://www.ppic.org/main/publication_quick.asp?i=1093.

4. John DiCosmo, email, October 16, 2016. In author's possession. I attach no greater importance to either incremental or fundamental changes. Both are

necessary in any institution serving the community. Each can (or cannot) be significant depending on the direction, say from teacher- to student-centered—and on available resources and the context. To make either kind of change requires enormous cooperation and heroic action on the part of participants.

5. In the introduction, I said that I avoid the word *stasis* as a synonym for *stability*. *Stasis* means no change, inertia, even torpor. In this study, I use the word *stability* to mean fluidity, a condition constantly in motion interacting with change. Too many reformers eager to make fundamental changes in schooling portray the system as inactive, inert, and in need of alteration, that is, to their version of change. Contrary to this common perspective on school improvement, I use *stability* throughout this study to make the obvious point that teachers, organizations, and environment are dynamic in their stability.

6. Naomi Oreskes, "Beyond the Ivory Tower: Scientific Consensus on Climate Change," *Science* 306, no. 5702 (2004): 1686; NASA, "Scientific Consensus: Earth's Climate Is Warming," April 2017, https://climate.nasa.gov/scientific-consensus/. On political polarization, see Pew Research Center, "The Politics of Climate," October 4, 2016, http://www.pewinternet.org/2016/10/04/the-politics-of-climate/.

7. European Council, *International Agreements on Climate Actions*, June 2016, http://www.consilium.europa.eu/en/policies/climate-change/international-agreements-climate-action/; Coral Davenport and Alissa Rubin, "Trump Signs Executive Order Unwinding Obama Climate Policies," *New York Times*, March 28, 2017.

8. Spencer Weart, *The Discovery of Global Warming* (Cambridge, MA: Harvard University Press, 2008).

9. Sources I used for this section are Michael Knowles et. al, "Roman Catholicism," *Encyclopedia Britannica*, 2016, accessed May 4, 2017, https://www.britannica.com/topic/Roman-Catholicism; Roger Finke and Patricia Wittberg, "Organizational Revival from Within: Explaining Revivalism and Reform in the Roman Catholic Church," *Journal for the Scientific Study of Religion* 39, no. 2 (2000): 154–170.

10. Henry Mintzberg and Frances Westley, "Cycles of Organizational Change," *Strategic Management Journal* 13 (special issue, 1992): 39–59.

11. Benjamin Bloom, *Stability and Change in Human Characteristics* (New York: John Wiley and Son, 1964); Avshalom Caspi et al., "Personality Development: Stability and Change," *Annual Review of Psychology* 56 (2005): 453–484.

12. Benjamin Bloom, "The New Direction in Educational Research: Alterable Variables," *Journal of Negro Education* 49, no. 3 (1980): 337–349; James Heckman, "Early Childhood Investments Substantially Boost Adult Health," *Science* 343, no. 6178 (March 2014): 1478–1485.

13. Robert Gordon, *The Rise and Fall of American Growth* (Princeton, NJ: Princeton University Press, 2015).

14. Ibid.

15. Claire Miller, "When Driverless Cars Break the Law," *New York Times*, May 13, 2014.

16. Sean Reardon et al., "Brown Fades: The End of Court-Ordered School Desegregation and the Resegregation of American Public Schools," *Journal of Policy Analysis and Management* 31, no. 4 (2012): 876–904.

17. Gary Sykes and Suzanne Wilson, "Can Policy (Re)form Instruction?" in *Handbook of Research on Teaching*, 5th edition, ed. Drew Gitomer and Courtney Bell (Washington, DC: American Educational Research Association, 2016), 851–916.

18. Lydia Saad, "Five Insights into U.S. Parents' Satisfaction with Education," *Education*, August 25, 2016, http://www.gallup.com/poll/195011/five-insights-parents-satisfaction-education.aspx. Challenges to these myths do exist; see, for example, Alan Krueger, "Reassessing the View That American Schools Are Broken," *Economic Policy Review* 4, no. 1 (1998): 29–43; Jack Schneider, "America's Not-So-Broken Education System," *The Atlantic*, June 22, 2016, https://www.theatlantic.com/education/archive/2016/06/everything-in-american-education-is-broken/488189/.

19. Clayton Christensen et al., *Disrupting Class: How Disruptive Innovation Will Change the Way the World Learns* (New York: McGraw Hill, 2008); Wendy Kopp, "Do American Schools Need to Change?" *The Atlantic*, October 25, 2013, https://www.theatlantic.com/education/archive/2013/10/do-american-schools-need-to-change-depends-what-you-compare-them-to/280768/; National Center for Educational Statistics, *120 Years of American Education: A Statistical Portrait* (Washington, DC: US Department of Education, Office of Educational Research, 1993); David Tyack and Larry Cuban, *Tinkering Toward Utopia* (Cambridge, MA: Harvard University Press, 1995); Larry Cuban, "The 'Failure' of New Technologies to Transform Traditional Teaching in the Past Century" (forthcoming).

20. "2017 Best School Districts in America," *Niche*, https://www.niche.com/k12/rankings/public-school-districts/best-overall/; Jay Mathews, "Top-Performing Schools with Elite Students," *Washington Post*, April 17, 2016, https://www.washingtonpost.com/local/education/top-performing-schools-with-elite-students/2016/04/12/1cd321d4-00d7-11e6-b823-707c79ce3504_story.html?utm_term=.e27e85efacf3; Alana Semuels, "Good School, Rich School; Bad School, Poor School," *The Atlantic*, August 25, 2016, https://www.theatlantic.com/business/archive/2016/08/property-taxes-and-unequal-schools/497333/.

21. Nikelle Murphy, "The Twenty 'Worst' Schools in America," *Money and Career CheatSheet*, May 12, 2017, http://www.cheatsheet.com/money-career/the-20-worst-public-schools-in-america.html/?a=viewall; William Julius Wilson, *The Truly Disadvantaged: The Inner City, the Underclass, and Public Policy* (Chicago: University of Chicago Press, 1990); William Julius Wilson, *Bridge over the Racial Divide* (Berkeley, CA: University of California Press, 1999).

22. Ray Rist, *The Urban School: A Factory for Failure* (Cambridge, MA: MIT Press, 1974); Richard Rothstein, "The Myth of Public School Failure," *American Prospect*, Spring 1993, 20–34; Frederick Hess, *Spinning Wheels: The Politics of Urban School Reform* (Washington, DC: Brookings Institution Press, 1999); Charles Payne, *So*

Much Reform, So Little Change (Cambridge, MA: Harvard Education Press, 2008).

23. Melanie Asmar, "A Turnaround in Denver," *The Atlantic*, February 5, 2016, https://www.theatlantic.com/education/archive/2016/02/a-turnaround-in-denver/460086/; Jane David and Joan Talbert, *Turning Around a High-Poverty School District: Final Report* (Palo Alto, CA: Bay Area Research Group, and Stanford, CA: Center for Research on the Context of Teaching, 2012).

24. William Galston, interview, *Frontline*, http://www.pbs.org/wgbh/pages/frontline/shows/vouchers/interviews/galston.html; Kristina Rizga, "Everything You've Heard About Failing Schools Is Wrong," *Mother Jones*, August 2012, 50–59; Jeffrey Snyder and Sarah Reckhow, "Political Determinants of Philanthropic Funding for Urban Schools," *Journal of Urban Affairs* 39, no. 1 (2017): 91–107.

25. Andrew Coulson, "District Consolidation: A Brief History and Research Review," Mackinac Center for Public Policy, 2007, https://www.mackinac.org/8663.

26. Sean Reardon et al., "Brown Fades: The End of Court-Ordered School Desegregation and the Resegregation of American Public Schools," *Journal of Policy Analysis and Management* 31, no. 4 (2012): 876–904.

27. Ashley Jochim and Paul Hill, "Street Savvy School Reform," *Education Next*, August 9, 2016, http://educationnext.org/street-savvy-school-reform-lessons-city-systems-politics/.

28. Peter Dow, *Schoolhouse Politics* (Cambridge, MA: Harvard University Press, 1991); Cathy Wissehr et al., "Looking Back at the Sputnik Era and Its Impact on Science Education," *School Science and Mathematics* 111 (2011): 368–375.

29. Suzanne Quick, "Secondary Impacts of the Curriculum Reform Movement: A Longitudinal Study of the Incorporation of Innovations of the Curriculum Reform Movement into Commercially Developed Curriculum Programs," (doctoral dissertation, Stanford University, 1978); George DeBoer,"What We Have Learned and Where We Are Headed: Lessons from the *Sputnik* Era," commissioned paper for the National Academy of Sciences' Symposium "Reflecting on *Sputnik*," Washington, DC, October 4, 1997; Peter Dow, *Schoolhouse Politics* (Cambridge, MA: Harvard University Press, 1991)

30. Larry Cuban, "Myths About Changing Schools and the Case of Special Education," *Remedial and Special Education* 17, no. 2 (1996): 75–82.

31. Mary Metz, "Real School: A Universal Drama Amid Disparate Experience," *Politics of Education Yearbook*, 1989, 75–91; Richard Elmore and Milbrey McLaughlin, *Steady Work* (Santa Monica, CA: RAND Corporation, 1988); John Meyer and Brian Rowan, "Institutional Organizations: Formal Structure as Myth and Ceremony," *American Journal of Sociology* 83 (1977): 340–363; Deanna Malatesta and Craig Smith," Lessons from Resource Dependency Theory for Contemporary Public and Nonprofit Managers," *Public Administration Review* 74, no. 1 (2014): http://onlinelibrary.wiley.com/doi/10.1111/puar.12181/pdf.

32. Charles Payne, *So Much Reform, So Little Change: The Persistence of Failure in Urban Schools* (Cambridge, MA: Harvard Education Press, 2008); Jeffrey Mirel, *The Rise*

and Fall of an Urban School System (Ann Arbor, MI: University of Michigan Press, 1999); Diane Ravitch, *The Great School Wars; A History of the New York City Public Schools* (Baltimore, MD: Johns Hopkins University Press, 2000).

33. See Larry Cuban, *Inside the Black Box of Classroom Practice* (Cambridge, MA: Harvard Education Press, 2013), chapter 6.

34. David Tyack, *One Best System* (Cambridge, MA: Harvard University Press, 1974), 25; Jody Wilgoren, "The One Room Schoolhouse," *New York Times*, August 6, 2000.

35. Tyack, *One Best System*, 44–45, 166; Larry Cuban, "What Happens to Reforms That Last: The Case of the Junior High School," *American Educational Research Journal* 29, no. 2 (1992): 227–251; William Reese, *The Origins of the American High School* (New Haven, CT: Yale University Press, 1999); Edward Krug, *The American High School* (New York: Harper and Row, 1964).

36. Robert Merton, "Bureaucratic Structure and Personality," *Social Forces* 18, no. 4 (1940): 560–568; Richard Scott, *Organizations* (Englewood Cliffs, NJ: Prentice Hall, 1981), chapter 13; Richard Mowday and Robert Sutton, "Organizational Behavior: Linking Individuals and Groups to Organizational Contexts," *Annual Review of Psychology* 44 (1993): 195–229; Stephen Raudenbush et al., *Contextual Effects on the Self-Efficacy of High School Teachers* (Washington, DC: Office of Educational Research, Center for Research on Context of Secondary School Teaching, 1990).

37. Rebecca Alber, "Six Ways To Avoid Feeling Isolated in the Classroom," *Edutopia*, January 9, 2012, https://www.edutopia.org/blog/avoid-teacher-isolation-stay-connected-rebecca-alber.

38. Patricia Cahape Hammer, *Effects of Disability Labels on Students with Exceptionalities*, report prepared by the West Virginia Department of Education, 2012, http://wvde.state.wv.us/research/reports2012/LitReview_EffectsofDisabilityLabelson StudentswithExceptionalities2012.pdf; Dana Shifrer, "Stigma of a Label: Educational Expectations for High School Students Labeled with Learning Disabilities," *Journal of Health and Social Behavior* 54, no. 4 (2013): 462–480.

39. Larry Cuban, "The Hidden Variable: How Organizations Influence Teacher Responses to Secondary Science Curriculum," *Theory into Practice* 34, no. 1 (1995): 4–11; Sara Deschenes et al., "Mismatch: Historical Perspectives on Schools and Students Who Don't Fit Them," *Teachers College Record* 103, no. 4 (2001): 525–547.

40. There are, of course, non-age-graded elementary schools that pop up in media reports. Ditto for competency-based learning where mastery is the outcome rather than time spent on a topic or in a grade. Both are newsworthy yet seldom lead to serious discussions of the links between age-graded structure, curriculum, and instruction. See, for example, Mallory Noe-Payne, "No Grades, No Problem: How One High School Is Transforming Learning," *WGBH News*, https://www.pri.org/stories/2015-06-18/no-grades-no-problem-how-one-high-school-transforming-learning.

41. Mary Metz, "Real School: A Universal Drama amid Disparate Experience," in *Education Politics for the New Century*, ed. D. Mitchell and M. Goertz (New York: Falmer Press, 1990), 75–91; for Gallup polls on education, see http://www.gallup.com/poll/1612/education.aspx; William Bushaw and Valerie Calderon, "Americans Put Teacher Quality on Center Stage," *Phi Delta Kappan* (October 2014, pt. II): 48–59, http://journals.sagepub.com/doi/pdf/10.1177/0031721714553411.

42. See http://aspirepublicschools.org/; http://www.kipp.org/; and http://www.successacademies.org/.

43. Claire Miller, "Class Differences in Child-Rearing Are on the Rise," *New York Times*, December 17, 2015; Theresa Julian et al., "Cultural Variation in Parenting: Perceptions of Caucasian, African-American, Hispanic, and Asian-American Parents," *Family Relations* 43, no. 1 (1994): 30–37.

44. Patricia Cohen, "Visions and Revisions of Child-Raising Experts," *New York Times*, April 5, 2003.

45. Pew Research Center, "Parenting in America," December 17, 2015, http://www.pewsocialtrends.org/2015/12/17/parenting-in-america/; US Census Bureau survey: https://contemporaryfamilies.org/child-rearing-norms-practices/; Paula Fass, "How Americans Raise Their Children," 27th Annual Lecture of the German Historical Institute, November 14, 2003: https://www.ghi-dc.org/fileadmin/user_upload/GHI_Washington/Publications/Bulletin54/bu54_007.pdf.

46. John Goodlad and Robert Anderson, *The Non-graded Elementary School* (New York: Harcourt, Brace and Company, 1959); Larry Cuban, "Ungraded Schools, Past and Present, pt. 2," *Larry Cuban on School Reform and Classroom Practice* (blog), https://larrycuban.wordpress.com/2012/02/04/ungraded-schools-past-and-present-part-2/.

47. David K. Cohen, *Teaching and Its Predicaments* (Cambridge, MA: Harvard University Press, 2011); Frederick Hess and Olivia Meeks, *School Boards Circa 2010: Governance in the Accountability Era* report published by the National School Boards Association, Thomas Fordham Institute, Iowa School Boards Association, 2010; Lisa Keegan and Chester Finn, "Lost at Sea," *Education Next* 4, no. 3 (2004), http://educationnext.org/lost-at-sea/.

48. Gary Sykes and Suzanne Wilson, "Can Policy (Re)form Instruction?" in *Handbook of Research on Teaching*. 851–916.

49. Ludy Benjamin, "A History of Teaching Machines," *American Psychologist* 43, no. 9 (1988): 703–712; Robert Reiser, "Instructional Technology: A History," in *Instructional Technology: Foundations*, ed. Robert Gagne (New York: Routledge, 1987), 11–48; Audrey Watters, "Education Technology and Skinner's Box," *Hack Education*, February 10, 2015, http://hackeducation.com/2015/02/10/skinners-box.

50. Richard Elmore and Diane Burney, "Investing in Teacher Learning: Staff Development and Instructional Improvement," in *Teaching as the Learning Profession*, ed. Linda Darling Hammond and Gary Sykes (San Francisco: Jossey-Bass, 1999), 263–291; David Cohen and Deborah Ball, "Instruction, Capacity, and

Improvement," (Philadelphia: Consortium for Policy Research in Education, 1999); Sykes and Wilson, "Can Policy (Re)form Instruction?"

51. For the science of fluttering butterflies, see Fenella Saunders, "What's All The Flap About?" *American Scientist*, 97, no. 1 (2009): 23; also see Phillip Lott, "Butterfly Flight Paths," *Phillip's Natural World* (blog), (August 2008), http://majikphil .blogspot.com/2015/08/butterfly-flight-paths.html.

52. Robert Shelton, *No Direction Home* (Milwaukee, WI: Hal Leonard Corporation, 2011).

APPENDIX

1. Robert Stake, *The Art of Case Study Research* (Thousand Oaks, CA: Sage, 1995); Matthew Miles and Michael Huberman, *Qualitative Data Analysis*, 2nd edition (Thousand Oaks, CA: Sage, 1994); Robert Yin, *Case Study Research: Design and Methods* (Thousand Oaks, CA: Sage, 2003).

2. Kendall Bronk et al., "An Introduction to Exemplar Research," *New Directions for Child and Adolescent Development* 142, no. 2 (2013): 1–12.

3. As part of the standards, testing, accountability movement, fueled by No Child Left Behind (2002–2015) and Race to The Top (2009–2016), evaluating teachers on the basis of student test scores spread rapidly across the nation, particularly in large urban districts. A backlash to these test-score based evaluations of teachers called for veteran teachers and principals to observe lessons to broaden the judgment about whether the teacher was effective or not by including other data than test scores. Observation protocols multiplied as this additional measure of teacher performance spread. Yet even the most exacting protocol, blessed with the most recent social science evidence, covering many facets of teaching and student learning ran into problems that undermined judgments about teacher effectiveness. See Rachel Garrett and Matthew Steinberg, "Examining Teacher Effectiveness Using Classroom Observation Scores: Evidence of the Randomization of Teachers to Students," *Educational Evaluation and Policy Analysis* 37, no. 2 (2015): 224–242.

4. Bernard Forgues,"Sampling on the Dependent Variable Is Not Always *That* Bad," *Strategic Organization* 10, no. 3 (2012): 269–275.

5. Stuart Purkey and Marshall Smith, "Effective Schools: A Review," *Elementary School Journal* 83, no. 4 (1983): 427–452; Brian Rowan et al., "Research on Effective Schools: A Cautionary Note," *Educational Researcher* 12, no. 4 (1983): 24–31. For businesses that are effective, see "Tom Peters's True Confessions: 'This Is Our Time to Lead,'" *Fast Company*, November 30, 2001, https://www.fastcompany .com/44077/tom-peterss-true-confessions; Bruce Neindorf and Kristine Beck, "'Good to Great,' or Just Good?," *Academy of Management Perspectives* 22, no. 4 (2008): 13–20.

6. The protocol is straightforward and subjective. I write out in longhand or type on my laptop what teachers and students do during the lesson. Each sheet of paper or laptop screen is divided into a wide column and a narrow column. In

the wide column, I record every few minutes what the teacher is doing, what students are doing, and teacher-directed segues from one activity to another. In the narrow column, I comment on what I see on the walls, ceiling, and whiteboards in the room, thoughts that occur to me as I observe teacher and students in activities, and questions and ideas that I need to pursue further.

7. Examples of the different definitions mentioned in text can be found at:
    http://www.definitions.net/definition/Technology%20integration
    https://nces.ed.gov/pubs2003/tech_schools/chapter7.asp
    https://en.wikipedia.org/wiki/Technology_integration
    http://www.education4site.org/blog/2011/what-do-we-really-mean-by-technology-integration/
    http://members.tripod.com/sjbrooks_young/techint.pdf
    http://fcit.usf.edu/matrix/matrix.php
    http://jan.ucc.nau.edu/~coesyl-p/principle3-article2.pdf

8. Rodney Earle's definition of integration concentrates on the teaching, not hardware or software: "Computer technology is merely one possibility in the selection of media and the delivery mode—part of the instructional design process—not the end but merely one of several means to the end." ("The Integration of Instructional Technology into Public Education: Promises and Challenges," *Education Technology Magazine* 42, no. 1 [2002]: 5–13); Khe Foon Hew and Thomas Brush define it this way: "[T]echnology integration is thus viewed as the use of computing devices such as desktop computers, laptops, handheld computers, software, or Internet in K–12 schools for instructional purposes" ("Integrating Technology into K–12 Teaching and Learning," *Education Tech Research Development* 55 [2007]: 223–252).

9. I took a definition originally in *Edutopia* and revised it to make clear that the integration of technology in daily lessons is harnessed to achieving curricular and instructional goals of the teacher, school, and district. The devices and software are in the background, not the foreground. I then stripped away language that connected usage of technologies to "success" or preferred ways of teaching. See "What Is Successful Technology Integration?" *Edutopia*, November 5, 2007, http://www.edutopia.org/technology-integration-guide-description.

Acknowledgments

My first book was published in 1964, and this one appears in 2018. After a half-century of writing, I can say with great confidence that writing about school reform and classroom practice has been most satisfying.

For me, the act of writing, frustrations and all, I have found wonderfully mysterious in how I eventually come to know what I want to say. As others have said, writing is thinking on paper and a way of continually learning. To me, writing is a form of teaching, and each blog post, article, chapter, and book has its own lessons embedded in it that I hope readers will note, agree or disagree with, but most important, learn from. So I continue to write for my blog, do short pieces or commissioned chapters, and yes, perhaps another book as long as I can lift a pen and click keys on my computer.

Make no mistake, however, writing a book is hard work.

Figuring out the right question to ask, doing research in archives and schools, analyzing what has been collected, and putting all of it into a coherent argument buttressed by evidence ain't easy. And that is before the writing even begins.

Then, I have to pull all these pieces together in clear, crisp language, across two hundred printed pages, that makes the question I ask, the answer I have constructed, and supporting evidence accessible to a broad audience of educational policy makers, practitioners, and academics.

Even though I have written many books over the past half-century, unlike riding a bicycle, when balance and road skills once learned become second nature, each new book has its own risks, tasks, and quirks that have to be finessed unlike the previous one. So while I have learned to become more efficient in knowing what has to be done in creating a book, that efficiency does not translate into writing the next one—with its different questions, core argument, and evidence—smoothly.

In going through all of the phases in writing *The Flight of a Butterfly or the Path of a Bullet?*, I found great satisfaction. And for that wonderful feeling, I owe thanks to many people who helped me along the way. I thank those teachers and administrators who identified exemplary teachers in their districts and schools: technology coordinator Dominic Bigue in San Mateo Union High School District, Teri Faught in Mountain View Los Altos, and Emily Garrison in Palo Alto Unified District. At Summit charter schools, Diane Tavenner and Adam Carter arranged for me to visit two schools in the network. In Milpitas Unified District, I thank Weller Elementary School's principal Raquel Kusunoki, Marshall Pomeroy Elementary School's principal Sheila Murphy-Brewer, assistant superintendent Norma Rodriguez, and director of technology Chin Song. They educated me about the district and its elementary schools.

The study could not have been completed without forty-one classroom teachers inviting me into their classrooms. While I have included vignettes of a half-dozen of these teachers' lessons, I have not yet identified all those who welcomed me to observe their classrooms and responded to my questions. I am most grateful for these teachers' cooperation and thank them publicly by listing their names (some requested pseudonyms so I cannot list their names here):

Sarah Press, Hillsdale High School
Nicole Elenz-Martin, Aragon High School
Will Colglazier, Aragon High School
Chris Kelly, Summit Prep
Ethan Edwards, Summit Prep
Aukeem Ballard, Summit Prep
Anne Giocondini, Summit Prep
Kristel Hsiao, Summit Prep
Katie Goddard, Summit Rainier
Edward Lin, Summit Rainier
Edwin Avarca, Summit Rainier

Jennifer Auten, Montclaire Elementary School

Mona Ricard, Sequoia Elementary School

Leslie Altman, Sequoia Elementary School

Michael Moul, Los Altos High School

Stephen Hine, Los Altos High School

Gabriel Stewart, Los Altos High School

David Campbell, Mountain View High School

Lyudmila Shemyakina, Mountain View High School

Kristen Krauss, Mountain View High School

Brendan Dilloughery, Mountain View High School

Carson Rietveld, Mountain View High School

John DiCosmo, Terman Middle School

Sue Pound, David Starr Jordan Middle School

Erica Goldsworthy, David Starr Jordan Middle School

Deanna Sainten, Marshall Pomeroy Elementary School

Liluma Bayanzay, Marshall Pomeroy Elementary School

Ashima Das, Marshall Pomeroy Elementary School

Jackie Dang, Joseph Weller Elementary School

John Duong, Joseph Weller Elementary School

Richard Hart, Joseph Weller Elementary School

Juhi Sharma, Joseph Weller Elementary School

Finally, I thank the director of the Harvard Education Press, Doug Clayton, for his steadfast confidence in me in both accepting and making possible the publication of this book.

About the Author

Larry Cuban is professor emeritus of education at Stanford University. He has taught courses in the methods of teaching social studies; the history of school reform, curriculum, and instruction; and leadership.

His background in the field of education before becoming a professor includes fourteen years of teaching high school social studies in big-city schools, directing a teacher education program that prepared returning Peace Corps volunteers to teach in inner-city schools, and serving for seven years as a district superintendent.

His most recent books are *Teaching History Then and Now: A Story of Stability and Change in Schools* (2016); *Inside the Black Box of Classroom Practice: Change Without Reform in American Education* (2013); *As Good as It Gets: What School Reform Brought to Austin* (2010); *Hugging the Middle: How Teachers Teach in an Era of Testing and Accountability* (2009); *Partners in Literacy* (with Sondra Cuban, 2007); *Against the Odds: Insights from One District's Small School Reform* (coauthor, 2010); and *Cutting Through the Hype: The Essential Guide to School Reform* (with Jane David, 2010).

Index